QUICK
Responses for Reducing Misbehavior and Suspensions

A Behavioral Toolbox for Classroom and School Leaders

Second Edition

QUICK Responses for Reducing Misbehavior and Suspensions

A Behavioral Toolbox for Classroom and School Leaders

Second Edition

Paul Gavoni
Anika Costa
Eric Gormley
Andrew Houvouras
Frank Krukauskas

KeyPress Publishing
www.keypresspublishing.com

This book is a work of nonfiction. Unless otherwise noted, the author and the publisher make no explicit guarantees as to the accuracy of the information contained in this book and in some cases, names of people and places have been altered to protect their privacy.

Copyright © 2025 by Paul Gavoni, Anika Costa, Eric Gormley, Andrew Houvouras, and Frank Krukauskas

All rights reserved. No part of this publication may be reproduced, stored in a retrieval system, or transmitted in any form or by any means, electronic, mechanical, photocopying, recording, or otherwise without the prior permission of the publisher or in accordance with the provisions of the Copyright, Designs and Patents Act 1988 or under the terms of any license permitting limited copying issued by the Copyright Licensing Agency.

First edition published by WND Press, LLC, August 2021

Authors: Paul Gavoni, Anika Costa, Eric Gormley, Andrew Houvouras, and Frank Krukauskas

QUICK Responses for Reducing Misbehavior and Suspensions: A Behavioral Toolbox for Classroom and School Leaders (2nd Edition)

Published by: KeyPress Publishing
Science Adviser: Thomas Freeman
Brand Integrity: Jana Burtner
Production Manager: Adele Hall
Editors: Mary Sproles Martin, Ashley Johnson, Stefanie Carr, Kelly Lee, and Gail Snyder
Designer: Kim Harding

ISBN 979-8-9922514-0-1

Library of Congress Control Number: 2025930394

Published in Melbourne, Florida

Distributed by:
ABA Technologies, Inc.
930 South Harbor City Blvd, Suite 402
Melbourne, FL 32901
www.abatechnologies.com

KeyPress Publishing books are available at a special discount for bulk purchases by corporations, institutions, and other organizations. For more information, please email keypress@abatechnologies.com.

Acknowledgments

Writing a book can be a difficult endeavor, especially when combining the knowledge and approaches of five different authors with many decades of collective experience. Most of us are or were educators; some of us were administrators; and each of us is a behavior analyst. While there are too many to list, we are grateful to those who have trained, coached, and mentored us along the way in effectively applying and disseminating behavior analysis.

Thankfully, we were all guided by the principles rooted in the science of human behavior. This anchored our writing, stories, and recommendations. Though widely misunderstood, behavior analysis has over a century's worth of research to support its effectiveness in producing socially valid outcomes. We are thankful to the researchers, educators, and practitioners who led the charge in making the world a better place through behavior analysis. Most of all, we are grateful to our families for their unconditional love and support.

Disclaimer

The environments in which problem behaviors occur are often complex, necessitating tailored evaluations to effectively address specific concerns. While the principles of behavior change are consistent across different settings, it is important to recognize that each environment has its unique aspects. Consequently, there is no universal "one-size-fits-all" intervention.

This book provides multiple examples of how behavioral principles and procedures can be applied in educational settings. These illustrations are intended to show possible ways to implement these strategies with students exhibiting challenging behaviors. However, please be aware that the authors and publisher are not responsible for the implementation or outcomes of the procedures described herein.

Should the problem behavior pose a risk to the individual or others, we strongly recommend seeking more personalized interventions. This may include consulting with a behavior analyst, who can conduct a functional behavior assessment and develop a tailored treatment plan. In cases where challenging behavior involves severe aggression, self-injury, or destruction, or constitutes a significant threat to life or health, we advise obtaining crisis management training for teams operating in such contexts.

The authors and publisher disclaim any responsibility for the use or misuse of the procedures and assessments detailed in this book, as well as for any injuries that might occur during related incidents.

Table of Contents

Acknowledgments v

Disclaimer ii

Preface xi

Introduction: Good Kid, Bad Behavior 13

Section I: Classroom Leadership for Reducing Misbehavior 16

    CHAPTER 1   Why Are We Here? What's the Problem? 17

    CHAPTER 2   Consequences of Behavior: Reinforcement, Punishment, and Misunderstandings . . . 23

    CHAPTER 3   You Can Run, but You Can't Hide! 31

    CHAPTER 4   The Quickest and Easiest Tool for Preventing Misbehavior 39

    CHAPTER 5   Good Teacher, Bad Behavior 43

    CHAPTER 6   Collaborative Classroom Management Through the ACT Matrix 55

Section II: School Leadership for Reducing Misbehavior 62

    CHAPTER 7   Changing Student Misbehavior Requires Good Leadership 63

    CHAPTER 8   Changing Student Misbehavior Requires Performance Diagnostics and Coaching . . 69

    CHAPTER 9   Suspending: The Good, the Bad, and the Ugly 75

    CHAPTER 10   The QUICK Response 81

    CHAPTER 11   The QUICK Room: An Alternative to In-School and Out-of-School
Suspensions or Out-of-Class Time-Outs 91

    CHAPTER 12   Crisis Management Versus Hands-Off Policies 97

    CHAPTER 13   Transforming School Culture: Principal Lack and the ACT Matrix 103

Appendices 109

References 197

Glossary of Terms 201

About the Authors 205

Preface

When we released the first edition of QUICK Responses for Reducing Misbehavior and Suspensions, our goal was simple: to provide educators, school leaders, and behavior interventionists with practical strategies that make a difference. The response was beyond what we imagined—reaching thousands of schools and showing us that the principles and procedures outlined in our book are truly valued in education.

In this second edition, we've added more real-life stories and updated examples to make the strategies even easier to use. We've also included more procedures in the appendices because the response to the original procedures was so positive. Our aim is to give you the tools you need to address everyday classroom and school challenges effectively.

We're also excited to introduce the ACT Matrix. It's a straightforward tool that you can use at both the classroom and school levels to help guide your actions and decisions. This addition aligns with our commitment to providing strategies that promote positive changes for educators, students, and schools.

Our mission with this book is clear: to support you in making lasting improvements in education. We know these strategies work, and we hope this edition empowers you to keep making a difference. Thank you for your dedication to your students and schools.

Here's to QUICK responses that lead to meaningful change.

Introduction

Good Kid, Bad Behavior

With many decades of experience, we authors have repeatedly encountered statements such as, "You have Ricky in your class? Wow, good luck. He's a really bad kid." We've heard countless tales from Ricky's previous teachers detailing his misdeeds, painting a vivid picture of his disruptive behavior. If you've ever made similar comments, don't feel singled out. Many of us have, especially before we fully grasped the complexities underlying behavioral issues.

Not only do students like Ricky suffer from the failure to manage their disruptive behavior, but it also has a significant impact on teacher well-being. Disruptive behavior can lead to exhaustion and contributes to the high attrition rates in the teaching profession. Studies indicate (e.g., Kollerová et al., 2023) that teachers frequently cite disruptive behaviors as a primary stressor that diminishes their job satisfaction and effectiveness in the classroom.

Classroom management is a challenge, with many expressing a need for more training and support (Greenberg et al., 2014). This issue could be addressed to enhance both teacher performance and student outcomes. In a study by Obee et al. (2022) aimed at professional development targeting classroom management and behavior support skills, the researchers found the training improved educators' practices, particularly in managing classroom behavior and implementing positive behavioral supports.

If you are like many other teachers, you likely feel inadequately trained in classroom management. This is a significant concern, given its impact on teaching effectiveness and student behavior. The National Council on Teacher Quality reviewed over 100 teacher preparation programs (Greenberg et al., 2014). While most programs cover classroom management in their curriculum, there is often a disconnect between the classroom management strategies taught and the practice opportunities provided to teacher candidates. Furthermore, the strategies taught are not always based on research.

Classrooms are dynamic environments, where learning is supposed to be the priority. Yet when students struggle with math or reading, our first instinct is to teach—to break down the problem and offer solutions until they grasp the content. But what happens when the challenge isn't academic? Why do we approach nearly every academic hurdle as a teachable moment yet fail to apply the same mindset to behavioral issues? Instead of guidance, there's often a rush to punish and label. This inconsistency not only undermines student growth but also misses the opportunity to shape behavior through teaching, just as we do with any other subject.

Labeling a student as a "bad kid" sends the message that the student is inherently flawed and not fixable, when in reality, it's the behavior that needs addressing. This approach makes it seem as though the problem lies within the student, rather than in their behavior, and can lead to a sense of hopelessness for both the student and teacher. Even when the focus is on behavior, it's often centered on eliminating undesirable actions, rather than fostering growth and reinforcing positive behaviors. This mindset prevents the opportunity to guide students toward the behavior we want to see. For educators aiming to effectively manage and mitigate misbehavior, it's essential to anticipate such challenges and view them as opportunities for instruction and growth. Common responses such as disciplinary referrals, admonishments, and suspensions may seem effective for immediate control of the situation or for most students, but they often fail to address the underlying causes of misbehavior, particularly in students who exhibit chronic issues. As we'll discuss, effective punishment should decrease the occurrence of unwanted behavior. If misbehavior persists, then our strategies are not only failing as deterrents but may inadvertently reinforce the behaviors we seek to discourage.

By concentrating on what students should avoid rather than what they should do, we miss critical teachable moments and could be setting up an escalation of behavioral issues. This is not the outcome we desire for any educator or student.

Addressing challenging behaviors is part of the job and requires us to work within the constraints we're given. Yet, if we can shift our perspective to see problematic behaviors as opportunities for intervention—much like a teacher adjusts their methods to meet the diverse needs of their students—we can begin to make real progress.

What you will learn in this book is that behavior is purposeful. Whether seeking attention, avoiding unpleasant tasks, or responding to other factors, each action a person takes serves a function that, if met with appropriate consequences, shapes future behavior. Recognizing this allows us to teach more suitable behaviors that fulfill the same needs, thereby transforming challenges into opportunities for positive change.

We also address common misconceptions and stigmas about reinforcement and punishment. More importantly, we provide actionable guidance on creating systems and leveraging procedures to minimize student misbehavior while promoting prosocial behavior and boosting academic achievement.

When implemented with fidelity, the strategies outlined in this book can lead to significant improvements across various domains, including

- enhanced focus on academic instruction
- boosted morale among students and educators
- increased instructional time
- higher student achievement
- reductions in misbehavior
- fewer classroom removals
- decreases in detentions and in-school suspensions
- fewer out-of-school suspensions
- less effort required from teachers and school leaders at all levels

Children learn from their environments and experiment with behaviors that, if successful, will likely be repeated. While we can't alter their genetics or their history, we can change their environment in a way that optimizes behavior and learning. Despite the significant influence of a child's home life and past experiences, the most immediate and influential environment is the school setting. Here, how attention is directed, tasks assigned, and behaviors managed play pivotal roles in shaping student actions.

When educators understand the function behind a student's behavior and tailor their own responses accordingly, they not only aid the individual student, but they enhance the overall classroom environment. As a result, students are more likely to adopt beneficial behaviors and contribute positively to their educational setting and society at large.

Addressing widespread behavioral issues demands a concerted, systematic effort from both classroom and school leaders. Breakdowns in any part of this system can have ripple effects, potentially creating a "behavioral avalanche:" that negatively impacts school climate and culture. Therefore, it's crucial to connect in-classroom events with broader school dynamics.

With this in mind, the book is structured into three distinct sections:

1. **Classroom Leadership:** This section provides teachers with evidence-based strategies and step-by-step protocols to effectively manage misbehavior and reduce its occurrence.

2. **School Leadership:** This section equips school leaders and their teams to address more significant behavioral challenges and reduce out-of-school suspensions through systematic, organizational behavior management techniques.

3. **Appendices:** The appendices include a number of procedures, including some that are not directly discussed in the book, offering additional resources for both classroom and school leaders.

While each section has its own focus, both teachers and administrators should read the entire book to fully grasp how classroom and school leadership work together to create a cohesive environment. The strategies we'll explore will empower you to address and amend these challenges effectively, which will significantly ease your professional journey and enrich your students' educational experiences.

SECTION I:

Classroom Leadership for Reducing Misbehavior

CHAPTER 1

Why Are We Here? What's the Problem?

The Perfect Storm

On the first morning of the school year, the earliest bus of the day arrives at its designated zone at the Title I school and unloads students into a scenario devoid of adult supervision. This lack of oversight allows the children's exit from the bus to devolve into a tumult of shoving and shouting. The bus driver's stern warnings to "Stop all that foolishness!" go unheeded as the students dash toward the cafeteria, their voices and curses reverberating through the courtyard and the front office. The disorder is not limited to noise disturbances; during breakfast, the chaos continues as students push in line and food frequently finds its way to the floor or is hurled across the room, leaving custodians to manage the ensuing mess.

By the second day, the staff member tasked with overseeing breakfast, already drained from the previous day's tumult, attempts to impose order with threats of silent lunches and calls home. Despite these efforts, the chaos persists throughout the day and permeates every transition—from classroom to classroom, and eventually back to the buses. Open defiance and frequent verbal abuse directed at adults is commonplace. Moreover, physical altercations become a regular occurrence and disrupt educational activities and common areas alike. Several incidents result in injuries to both students and staff, one of which is severe enough to require hospitalization. This ongoing upheaval drains valuable instructional time and compels school leaders to divert their focus from academics to managing behavioral crises.

As the weeks turn into months, the narrative of student behavior dominating the campus solidifies. The continued struggles indicate an escalation of chaos, which leads to increased suspensions, more entrenched behavioral problems, and a cycle that culminates in a fatigued staff, diminished academic performance, and a faculty overwhelmed by the relentless demands of managing such disruptions.

Despite the evident issues, our consultancy was only brought in to assist at the year's end. Upon initial evaluation, we observed that school administrators and instructional coaches were continually being pulled away from their primary educational responsibilities to address the waves of misbehavior that overwhelmed the school. Teachers lost critical instructional time, and student academic achievement plummeted. The discipline referral data suggested there were about 10 major behavioral incidents daily, but the logs of calls for administrative intervention often exceeded 40 per day.

Early in the school year, administrators had attempted to mitigate these issues by asking teachers to identify their most challenging students for referral to problem-solving team meetings. This initiative resulted in nearly 300 students' names being added to the problem-solving team list—a staggering number considering the school held only 600 students. Regrettably, the sheer volume of referrals and the limited number of school days meant that most of these scheduled meetings never took place, and so the misbehavior was allowed to continue largely unaddressed.

This dire situation was the result of several systemic failures, which together created what can be described as the perfect storm. One significant factor was the cessation of a bussing program designed to diversify the student body socioeconomically. Studies support the benefits of such diversity on student achievement and school success, as students are positively influenced by the behaviors, hopes, dreams, and aspirations of their peers (e.g., Balfanz & Legters, 2004; Basile, 2012; Palardy, 2008). The removal of the bussing program—deemed necessary due to budget constraints—had a markedly detrimental effect.

Moreover, the school experienced a complete overhaul in leadership at a critical time. A new administration took the helm, including both a principal and an assistant principal in their first year. These individuals, while well-intentioned and desiring to provide robust instructional leadership to support their teachers and foster student success, quickly found themselves outmatched by the escalating behavioral crisis. Furthermore, 80% of the teaching staff was new, with most in their first or second year of teaching. These educators, many of whom had neither work experience nor training to help them handle the complex challenges associated with Title I school environments, found themselves ill-prepared for the behavioral issues they encountered. This gap in preparation is not entirely their fault; most university education programs lack dedicated courses on classroom and behavior management, and thus many teachers are unequipped to deal effectively with such challenges.

The absence of basic routines and procedures for managing student behavior systematically meant that misbehavior often went unchecked. This led to a decline in collective teacher efficacy. As misbehavior escalated, teachers' beliefs in their ability to prevent or manage it diminished, which in turn impacted their collective efforts to even attempt to manage these challenges. By the end of the school year, the school had recorded over 900 suspensions—a drastic increase from the 23 reported the previous year. The school's grade plummeted from an A to an F as a result.

This case exemplifies the critical need for a focus on systemic issues rather than on individual student misbehavior. Schools such as this require a well-designed system to prevent and manage misbehavior effectively. Without strategic changes to address these systemic issues, educational institutions will continue to struggle and will remain caught in a perpetual cycle of behavioral crises that detracts from their primary educational missions. This narrative not only highlights the severity of the situation but also demonstrates the urgent need for educational reforms that prioritize effective behavior management and systemic process improvements that will stabilize the educational environment and ensure academic success for all students.

Let us be clear, it is not that these educators lacked initial enthusiasm or that the schools were devoid of robust plans. Indeed, most educators were highly motivated, and several of the plans were well conceived. However, successfully activating these plans and cultivating an environment that enhances motivation often necessitates a precise behavioral strategy that begins with the leadership team—a theme we will explore more thoroughly in Section II.

In this school system, the subsequent year brought about notable changes: The same cohort of students (albeit a grade older) remained, but there was a new administrative team and, once again, a staff composed of 80% new teachers. As we moved into the new school year, we contributed to transforming the school into a more effective learning environment. The school's climate, or shared perception, saw substantial improvement, which in turn positively influenced the culture, or shared behavior, within the school. Remarkably, the number of suspensions plummeted from the previous year's record of over 900 to fewer than 100. This drastic reduction was not solely the result of implementing a dedicated room as an alternative to suspension (i.e., a QUICK Room)—although we will explain this initiative in more detail later—it was also due to the systematic application of strategies grounded in the science of human behavior.

While we take pride in these achievements, the real accolades belong to the teachers and school leaders. It was their diligent effort that made the difference. Our role was simply to guide them by employing the scientific methods detailed in this book, thereby making their challenging tasks more manageable. Before we explore the specific approaches and tools that can foster positive change, let us briefly review some research to further underscore the importance of the evidence-based methods we advocate and will elaborate on in the later chapters.

What the Research Says

Safe and orderly schools and classrooms provide the fundamental structure for improving student achievement. Disruptive student behavior impacts student performance, as critical instruction time is redirected toward behavior management (Musti-Rao & Haydon, 2011). Westling (2010) suggested, "There may be no greater hurdle in public schools today than that presented by students who exhibit challenging behavior" (p. 48). As a result, educators continue to search for workable solutions to deal with the problems created by challenging student behaviors within the school setting (Sailor et al., 2009; Valenti & Kerr, 2015). Oliver et al. (2011) found that educators who are challenged with misbehavior in the classroom are more likely to experience stress and burnout. Even with an abundance of research supporting effective behavior management and classroom management strategies, educators overwhelmingly cite discipline and behavior problems in school as a major concern and determining factor for leaving the field (Liu & Meyer, 2005; Martella et al., 2012; Westling, 2010).

Poorly conceived, traditional reactive consequences to misbehavior include student removal from the classroom without solid procedures and out-of-school suspension. These have proven ineffective and even counterproductive to managing and reducing problem behaviors (Hirschfield, 2008; Martinez, 2009; Morris & Perry, 2016; Mosca & Hollister, 2004; Perry & Morris, 2014). Many school systems have used (and use) unsystematic approaches that are not rooted in behavioral science. Subsequently, school-wide proactive and systematic behavior management systems such as School-Wide Positive Behavioral Interventions and Supports (SW-PBIS) have emerged in an effort to prevent misbehavior from occurring (Childs et al., 2015; Lewis & Sugai, 2017; Skiba & Peterson, 2000). These approaches have widely documented success. However, even with the best preventative initiatives in place, misbehavior is still likely to occur, especially in the initial stages of any system change. When misbehavior does occur, it is important for consequences to be in place that reduce the likelihood that the misbehavior will reoccur. Sadly, with so much focus on prevention, consequences intended to correct misbehavior often inadvertently reinforce and increase the undesired misbehaviors. The result is more misbehavior and the false belief that all of this positive reinforcement mumbo jumbo doesn't work.

To complicate matters, people come into schools with existing biases regarding behavior and how to manage it based on their own learning histories (McIntosh et al., 2014). Some of these biases are overt and recognized by the individuals holding them; however, other biases are implicit (McIntosh et al., 2014) and lurk under the surface, where they shape individual perception and behavior. For instance, consider the teacher who believes a student remains "bad" throughout the school year. Though the student may be improving behaviorally (e.g., calling out 10 times instead of calling out 20 times), the teacher is understandably tired of the student regularly disrupting the classroom. Consequently, the teacher tends to only recognize the student's misbehavior rather than any progressive improvement. This is known in some circles as the "horn effect." Recognizing progress under these conditions can be difficult for anyone! The same can occur in reverse. For example, there are teachers or leaders who can "do no wrong" because of their history of success. These people tend to be inflexible and ignore errors and shortcomings; this is known as the "halo effect."

Because people enter schools with existing beliefs and responses to certain stimuli in the environment, misbehavior especially tends to catch their attention and reinforce those beliefs. As they recognize the stimuli (specific misbehaviors), this tends to confirm their beliefs, a phenomenon called "confirmation bias."

Research to Practice

While rooted in behavior science, this book is purposely application based. Our goal is to translate research into practice by presenting school administrators, teachers, and stakeholders with simple procedures that will provide the most effective methods for correcting misbehavior. We present procedures we have used ourselves to achieve positive outcomes. As such, we focus on bringing the science of human behavior to life through real stories to illustrate the application of concepts and procedures within the school setting. To support you in this area, Appendix 1 includes a simple menu that categorizes misbehavior and recommends specific and practical ways to correct it.

Remember, this book is intended to complement preventive systems such as School-Wide Positive Behavioral Interventions and Supports (SW-PBIS) by helping educators understand, apply, and help each other employ effective, proactive strategies to increase positive and prosocial behavior alongside effective reactive strategies. Specifically, we aim to provide strategies that reduce misbehavior, even in "frequent fliers" who have historically not responded to discipline strategies outlined in the school's typical code of conduct manual. Not only do we provide easier-to-follow systems for quickly responding to and managing misbehavior in and out of the classroom, but we also provide strategies rooted in organizational behavior management (OBM), which is the application of behavior science to groups and organizations to rapidly get these systems up and running.

We have intentionally focused on making interventions quick and practical because we recognize that the complexity and effort required is directly related to the likelihood an educator or school will adopt a new approach. In Appendices 2–14, we've highlighted strategies for addressing behaviors. Based on the type of behavior, you can use our examples of consequences listed in Appendix 1 in combination with the strategy or procedure chosen to address it. For example, if a student is being mildly disruptive, you can follow our procedures for verbal redirection and/or setting limits (Appendices 4 & 5).

QUICK responses include the following elements:

- **Q**uestioning
- **U**nconditional positive regard
- **I**ntermittent reinforcement
- **C**onstructive
- **K**eep it brief

This book and the examples within are certainly not a knock on educators. The frequency, duration, and intensity (effort) required of any behavior in relation to the valued outcomes it produces are critical to the success of any initiative, anywhere. Think about this. If we asked you to dig a ditch, would you? The answer is likely no—unless you knew us, maybe liked us, or if digging the ditch produced some valued outcome. If you were a missionary, for example, the outcome of digging a big ditch might be access to life-giving water for a community of people who had to walk an hour to the river every day to obtain it. If you valued helping people and making their lives easier (and we know you do because you are reading this), that outcome might be enough to sustain your behavior of ditch digging, even if, like us, you hate digging ditches!

But what if there were some other variables? For example,

- The ditch needed to be 100 feet deep.
- You were only given a spoon to dig it.
- You were doing it alone.
- You estimated the time required to dig the ditch with the spoon would be 3 months.
- You had physical ailments that made ditch digging hard.
- The daily temperature was typically in the 90s, with high humidity.
- Nobody brought you additional water to compensate for the excessive sweating.
- No one recognized your progress—even if it was small.

Would you dig the ditch under these conditions? Maybe. Maybe not. The point is that the amount of effort required to achieve an outcome is critically important. And people often highlight that one school that was successful, that one year. And they say, "Well they did it, so you should be able to do it too." This neglects the superhuman—and typically unsustainable—behavior required to do it. It's easy to point fingers at educators when they fail, until you've walked in their shoes and had to dig that behavioral ditch armed with a spoon. Sure, it can be done. But at what cost? But we digress, and we know we are preaching to the choir!

Here's the promising aspect of our approach: The foundational principles we propose for removing students from the classroom and implementing alternatives to traditional suspensions require less effort than you might expect. Ultimately, these methods could prove to be the most viable and effective replacements for well-intentioned, yet often ineffective, in-class corrections, out-of-class time-outs, detentions, and both internal and external suspension programs. Of course, the decision to adopt these strategies rests with you.

As you begin to steer your "behavioral ship" in the right direction, it's important to recognize that misbehavior won't pause while you adjust your course. The transition to effective prevention strategies takes time to embed within the school culture. During this transitional phase, it's crucial to ensure that the consequences assigned for misbehavior don't exacerbate the problems. This means establishing robust and efficient systems that enable consistent and effective responses to behavioral issues.

Implementing these systems involves more than just a temporary fix; it requires a strategic overhaul that addresses the immediate needs, while fostering a long-term environment conducive to positive student behavior. Such systems not only provide immediate responses to issues as they arise but also build a framework that supports the gradual adoption and effectiveness of preventative measures. This dual approach ensures that while the necessary adjustments are being made, the school maintains a functional and constructive learning environment for all students.

Key Points

- System failures significantly impact student achievement and behavior.
- A perfect storm of events and system failures can contribute to increased misbehavior and suspensions, decreased academic performance, and a school's inability to retain faculty and staff.
- Many teachers leave the profession, citing student discipline problems as one of the top reasons.
- New teachers are often underprepared to meet the challenges and demands of the classroom.
- Most college and university programs do not provide adequate training to teachers in classroom management.
- Most teachers are not trained to support students navigating behavioral challenges.
- Administrators are pulled into managing student discipline and, as a result, are not able to attend to their instructional leadership duties.
- Schools must have basic routines and procedures in place to systematically guide the collective behavior of the teachers, staff, and school leaders.
- Educators must believe in their abilities to prevent or manage student misbehavior. If educators are working hard and not producing the desired impact on student behavior, they are more likely to stop trying.
- Disruptive student behavior negatively impacts student performance, as instruction time is redirected toward managing problem behavior in the classroom.
- The frequency, duration, and intensity (effort) required of any behavioral intervention in relation to the valued outcomes it produces are critical to its success.

Reflect on It

- What are some of your concerns about managing student behavior in your classroom?
- When and where did you receive training or preparation in classroom management? Was it sufficient training? What questions do you still have about classroom management and student misbehavior?
- How prepared do you feel to meet the demands of the classroom? What have you done to prepare? What else do you need to do to expand your knowledge?
- Does your school have a school-wide behavior-management system? If so, how is it working?
- Do you have a classroom management plan? If yes, how is it working? If not, what do you need to consider in creating an effective classroom-management plan for your classroom?
- If you are a school administrator with a school-wide behavior-management plan, how confident are you in it? Have your staff been well trained in the procedures outlined? Do they receive regular coaching to ensure habit development?

CHAPTER 2

Consequences of Behavior: Reinforcement, Punishment, and Misunderstandings

While this book is dedicated to reactive procedures for decreasing the future occurrence of misbehavior, we think a reminder of the obvious is warranted here. Engaging curriculum and instruction presented at the student's skill level is the first and most effective strategy for preventing misbehavior. This, paired with consistent positive reinforcement (more on what this really is shortly), will prevent many misbehaviors from occurring. If the student truly feels that the classroom is of little value to them, it is important to make adjustments (e.g., increase positive attention, differentiate instruction, use active student responding strategies) to increase the reinforcement available (e.g., enjoy interacting with the teacher more, enjoy learning and getting good grades) so the student is more likely to learn and remain on task within the classroom. No student wants to attend a school where they do not feel safe, valued, and that they are doing something meaningful. The same can be said for adults and their work environments. It seems like common sense. But common sense can get lost under the stressful conditions often produced by chronic misbehavior.

The Good

OK, back to the term "positive reinforcement." Unfortunately, there are many misconceptions about positive reinforcement. In fact, there are several arguments against using positive reinforcement in the classroom. Have you ever said or heard, "I've tried positive reinforcement and it doesn't work!" or, "Why do students need rewards to do their work?" These arguments about incentives or rewarding behavior frequently equate positive reinforcement to bribery. It is thought that somehow using positive reinforcement isn't equitable to students not receiving the rewards, and that it only serves to harm motivation. There's also fear that students will get "hooked" on praise and tangibles. Indeed, dependence on reinforcers does necessitate monitoring. Good behavior should include plans for fading as well as pairing positive feedback with delivery of more concrete reinforcers. The problem with reinforcement is that these misconceptions are stated as facts, and they undermine an approach with decades of research supporting its effectiveness. All behavior (apart from reflexes—automatic physiological responses to stimuli) occurs as a result of the reinforcing consequences it produces. When we say consequences, we are not referring to the application of a disciplinary measure intended to stop or decrease misbehavior. Behavioral consequences are things that follow a behavior and increase or decrease the likelihood the behavior will happen again in the future (Daniels, 2016). In other words, we are simply referring to something occurring after a behavior, as a result of the behavior.

Reinforcement and Reinforcers

If a consequence serves to strengthen or maintain a behavior, we call the consequence a reinforcer. The goal is to strengthen the behavior we want to see. There are times we inadvertently reinforce misbehavior when the consequence produced increases the likelihood the student will engage in the behavior again in the future. But let's dig a little deeper, as this concept is very important and at the root of successful behavior improvement.

Positive Reinforcement

Many well-intended people attempt to apply positive reinforcement. Positive reinforcement, though, cannot be measured by intent, only by its impact on behavior: Did the behavior continue or increase? So, what exactly is positive reinforcement? Think about it this way: Positive reinforcement is what gets you to do something or engage in a particular behavior, such as going to work. What do you get out of going to work, and why do you continue to do it? Well, we would guess that one reason you go to work is to get paid. By showing up for work and staying for the required amount of time, the consequence you receive is a paycheck (see Table 2.1).

Table 2.1. Positive Reinforcement at Work

Antecedent	Behavior	Consequence
I have bills to pay.	I show up for work and stay for the required amount of time.	I get a paycheck (reinforcer).
If I continue to show up for work or increase my work attendance, the paycheck can be said to be a reinforcer. More specifically, a positive reinforcer.		

The paycheck is just one positive reinforcer for working. If you are like most educators, you likely find true value in helping students achieve. The positive reinforcement or "pay," so to speak, isn't just financial. It comes from facilitating achievement. This is where people get confused, as they think of positive reinforcement as transactional in nature. In other words, they think it's about somebody giving something to somebody else for what they've done or perhaps to get them to do more of what they've done. There is no money for student achievement, just that great feeling you get by fostering it. And it makes you want to do it again, and again, and again! This is to say that your behavior of helping students achieve has been positively reinforced by the outcomes it produced. Now, of course, if you didn't get paid, would you continue to show up? What if you only got paid in verbal praise from your boss—would you continue then? As much as you might enjoy teaching and want to help students learn (two big positive reinforcers for educators), there is a good chance you wouldn't show up to work, as there are several bad outcomes associated with not having money to pay the bills!

Let's continue to dive deeper into this all-important concept. Positive reinforcement is a stimulus, something added to the environment that increases behavior. Positive reinforcement works when a person comes into contact with a motivating or preferred stimulus after engaging in a behavior, making it more likely that the behavior will occur again in the future. Basically, if I do this (whatever "this" is), something good (something I like) happens, and I'll probably do whatever that was again. When attempting to improve or increase some behavior, many people say, "We are giving him positive reinforcement, but he's still calling out instead of raising his hand." While these folks are well-intentioned and are likely delivering something in a "positive" way, the only way to determine if that something is a reinforcer, and in this case a positive reinforcer, is to assess the impact on behavior. Is the behavior occurring more as a result? If it is, then the "something" serves as a positive reinforcer. In this example, if the student is not raising his hand more, whatever was being delivered, no matter how nice it was, did not serve as positive reinforcement for hand raising.

In the example above, if a student is calling out to gain attention (a positive reinforcer) from the teacher, each time the teacher addresses the student in an attempt to correct the calling out, even providing a reprimand may inadvertently reinforce the calling-out behavior. This is where things can get warped: People often inadvertently reinforce the very behavior they would like to limit. This unknowingly creates a ripple effect of problems for them. What eventually proves to be the most effective tool for educators—the widespread, liberal use of positive reinforcement—can initially work against educators if it is not well understood and deliberately applied.

Now think about your reinforcers again. What are some of those reasons you show up for work? Helping kids, imparting knowledge, interacting with or helping other educators, and getting paid! Reinforcers are idiosyncratic, they are highly individualized, and your reasons for showing up for work may not be the same as your colleagues'. And sometimes, your reasons—your reinforcers—might change. If you won the lottery, for example, perhaps money would not be as motivating as helping students or your peers. And the same goes for your students. Just because some students are motivated to earn stickers doesn't mean all students will work for them, or even that the same student will work for them all the time.

It is essential to remember that it's the student's behavior that decides what's reinforcing. Just because you think the student should like the item or activity doesn't necessarily mean it will get them motivated to do their work or behave appropriately. Their behavior will tell you. Just remember that some things are more or less motivating on a given day! For example, you don't always carry an umbrella with you, but if you have ever been caught in a torrential rainstorm, we bet you wish you had one. On that day, that umbrella would be very reinforcing. The value of having an umbrella under these conditions is much higher than having it on a sunny day.

One last example before we move on. How many people would say a glass of water is an effective potential reinforcer? We could say with certainty that if you were in the desert for days without water or food, the glass of water, which on most days would possibly not be that important, would be more valuable than any amount of money. Now let's move on to another term that confuses a lot of people: negative reinforcement.

Negative Reinforcement

So, what exactly is negative reinforcement? Well, here is a hint: It has nothing to do with bad or good. It is not a value judgment. Think about a young child. When her diaper is dirty, she cries. Her parent hears her crying and changes her into a clean diaper. As a result, she stops crying and smiles. Now every time the child has a dirty diaper, she cries. The dirty diaper is aversive (disliked, producing discomfort and the need for alleviation) to the child, and she has learned that crying (the behavior) will remove the aversive stimulus (the dirty diaper). In this case, the child's crying behavior is being negatively reinforced. Specifically, the dirty diaper or discomfort is being removed. The crying behavior is likely to recur when the child's diaper is dirty. This is negative reinforcement (see Table 2.2). And in this case, it's probably a good thing!

Table 2.2.
Negative Reinforcement for a Young Child

Antecedent	Behavior	Consequence
Young child has a dirty diaper.	Child cries.	Parent removes the dirty diaper (removes an aversive).
If the child continues to cry or cries more often when she has a dirty diaper, then the removal of the dirty diaper can be said to be a reinforcer. More specifically, a negative reinforcer.		

The parent in this example is also experiencing negative reinforcement. When the parent hears the child crying, stopping the crying becomes motivating to the parent. Changing the dirty diaper stops the crying. This would make any parent happy. It also means the parent is more likely to change the baby's diaper in the future.

Negative reinforcement isn't punishment. Negative reinforcement occurs when an aversive stimulus is removed after a behavior and increases the likelihood that behavior will occur again in the future. When we discuss the things people generally do to avoid, escape, prevent, or remove themselves from situations, we are talking about negative reinforcement. Reinforcement increases behavior, whether it is positive or negative. The terms "positive" and "negative" simply mean that something is added to the environment (positive) or removed from the environment (negative). A meaningful consequence occurs as a result of behavior—like showing up for work or crying. Specifically, attention or an item is added (positive reinforcement) or discomfort is subtracted (negative reinforcement). In any event, this adding or subtracting of stimuli that increase occurrences of behavior (be it desirable or undesirable) is known as positive or negative reinforcement. This is a key element for understanding reinforcement and using it effectively (see Table 2.3).

Table 2.3. Positive Versus Negative Reinforcement

What is the effect or outcome of the behavior?	Behavior increases
	The behavior continues or is used more frequently than before the person experienced the consequence.
Behavior results from something being **added** (+) to the learner's environment.	Positive reinforcement (+)
Behavior results from something being **subtracted** (-) from the learner's environment.	Negative reinforcement (-)

- **Reinforcement** always means an **increase** in behavior.
- **Positive** simply means we **added** something after the behavior.
- **Negative** simply means we **removed** something after the behavior.

Because words like "consequences," "extinction," "positive," "negative," and "punishment" are borrowed from everyday language, the general public assigns a meaning different from the meaning used in the science of behavior (Foxx, 1996; Ledoux, 2014). This type of verbiage has served as a source of confusion because people use words like "positive" or "negative" in everyday language to describe something as being "good" or "bad." So if you've been confused, don't worry. You aren't alone! In the science of human behavior, positive or negative are not value judgments. They simply mean, as illustrated by the paycheck and crying examples above, that something (a stimulus) is added (positive) or subtracted (negative).

Misconceptions

A pervasive fallacy is that using positive reinforcement is akin to bribery. While bribery may happen when people do not understand how to use the power of positive reinforcement, there is a major difference between the positive reinforcement and bribery. Bribes occur before a behavior. They are given to try to motivate a person to engage in an action. Reinforcement occurs contingent (i.e., depending) on a behavior as a consequence following the action. It is focused on strengthening or increasing the future occurrences of that behavior. For example, if an elementary school student begins using a mathematical concept correctly for the first time, the teacher might say, "Johnny, I noticed you carried the 2 over. As a result, you got the answer correct. Great job!" Johnny is likely to continue carrying the 2 and may also make more attempts to produce correct answers. Beyond these two major differences noted here, bribes often have immoral or illegal implications and fail to produce long-term behavior change.

Another misconception is that positive reinforcement must be delivered by somebody, or what is referred to as social mediation. For example, when a teacher gives a student a sticker for behaving appropriately, we call that socially mediated positive reinforcement. In the example above, the math teacher praised Johnny for using a new concept. The teacher also pointed out that by using the concept, Johnny got the problem correct. If Johnny finds it valuable to get problems correct, he will be more likely to use the mathematical strategy again, even in the absence of teacher praise or a sticker. The feedback from the teacher, as well as the affirmation of getting an answer correct, has important, lasting implications for both the teacher and the student. One of these implications may be the attempt to learn and the production of correct answers without the need to always have the teacher mediating the reinforcers.

This type of reinforcement, occurring without the presence of the teacher, is known as naturally occurring reinforcement, which is the holy grail for educators. The only way to get students to go above and beyond even when no one is looking is to get them in touch with naturally occurring positive reinforcement. Some folks call this "intrinsic" reinforcement. It essentially means the reinforcement is inherent to the activity (e.g., I like reading, so reading is reinforcing; I like to help people, so helping people is reinforcing; I like doing math, so solving math problems is reinforcing). An adult or other person is not necessary for me to continue these activities. The activity itself is the reinforcer. The more that students find an activity engaging, the more likely they are to do it, even if nobody tells them to do so.

The goal of the teacher should always be to get students in touch with this kind of natural reinforcement. However, if reading, doing math, or helping others is not reinforcing to the individual, the goal is to get them there through what is sometimes called "extrinsic" reinforcement. By pairing something of value (e.g., a sticker, verbal praise) with the behavior of helping people, for example, the goal is that the impact of helping the person eventually replaces the extrinsic reinforcement with naturally occurring reinforcement. In other words, students may think, "I like helping people. It's a great thing. It positively impacts others, and it makes me feel good and valued." The goal should be for the educator to help the students see the positive impact of their helping behavior on others, their environment, and themselves and then to gradually reduce the delivery of extrinsic reinforcement such as a sticker, praise, and so forth. When students expect to receive something for an expected behavior, it is a problem. This problem usually lies in a failure to pair reinforcement and behavior or a failure to reduce/fade the reinforcement over time.

Potential Drawbacks to Positive Reinforcement

We would be remiss if we did not speak briefly on the potential negative effects of positive reinforcement. In his play *As You Like It*, Shakespeare asks, "Can one desire too much of a good thing?" (1623/2012). The answer here is emphatically, "Yes!" Remember, "good" is subjective—reinforcement is not. Because behavior tends to go "where reinforcement flows," as Aubrey Daniels (2000, p. 55) notes, when reinforcement is abundant during activities considered detrimental, then reinforcement can be bad. Behaviors such as overeating, drug abuse, stealing, and cheating are detrimental behaviors being maintained by contingencies of positive reinforcement. Positive reinforcement, as you now know, is not "good." It is simply a desirable consequence that follows a behavior, and the behavior is likely to recur, regardless of whether the behavior is perceived as adaptive (prosocial, desirable, functional actions) or problematic.

In some cases, the removal or absence of reinforcement under conditions where a behavior has previously contacted reinforcement can lead to unintended outcomes. Michael Perone (2003), in his article "Negative Effects of Positive Reinforcement," provides an illustrative example from his experience as a university professor. To encourage attendance, he awarded additional points to students who attended every class. As Perone explains, "Whenever a reinforcer is contingent on behavior, it must be denied" (p. 7). Students who did not attend every class were not penalized, but they also could not earn the additional points.

While this contingency was designed to increase attendance by positively reinforcing it, some students perceived the lack of points as a form of "denial" or punishment. This perception likely arose because access to the additional points was contingent on their presence in class. Thus, what was intended to promote attendance inadvertently created negative feelings among some students who missed classes. Perone's example highlights how the absence of reinforcement, though not a punishment in the technical sense, can be misinterpreted as such, leading to undesirable side effects.

We see similar effects in schools where students who received reinforcers in the past become upset when they cannot access their usual, expected positive reinforcers. Moreover, when an abundance of positive reinforcement is available but is far beyond the natural environment, generalization of these behaviors (i.e., behaving appropriately under normal conditions) becomes an issue. Consider the following example: A teacher makes $200,000 a year (and we believe they deserve it!) in one district and then moves to another district where they make $100,000. Even if this was twice the national average, the teacher may not find this amount suitable because of their previous salary. This can cause strife and demotivate the teacher who desires their previous salary, or the student who desires the previously high rate of preferable activities, attention, and so forth.

This is one reason why positive reinforcement should be supported by reasonable forms of correction intended to teach students adaptive behavior. In other words, there typically should be a reasonable amount of positive reinforcement within the environment to create a suitable want for students as well as a reasonable amount of punishment available that serves as a deterrent—something most students want to avoid. For example, teacher reprimands often function to reduce in-class problem behavior. Students in classrooms where positive reinforcement is plentiful often engage in actions to produce that reinforcement and avoid punishment.

Punishment

In many cases, the topic of punishment has become so taboo that people refrain from even using the word. When you saw us use the word above, you might have even felt a little uncomfortable. While punishment has become a "naughty" word in education, it is, in fact, not. As described earlier, there is a misconception of what punishment actually is because the word is borrowed from everyday language (Foxx, 1996). A true punisher is something added (positive punisher) or subtracted (negative punisher) that decreases the future occurrence of a behavior (see Table 2.4). If this is misbehavior, then punishment can be beneficial. Like reinforcement, we only know something serves as a punisher if it decreases the future occurrence of a behavior (Cooper et al., 2020).

Table 2.4. Positive Versus Negative Punishment

What is the effect or outcome of the behavior?	Behavior decreases
	The behavior ceases or is used less often than before the person experienced the consequence.
Behavior stops from something being **added** (+) to the learner's environment.	Positive punishment (+)
Behavior stops from something being **subtracted** (-) from the learner's environment.	Negative punishment (-)

- **Punishment** always means a **decrease** in behavior.
- **Positive** simply means we **added** something after the behavior.
- **Negative** simply means we **removed** something after the behavior.

The problem isn't about correcting misbehavior. The problem usually involves how, when, and how frequently we attempt to correct it relative to the amount of positive reinforcement being experienced by the student. If you are following a 4:1 ratio of positive reinforcement to correction (Madsen & Madsen, 1974, as cited in Daniels & Rosen, 1989), you are probably in good shape. For example, if a student is off task, a teacher may have to say, "Rebecca, please turn to page 57 and read quietly." This should serve as a prompt to find students who are on task and offer them positive feedback and perhaps even circle back to the redirected student if she is back on track: "Preston, I like the way you are focusing on reading"; "Kooper, your handwriting looks excellent"; "Jane, your concentration is outstanding"; and "Rebecca, thank you for getting back to work." Just be aware of how you are delivering that 1. If you speak to someone in a way that is mean or coercive (i.e., using pressure or intimidation to influence behavior), the ripple effects can be devastating to your relationship with the student and even with other students in your classroom. It can actually make students want to avoid you and can lead to a reduction in learning and increases in disruptive, unpredictable, and even aggressive behavior (Cooper et al., 2020).

When we say "punishing," we are not suggesting corporal punishment nor typical reactionary strategies such as discipline referrals and suspensions. Instead, we are referring to procedures designed to reduce the likelihood that problem behaviors will recur. By definition, punishment decreases behavior (if it doesn't, it's not punishment). While punishment is effective, it also comes with potentially problematic side effects (Lerman & Vorndran, 2002). For example, a teacher who successfully reduces problem behavior through punishment may be reinforced for using it, increasing the likelihood they will rely on punishment more frequently. This can lead to an overuse of punishment, often in the absence of reinforcement-based strategies.

It can become an ugly, vicious cycle. Oftentimes, the same people who view themselves as winning the battle end up losing the war, as they become dependent on the use of punishment and create aversive learning environments marred by reduced learning under the constant threat of coercion. While punishment should be understood and examined, it must be utilized sparingly and only within the context of a balanced, reinforcement-focused strategy to support lasting behavior change.

It is often said, "One lie can undo a thousand truths." We think this can be applied to the poor application of punishment. One highly coercive interaction can undo a thousand positive ones. Be careful of the tone, volume, and cadence of your voice, as well as your nonverbal behavior (Matsumoto et al., 2013). Make sure that punishment is directed at the behavior, not the student. For example, you wouldn't say, "Johnny, you are a bad boy." But you might say "Johnny, X, Y, and Z were bad behaviors, and here's why." The goal is to address the behavior and its associated outcomes, and to encourage appropriate behavior while refraining from criticizing the student. It's all about the behavior!

Many people threaten to punish but do not actually apply a reasonable consequence to effectively decrease or stop behavior. Suffice it to say, threats are not punishment. In fact, threatening can make behavior worse. If a parent threatens to take away their child's video games for throwing their clothes on the floor and the child doesn't correct their behavior (picking up the clothes), the threat does not serve as a punisher. If the parent takes away the video games but the child continues to throw their clothes on the floor, the video game removal being applied as if it were a punisher is, in fact, not a punisher. Only the impact on the child's behavior can dictate if the consequence is punishing. If the parent takes away the video games and the child stops throwing their clothes on the floor, then it could be considered a punisher.

This is why we prefer to use the term *correction*, as it encompasses a range of strategies that can serve multiple purposes. Correction refers to interventions designed not only to reduce the likelihood of problem behavior but also to promote skill acquisition, clarify expectations, and guide students toward appropriate alternatives. It is a more comprehensive approach than punishment, which simply decreases unwanted behavior without providing direction for what to do instead.

Correction can take many forms, such as prompting, modeling, redirection, or feedback. It serves to both interrupt undesired behavior and explicitly teach or reinforce desired behaviors. For example, punishment used by itself is insufficient because it does not instruct the student on the desired behavior. Consider the example above. The parent did not tell the child where to put their clothes, only that they should stop throwing them on the ground. So, what if the child began throwing their clothes on the bed? On the couch? In the sink? These examples highlight why teaching and reinforcement are critical.

Effective punishment reduces the problem—it teaches students what not to do. However, it is only a starting point. Reinforcement, on the other hand, establishes and maintains desired behaviors. Effective educators understand this distinction and leverage both strategies to support meaningful and lasting behavior change.

Exercise 2.1

Let's see if you can determine which is potentially the result of reinforcement or punishment as illustrated in the examples below. Think R for reinforcement, P for punishment, and N for not enough information. You can find the answer key at the end of the chapter, but try not to look at it until you've considered each example.

1. Miles's swearing behavior increases after the teacher praises him.
2. Ms. Von Thaden uses a random picker to choose students when asking questions. As a result, there is an increase in on-task behavior.
3. Ms. Goulbourne praises a student for raising their hand.
4. Each Monday during morning meetings, Mr. Hawkins "shouts out" the students who completed all of their daily 2-minute practice drills for the prior week. As a result, all of Mr. Hawkins's students complete their drills each week.
5. Pierre's calling out decreases after his teacher stands by his desk and continues to teach the lesson.
6. Scarlett's swearing stops after she receives a time-out from swearing from the coach during the soccer game.

Key Points

- Reinforcement is going on around us all the time, both positive and negative; planned or unplanned.
- Reinforcement is defined by its effect: It increases behavior.
- Positive reinforcement occurs when something that is added to the environment increases behavior.
- Negative reinforcement occurs when something that is removed from the environment increases behavior.
- Positive reinforcement cannot be measured by intent, only by its impact on behavior. If a consequence does not increase behavior, then it is not reinforcement.
- The holy grail for educators is reinforcement occurring without the presence of the teacher. This is known as naturally occurring reinforcement.
- The only way to get students to go above and beyond, even when no one is looking, is to get them in touch with naturally occurring positive reinforcement.
- Items and activities that function as reinforcers are idiosyncratic: What may be reinforcing to one student may not be reinforcing to another. Just because some students like stickers doesn't mean stickers will necessarily work for all students.
- The statement "positive reinforcement doesn't work" is a fallacy. If the consequence (in this case, reward, item, activity, or praise) does not strengthen or increase the student's behavior, then that consequence isn't reinforcement.
- Remember, bribery is not reinforcement. Bribery is unplanned and offers to do something for someone for the express purpose of receiving something in exchange.
- As with any other behavior, some students need to be taught how to engage in appropriate behavior in the classroom.
- Reinforcement of expectations and of appropriate classroom behaviors teaches students what to do.
- Being sensitive to how reinforcement and punishment impacts your students' behavior will help you teach more effectively, implement proactive strategies, and address problematic situations as they arise.
- A true punisher is something added (positive punisher) or subtracted (negative punisher) that decreases the future occurrence of a behavior.
- One highly coercive interaction can undo a thousand positive ones. This is the poor application of punishment.

Reflect on It

- What is the benefit of using reinforcement over punishment?
- What are some potential side effects of using punishment in the classroom?
- What are some potential added benefits of increasing classroom management by reinforcement rather than punishment?
- Is your ratio of praise to correction at least 4:1?

Exercise 2.1 Answer Key

1. **R.** There was an *increase* in swearing as a result of the teacher's praise. This one is tricky because when we hear praise, we tend to automatically place a value judgment on it (e.g., praise is good). But remember, reinforcement is about what happens to behavior, whether it's behavior we want or not. If Miles's behavior increased as a result of the teacher's praise, then the teacher's praise served to reinforce Miles's swearing.

2. **R.** There was an *increase* in on-task behavior as a result of using the random picker.

3. **N.** We need to know what happened as a result of the praise. Remember, it's about the impact on behavior. If the student raises their hand more as a result of the praise, we could say the praise is a reinforcer. If they raise their hand less as a result of the praise, we could say the praise is a punisher.

4. **R.** As a result of Mr. Hawkins's "shout outs," there was an *increase* in students completing their drills each week.

5. **P.** There was a *decrease* in Pierre's calling out, so his teacher's behavior served as a punisher. You see, in this case, the punisher "standing by the desk" can probably be considered acceptable. It resulted in behavior reduction and is not heavy-handed!

6. **P.** The behavior *stopped* as a result of the time-out. If the behavior of swearing increased, then the time-out would have actually been a reinforcer. For example, if Scarlett didn't like soccer, the time-out may have provided her with a break away from something she considered aversive.

CHAPTER 3

You Can Run, but You Can't Hide!

The Function of Behavior

It's a common observation that even excellent teachers can struggle with managing misbehavior, often due to inconsistencies in applying effective consequences. We don't want them—or you—to work harder than necessary. Teaching is inherently complex, and additional distractions or drains on your time and attention can further complicate your role. This brings us to the crucial concept of understanding the function of behavior, which is essential for addressing it appropriately.

The function of a behavior essentially refers to what the behavior achieves for the individual. It's about understanding why the behavior is happening. For instance, if escaping math is the function of a student tearing up a math sheet, ignoring the student, as opposed to providing another sheet and prompt to begin, would likely increase the likelihood the student might tear sheets in the future. This illustrates how picking an intervention cannot be arbitrary; rather, it should be based on the behavioral function so as not to inadvertently reinforce the undesired behavior.

Generally, behavior occurs for one of two fundamental reasons:

- to obtain something desirable (e.g., attention, a specific item, sensory stimulation)
- to avoid something undesirable (e.g., an unpleasant task, a stressful situation)

Drilling down from these reasons, we get to the common functions for students' misbehavior with the EATS acronym:

- Escape/avoid or delay (skill deficit or motivational deficit)
- Attention (from peers or staff)
- Tangible (access to things or activities)
- Sensory (feels good)

Grasping these functions allows you to strategically increase learning and prosocial behaviors while effectively reducing behavioral challenges. It's important to remember that these functions also apply to maintaining the behaviors you want to encourage. Table 3.1 provides simple examples to help you think about behaviors in terms of their functions.

Table 3.1. EATS: Escape, Attention, Tangible, and Sensory Behavior Functions

	Escape	Attention	Tangible	Sensory
What the Person Wants	Escape from person, task, environment, etc.	Attention from peers, adults	A specific item or activity	To feel good or lessen discomfort
When	In response to a specific person, event, or requests to perform an activity	When specific individuals are present (peer attention) Person-specific, not event- or location-specific	When the person wants access to some tangible object Not person-, event-, or location-specific	Anytime, anywhere Not person-, event-, or location-specific May occur more often when under stress
Example	Tasha screams at the teacher to be sent out of class to escape the reading assignment.	William tells a joke loudly to make his peers laugh.	Isaiah leaves his seat to grab his favorite toy from behind the teacher's desk.	Benjamin taps on the desk when he is bored.

By aligning your behavioral strategies with the identified functions, you create a more conducive learning environment that not only addresses misbehavior more effectively but also enhances the overall classroom dynamics. As illustrated in Table 3.2, this approach ensures that interventions are tailored to the specific needs and motivations of each student, leading to better outcomes and a more harmonious classroom.

Table 3.2. Behavioral Strategies According to Function

Example	Behavior	Apparent Function	Strategy
Escape	Student doodles during math class.	Avoiding difficult math problems	Provide step-by-step guidance and break tasks into manageable parts.
Attention	Student frequently shouts out answers.	Gaining teacher's and peers' attention	Teach the student appropriate ways to gain attention, such as raising their hand.
Tangible	Student steals a classmate's snack.	Obtaining a desired item	Teach social skills for requesting items they want and reinforce sharing behaviors.
Sensory	Student taps pencil loudly during tests.	Sensory feedback or stress relief	Provide alternative sensory tools such as stress balls, or allow for movement breaks.

The ABCs

Behavior occurs and persists over time primarily because of what transpires in the environment immediately following the behavior—the consequence—which often serves to reinforce the behavior. Additionally, behavior is influenced by physical and emotional states, and it evolves as children grow and develop new knowledge and skills. When analyzing behavior, it's important to consider not only the form of the behavior—how it manifests—but also its function.

You may be familiar with or have been tasked with collecting ABC data for a student's academic or behavioral assessment. ABC stands for antecedent, behavior, and consequence:

- **Antecedent** refers to the event or circumstance that precedes the behavior.
- **Behavior** is the action or interaction between the individual and the environment, which includes the people within that environment.
- **Consequence** is what follows the behavior.

Collecting ABC data can be critical because it can help identify patterns and potential functions of problem behaviors (refer to Appendix 15 for detailed guidance). Understanding the sequence of antecedents and consequences allows for the implementation of strategies that manage the effects of a behavior more effectively. When we learn to do this, rather than merely reacting in ways that may exacerbate the problem, we can make effective changes in our management of problem behaviors. Given the demanding nature of teaching, utilizing our time efficiently and avoiding counterproductive responses is essential.

Consider this scenario:

During independent math work, Joey draws pictures instead of completing his assignment. When his teacher prompts him to "get on task," Joey reacts by cursing and throwing his pencil, which leads to him being sent out of the classroom. This sequence has become a routine during math sessions.

Breaking it down
- **Antecedent:** The teacher tells Joey to get on task during math work.
- **Behavior:** Joey curses and throws his pencil.
- **Consequence:** Joey is sent out of the classroom.

Given that Joey's disruptive behavior persists, it is clear that it is being reinforced, not punished. If the behavior were being punished effectively, it would decrease. However, Joey's consistent removal from the classroom suggests that this consequence may actually be reinforcing the behavior. Why? In the alternative setting, Joey might receive more attention from staff, spend time with peers, and engage in preferred activities—all of which are more appealing than the math work he escapes.

The Inadvertent Reinforcer

Let's examine what typically happens when students are removed from the classroom. These students are often escorted to an alternative location, where they receive considerable attention from well-meaning staff and sometimes receive counseling sessions. They might also be asked to sit in the front office with two or three of their "frequent flier" friends—students known for their chronic misbehavior. Sometimes, to keep them occupied while administrators handle the necessary paperwork, they are given tasks or activities. If the student is particularly upset, they might be offered physical activities, such as doing push-ups or shooting basketballs, to help them calm down or release energy. In this way, misbehavior becomes a means to escape the classroom and the tasks at hand, engage in conversations with valued adults and peers, and gain access to enjoyable activities that aren't available during class.

From a functional perspective, this setup can inadvertently create a problematic incentive. If a student prefers not to engage with classwork, follow staff instructions, or stay in the designated area, misbehaving becomes a strategic option for removal from the classroom—a scenario that might be perceived as more appealing, akin to an escape to a paradise. This avoidance of what they perceive as aversive situations, or like being in a "pit," is counterproductive not just for the student but also for teachers and school leaders. In fact, it compounds the problem by reinforcing the very behaviors we aim to diminish. It's important to recognize that these students are not sent into a void; instead, our experience shows that frequent fliers are often removed to an environment that proves more reinforcing—a dynamic we describe as moving from "the pit to paradise."

For many students, removal from class as a consequence of misbehavior would serve as a deterrent, significantly reducing the likelihood of future disruptive behavior. However, for frequent fliers, this tactic clearly isn't effective, as evidenced by the continuous nature of their misbehavior. Let's delve deeper into understanding why these responses may be problematic and explore the broader issues they generate.

Consider this scenario:

As a self-described "inadvertent reinforcer," school administrator Mark Doe once believed he was aiding students and staff. However, he eventually realized his actions were compounding issues rather than resolving them. Below is a typical example of this cycle of student behaviors and Mark's habitual response.

Zach has just been handed a writing assignment that he is unwilling to tackle. Shortly after receiving the assignment, he starts making disruptive noises, which elicit chuckles from his classmates. Reacting to Zach's disruptions, his teacher gives a verbal reprimand: "Zach, be quiet."

For Zach, this reprimand signals that attention—which he perceives as reinforcement—is imminent. His response is to escalate the behavior by making more noises and even leaving his seat. After another warning, Zach defiantly declares, "I'm not doing this stupid stuff," which leads to a call for his removal from the classroom.

Here, Mark sees an opportunity to step in and "save the day." He envisions a scenario where he can fix Zach's behavior, return him to class, and emerge as a hero who alleviated the teacher's stress and helped Zach overcome a rough patch. He picks Zach up from the classroom, and as they walk and talk, Mark senses Zach is having a tough day; and he already knows of some family issues in Zach's home. Believing that a few basketball shots will remedy the issue, Mark takes Zach to the basketball court.

After some time shooting hoops, Zach seems in better spirits, prompting Mark to decide it is time to head back to class. However, on their way back, Zach's demeanor shifts to sad and irritated. Mark quickly concludes that Zach hasn't fully released his pent-up frustrations. "I know swhat to do," he thinks. "I'll take him to the weight room since he loves it there!"

After a 30-minute session in the weight room, a now-smiling Zach is transitioned back to his classroom, with Mark feeling triumphant, believing he has successfully turned the situation around.

In this scenario, several critical errors were made:
- Counseling Zach under these circumstances could inadvertently reinforce his behavior, if he perceives attention as a valuable commodity.
- Allowing Zach to play basketball likely served as significant reinforcement.
- Taking Zach to the weight room was almost certainly a treat rather than a deterrent.
- Removing Zach from the classroom allowed him to successfully avoid completing his assigned task.

This type of scenario is not uncommon across schools and districts, and it is a pattern we too followed before recognizing through a behavioral lens that our responses were likely reinforcing the behaviors we aimed to eliminate. Although unintended, such actions reduce students' learning opportunities and compound the challenges teachers face due to misbehavior that is inadvertently reinforced by well-intentioned individuals who provide access to enjoyable activities outside the classroom following misbehavior.

Boredom can be strategically employed here. If a student is motivated by escape, the most significant reward we can inadvertently offer is an out-of-school suspension. If students are frequently removed from class and the out-of-class environment replicates the rewards listed above, a deeper assessment within the classroom is necessary to identify the true function of the behavior so that appropriate adjustments can be made. For administrators, this involves reviewing and observing the classroom management plan for fidelity. For teachers, it is crucial to have a robust classroom management plan that outlines expectations, routines, and procedures and details how behaviors will be reinforced or corrected. Developing a comprehensive classroom management plan is a vital first step in fostering a positive learning environment that reflects your educational goals. For your convenience, the Effective Classroom Management Planning Guide is provided in Appendix 16 to assist in this process.

Addressing misbehavior effectively requires ensuring that the consequence provided doesn't grant students access to desired outcomes, facilitate escape from undesired situations, or result in placement in an environment that might appear more appealing than the classroom. It's important to recognize that not all escape behaviors in class stem from challenging tasks or teacher demands. Often, students may find stronger reinforcement outside the classroom due to the availability of more attractive reinforcers (e.g., interacting with a favored staff member) or a lack of reinforcement within the classroom setting itself.

For administrators who are evaluating the dynamics of a specific classroom, a grade level, or an entire school, it's useful to track the frequency of visits to the front office and analyze these data critically. For teachers, it's beneficial to inquire with administrators about where students are typically sent during disciplinary actions and whether data on these incidents are available. Data provide an objective basis for understanding patterns; if the numbers are consistent or if certain students are frequently sent to the office, it might indicate that an alternative approach is necessary.

We advise against routinely sending students to the lobby or front office, where they might congregate with other frequent fliers and engage in stimulating observations of people and activities. Instead, fostering a sense of boredom with the consequence can be strategically advantageous, as it decreases the appeal of being removed from class. Ideally, we want students to feel as though they are not moving from "the pit to paradise," but rather from "paradise to the pit." The pit should appear far less appealing than paradise, making the classroom the more desirable environment.

In subsequent chapters, we will discuss the implementation of an alternative setting, referred to as the QUICK

Room, for removing students more effectively. Additionally, we will provide essential classroom behavior management strategies that are practical yet pivotal for cultivating positive behaviors and reducing instances of misbehavior. These strategies are designed to enhance the classroom environment, making it a place where students are motivated to behave appropriately and to engage positively with their lessons and peers.

Use Positive Reinforcement

The strategies discussed in this book are designed to help you conceptualize function-based consequences as reactive interventions to misbehaviors that disrupt the classroom environment. It is essential to pair these strategies with positive reinforcement. Positive reinforcement must be provided for appropriate (replacement) behaviors that serve the same function as the misbehaviors targeted for reduction. Implementing consequences without a strong emphasis on positive reinforcement (maintaining a 4:1 ratio of positive to negative interactions) will likely increase disruptive behavior. At best, the student might not fully benefit from their education; at worst, they may develop a disdain for education altogether, increasing the risk of dropout.

Use Feedback

Specific feedback as a form of reinforcement is necessary for effective teaching and behavior change. We believe the best reinforcement occurs naturally through meaningful work and strong, daily nurtured student-teacher relationships. If students enjoy the work and like their teacher, misbehavior will likely be minimized, and the effectiveness of the strategies we propose will be maximized.

Avoid Unintentional Reinforcement

You might think that most students would dread the idea of the school calling their parents, and of them having to visit the front office, seeing it as a distressing experience and an effective deterrent—a consequence designed to reduce the likelihood of repeating undesirable behavior. However, for students who frequently find themselves in this situation, especially when parental involvement with the school is scant, this process often acts as a reinforcer for their misbehavior, providing them with attention and a respite from classroom demands.

Behavior does not occur in a vacuum; it is shaped by various factors in the environment, whether immediate or delayed. While we cannot alter a student's genetic makeup or change their past, we can modify the environment to better support behavior and learning. Acting like astute behavior detectives and identifying what reinforces misbehavior is key to reducing it and enhancing educational opportunities.

We recognize that all behavior, aside from reflexes (e.g., the blink or startle reflexes), occurs either to obtain something (positive reinforcement) or to avoid something (negative reinforcement). If Zach resists following instructions, wishes to escape a particular task, relishes the reputation of being seen as the "bad boy," or finds the front office environment engaging, his misbehavior is fulfilling one or more of these needs. The principles of behavior science show us that if Zach finds something reinforcing, the misbehavior leading to it is likely to be repeated and to pose ongoing challenges for the teacher, consume more time for administrators, disrupt the class, and reduce instructional time for all students.

Many educators default to two or three strategies for most misbehaviors, regardless of their function—such as reprimands, in-class time-outs, or calling for a student to be removed. While sometimes effective, the overuse of these strategies can be counterproductive, especially if the consequences fail to compete with the reinforcing aspects of misbehavior, such as peer attention or avoiding work. For instance, if a teacher tells Johanne to remain quiet, but she continues making noises because her peers laugh, her behavior serves to provide her with powerful social reinforcement (peer attention) that outweighs the effect of the teacher's use of a reprimand or classroom removal. As a result, these consequences are often ineffective and may even reinforce the undesirable behavior.

We recommend developing a list of misbehaviors in your classroom and categorizing them into three groups to improve the consistency of your responses and to reduce emotional reactions (for help on emotional regulation for your students, see Appendix 17):

- Low-Magnitude Misbehaviors include behaviors such as pencil tapping, talking out of turn, being out of seat, or refusing to start a task. While annoying, they don't severely disrupt the flow of instruction.
- Moderate-Intensity Misbehaviors include behaviors such as task refusal, yelling out, or running around the classroom. These behaviors disrupt the student and the classroom environment but are not dangerous.
- High-Intensity Misbehaviors include behaviors that are addressed in the school code of conduct, such as physically dangerous acts, threats, or open defiance.

> A word of caution: Out-of-school suspension (OSS) is often used for these behaviors but may inadvertently reward frequent fliers. If a student is motivated by escape, the most significant reward we can inadvertently offer is an OSS. Alternatives like lunch/after-school detention or internal school suspension should be considered if OSS is ineffective.

In the upcoming chapters, we'll explore strategies related to suspension in depth. But for now, think about the functions behind the misbehaviors you observe. This understanding is vital, as you or the teachers you support may inadvertently be reinforcing these misbehaviors through your responses. For instance, giving a time-out to a student trying to escape work likely won't be effective. Reprimanding a student who seeks teacher attention might as well be an invitation for more misbehavior. Understanding that even unintentional or impulsive behaviors serve a function for the student is key to addressing them effectively. We'll discuss this further and provide practical tips for creating a conducive learning environment.

For students who try to avoid academic tasks for reasons other than a skill deficit, it's essential that they are eventually required to complete the assignments. While this approach may still permit some delay, it effectively prevents a complete evasion of the task. It might seem like basic common sense, but too often, we observe students being inadvertently rewarded for their avoidance behaviors by actually escaping the work they dislike. A practical strategy to counteract this is what we term a work-out, where access to preferred activities or items is withheld until the student completes the required work or at least part of it. Rather than removing the student from a potentially reinforcing environment (such as during a time-out), this approach restricts access to reinforcers until the task is accomplished.

Set Clear Expectations

Remember, while we can't force someone to perform a task, we do have significant control over many environmental factors that can influence behaviors. For instance, nobody can make you attend work, but your employer might outline the consequences clearly: "If you come to work, you'll get paid; if you don't, you won't. I hope to see you there." This isn't coercion; it's simply setting clear expectations and reminding employees of the natural consequences of their choices—both positive and negative.

A related example in an educational setting involves a high school student who refuses to complete her assignments. Given that social interaction is highly valued among teenagers, a suitable approach might be: "Maddie, if you turn in your work, you'll be able to have lunch in the cafeteria with your friends. If not, you'll need to stay in class to finish your work during lunch." Removing personal emotions from these interactions allows the natural consequences of the students' choices to be the primary motivator. Clearly stating expectations and patiently waiting for the desired behavior to manifest proves effective in managing classroom behavior. This method also underscores the importance of collaboration between teachers and school leaders to ensure consistency and fairness in applying these strategies.

Exercise 3.1

Let's help you deepen your knowledge a little more through application. Read the following scenarios and complete the ABC form (Table 3.3). We've provided an answer key at the end of this chapter, but please attempt the exercise before jumping ahead.

1. Mr. Kendorski is giving a whole-group lesson, and the students will not stop talking during his instruction. He stops teaching to ask the students

Table 3.3. ABC Form

	Antecedent	Behavior	Consequence
1.			
2.			
3.			
4.			
5.			

to be quiet. The behavior stops briefly and starts again. Mr. Kendorski stops teaching to correct the students again. This pattern continues until the end of the whole-group lesson, preventing Mr. Kendorski from giving the written assignments.

2. Miranda throws a book on the floor during the math lesson. The teacher continues to teach, but other students laugh.

3. Ms. Jones asks her students to get ready for reading groups and centers. Allison gets under her desk and starts screaming, "I hate centers." The teacher calls for the assistant principal to remove Allison from the classroom.

4. After the social studies lesson, Ms. Adams asks her students to take out their notebooks in preparation for independent seatwork. During this time, Alec sharpens his pencil every couple of minutes, resulting in Alec not finishing his work on time.

5. Olivia taps her pencil while doing a reading assignment.

Key Points

- Behavior happens for two reasons: to get something or to get away from something.
- All behavior serves a purpose or has a function.
- The typical functions of behavior are EATS: Escape, Attention, Tangible, and Sensory.
- When observing student behavior, it's important to understand the form and the function of the behavior by identifying what the behavior looks like, when it occurs, with whom, and under what context.
- To further understand the function of student behavior, you must be aware of what happens after the behavior—the consequence.
- The consequence will either reinforce behavior (strengthen or increase the likelihood it will occur), punish behavior (weaken or make it less likely the behavior will occur), or not reinforce behavior (in which case the behavior will decrease over time).
- Behavior occurs as a result of past behavior that produced valued outcomes.
- Teach the student what you want them to do instead of misbehavior based on the identified function.
- Focus on providing reinforcement for what you want to see the student do, and avoid allowing the student's problem behavior to receive reinforcement.
- Changing behavior takes time, consistency, and patience.

Reflect on It

- Do you have frequent fliers?
- What are some common classroom situations that cause misbehavior?
- Think about a student in your class who engages in problem behavior:
  - How would you define or describe the student's behaviors?
  - Which of these behaviors are the most disruptive to instruction?
  - What do you think the function of these behaviors is? There may be multiple.
- To understand the function of behavior, ask yourself what came after the behavior. Was the student given attention (e.g., reprimand or praise)? Was the student removed from a task, activity, or classroom? Did the student receive an item? Was the behavior sensory based?
- If you are an administrator, do your staff members understand the functions of behavior and are they applying function-based consequences?

Exercise 3.1 Answer Key

	Antecedent	Behavior	Consequence	The Breakdown
1.	Mr. Kendorski is giving a whole-group lesson.	Students will not stop talking during his instruction.	Mr. Kendorski stops teaching and asks students to be quiet (this pattern is repeated several times throughout the lesson). No written assignments were given to the students at the end of the lesson.	If there is a pattern of the students talking during whole-group instruction, it is likely that the students are trying to escape the written assignment. What the students have learned is that the more they talk, the more the teacher will stop teaching, thereby delaying the assignment.
2.	The teacher is giving a math lesson.	Miranda throws a book on the floor.	Students laugh and the teacher continues to teach.	If Miranda's book-throwing behavior continues to occur during math after her peers have responded by laughing (the consequence) and there is a pattern of Miranda receiving a similar response from her peers, it is likely that receiving attention from her peers is the function of the behavior.
3.	Ms. Jones asks her students to get ready for reading groups and centers.	Allison gets under her desk and screams, "I hate centers."	The teacher calls for the assistant principal to remove Allison from the classroom.	If Allison's problem behavior persists every time Ms. Jones transitions to centers and small reading groups, the behavior is likely escape, as Allison is being removed from the classroom after the behavior occurs—she is going from a less-preferred to more-preferred environment.
4.	The teacher asks students to get ready for independent work during social studies.	Alec sharpens his pencil every few minutes.	Alec does not finish his independent work.	The function of the pencil-sharpening behavior could be escape, though more information about the consequence may be needed to see if there is a pattern established to determine the function.
5.	The class has a reading assignment	Olivia taps her pencil.	Unknown.	Here you need more information about the consequence. What happens after Olivia taps her pencil? To determine the function, you need to know if there is an established pattern of the behavior and the consequence.

CHAPTER 4

The Quickest and Easiest Tool for Preventing Misbehavior

Educators are amazing. They have so many tools in their toolbox, and many don't even know it or perhaps do not recognize how powerful their tools can actually be! In fact, every educator possesses the most powerful tool for influencing student behavior, and the incredible thing is it's been right under their nose the whole time: It's their mouth. The simplest and quickest strategy for improving student behavior is through effective communication. Communication, while relatively complex, can be used to start, stop, prevent, increase, and decrease behavior. Even our proximity to students (see Appendix 3), our smallest facial expression, the slightest change in the tone of our voice, or the tiniest of gestures can communicate so much meaning to a student. One of the keys to effectively influencing behavior through communication is to remember it's not what you say but how you say it, and when you say it (delivery).

Cues, such as tone of voice (paraverbal), volume, and cadence (rate of speech), whether purposeful or not, play a role in effective communication. These cues assist others in understanding and decoding what we are communicating. They also help us in understanding and decoding what others are communicating to us.

While the importance of verbal and written communication skills is well recognized, research continues to highlight that a significant portion of our daily interpersonal communication is nonverbal (Matsumoto et al., 2013). A person's body language—whether they are the speaker or the listener—often gives us an idea, or at least a good guess, of their moods and emotions. If we pay attention, we can enhance our understanding of students' and coworkers' reactions to what we say and how we say it. Body language is nonverbal communication where our physical behaviors, as opposed to spoken words, convey information. Such behaviors include facial expressions, body posture, gestures, eye movement, touch (haptics), and the use of space (proximity). Body language exists in both animals and humans and it can—and does—communicate a lot.

While there is often an agreed-upon interpretation of certain body language, it is always open to interpretation, which can vary for many reasons. A person's culture or upbringing, their history of reinforcement and punishment, and so forth all affect how body language is perceived. This subset of nonverbal interactions can complement or confuse what is spoken during social interaction. Some researchers conclude that nonverbal communication accounts for most of the information transmitted during interpersonal interactions. Although body language is an important part of communication, much of it happens without us being conscious of it. Let's take a deeper look at verbal and nonverbal communication in the context of relationships.

Communication and the Relationship Bank

Have you ever been urged to do something by someone using a tone that felt condescending or that seemed agitated? Think about your reaction to that interaction. Were you more or less likely to follow their suggestion? How did it affect your relationship with them—did it bring you closer, or did it drive a wedge between you?

Consider the scenario where it was a supervisor speaking in such a tone: Did it inspire you to increase your efforts, or did you find yourself only appearing diligent when they were around to avoid their criticism?

It's widely recognized that students tend not to engage well with educators they don't respect or like. As such, it is critical for teachers and staff to align themselves with positive reinforcement methods. Consider every interaction a teacher has with a student as either a deposit into or a withdrawal from a relationship bank. The aim for teachers and school leaders should be to enrich and support students by making deposits into their relational accounts through as many meaningful interactions as possible, while ensuring that any correction of misbehavior represents only a minor withdrawal.

It's essential to maintain a balance of four positive interactions for every one corrective interaction, with the corrective interaction conducted in a manner that respects the student's dignity and promotes improvement. If an interaction from a teacher or staff member feels coercive (i.e., they are using pressure or intimidation to influence behavior), it's akin to making a substantial withdrawal from the relationship bank. Without sufficient positive deposits, this can lead to "overdraft fees" manifested as increased misbehavior.

One way we see this in action is when we fall into a pattern of addressing misbehavior through coercion more than by acknowledging appropriate behavior. Misbehavior naturally tends to draw more attention than positive behavior for a variety of reasons, but importantly, in educational settings, you often end up seeing more of the behaviors you focus on. If that focus is on misbehavior, the consequences are clear—the misbehavior increases—and if you are addressing it through coercion, it creates withdrawals from the relationship bank.

The concept of the relationship bank is equally applicable to administrators in their work with their staff. Administrators who employ this strategy not only set an example but are also more likely to foster positive classroom and school environments that boost student achievement and staff retention. They achieve this by demonstrating respect and appreciation for their staff, while also reinforcing positive behaviors. This approach also ensures that recognition of good performance is paired with positive reinforcement, which leads to better overall behavior, enhanced performance, and stronger relationships.

We will explore the importance of administrators building relationships with faculty and staff further in the final two chapters of this book. However, it's worth noting that effective communication skills are essential, in both personal and professional contexts. For educators looking to improve their nonverbal communication skills, here are several tips that can significantly enhance their ability to effectively engage with students or staff:

- **Maintain eye contact:** Eye contact can convey trust, clarity, and respect. It shows you are engaged and value the interaction.
- **Be mindful of your body language:** Open body language can make you appear more approachable and receptive, which is inviting to students and colleagues alike.
- **Monitor your facial expressions:** Your facial expressions can communicate a wealth of emotions. Ensure they match the message you intend to convey.
- **Consider your tone of voice:** The tone of your voice should be consistent with your message. A supportive tone can reinforce a positive message, while a harsh tone might undermine it.

These strategies not only aid in reducing misunderstandings but also play a pivotal role in building trust and openness in relationships.

Making Deposits to the Bank

Consistently engaging with students in a positive, noncontingent manner helps to build the relationship bank. Noncontingent attention, which means giving attention without requiring specific actions or behaviors in return, shows students that they are valued as individuals, independent of their performance or behavior. By establishing a positive rapport and engaging in supportive social interactions, you create an environment where students are more likely to feel connected and motivated to exhibit appropriate behaviors. Simple actions such as greeting students warmly, encouraging them to seek help, and taking an interest in their activities are ways educators can make positive deposits into this bank.

Effective communication also involves mastering nonverbal cues—what you don't say can be just as powerful as what you do say. Ensuring that your body language supports your verbal messages is critical. Correcting misbehavior should be done consistently, calmly, immediately, and succinctly to maintain a healthy teacher-student relationship.

It's imperative to remember that no matter the severity of the misbehavior, corrective actions without sufficient deposits into the relationship bank will likely backfire over time.

Key Points

- Behavior is communication.
- The simplest and quickest strategy for improving student behavior is through effective communication.
- Communication, while relatively complex, can be used to start, stop, prevent, increase, and decrease behavior.
- Even proximity to students, the smallest facial expression, the slightest change in tone of voice, or the tiniest of gestures can communicate so much.
- You must focus on making deposits in the relationship bank. Students are unlikely to maximize learning from people they don't like.
- One of the keys to effectively influencing behavior through communication is to remember it's not just what you say, but how you say it (and when).
- Brief, meaningful interactions tend to be more effective when attempting to influence behavior, especially when the goal of the conversation is correction.
- Correcting misbehavior consistently, calmly, immediately, and briefly is an effective and powerful way of keeping the teacher-student relationship intact.
- Oftentimes adult behavior needs to change in order to support students' behavioral improvement.

Reflect on It

- What does your students' behavior tell you?
- Is there an awareness deficit?
- A motivational deficit?
- A skill deficit?
- Are they trying to get something?
- Get away from something?
- Does problem behavior persist?
- What do your nonverbal behaviors say to your students?
- Do you correct behavior calmly?
- Do you correct behavior briefly?
- Are you giving correction immediately?
- How are you making deposits in the relationship bank?

CHAPTER 5

Good Teacher, Bad Behavior

Throughout our many years supporting students and instructional staff in educational settings, we've witnessed many educators effectively employing a variety of effective classroom management skills, despite receiving little to no behavioral training during their teacher preparation programs. This is an amazing testament to the grit possessed by so many determined educators, and it tells us that many educators either use strategies taught by their school or district or they actively research and apply what they have learned independently. Instead of wishing behaviors will just go away, they adapt and overcome, and we have considerable respect for them!

Common Strategies for Correcting Misbehavior

Regrettably, some educators use a strategy that, in many cases, tends to cause more misbehavior from the very students who already make educators want to pull their hair out. With all of the obstacles they must navigate, this is the last thing teachers or school leaders need! Public posting of misbehavior (e.g., writing a student's name on the board) is an often-used, surefire way to set students off, especially your frequent fliers—the challenging students who rarely miss school and when they finally do, the teacher feels like they have been given a week's vacation.

But let's think about this situation more critically. Who wants to be called out in front of their peers? Can you imagine sitting in an all-staff meeting somewhere and the principal or superintendent writes your name on the board or yells across the table for you to pay attention? What might your reaction be? Would it create an environment you'd want to be a part of or one you'd want to escape from? Does this approach bring out the best in you? Likely, it does not.

If this were the culture of your work environment, you would eventually seek greener pastures if the reinforcement available (pay, benefits, job satisfaction, etc.) did not compensate for the negativity. Leaders, this is one reason for high turnover at schools. Unfortunately, students do not have the option of moving away, and they must experience this negativity day after day with little to no possibility of their own greener pastures for an entire school year. Under these conditions, students, teachers, or school leaders are going to be unhappy as misbehavior increases and student achievement decreases.

Improving Public Posting

Balance is key for teachers who find success with public posting. We have observed this old-school strategy working in classrooms with relatively few problem behaviors, where students are engaged by the instruction and have reported they feel safe and cared for by teachers. If it is working for you, and you have engaged and happy students with few behavior problems, then you probably shouldn't change it. A good guide to measuring the effectiveness of public posting is to observe what occurs immediately after publicly calling out a student or marking a student's name on the board for misbehavior. Do other kids laugh? Does the student interrupt the instructional flow? Does it improve the student's behavior? Does it improve the behavior of other students? Or does the student continue the misbehavior or maybe even take it to the next level?

If you are using this strategy, we would highly recommend you use a misbehavior/prosocial behavior recording sheet. This allows you to record instances of misbehavior more discreetly and creates the opportunity to recognize and reinforce student behaviors that benefit peers. This recording sheet can just be a piece of paper with student names on it on which teachers can keep a tally of misbehavior and exceptional helpful behavior as demonstrated in Figure 5.1.

Student	(/) = Misbehavior (e.g., calling out)	(+) = Prosocial Behavior (e.g., helping)
Malik	///	+++++ +++++ ++
Murray	///// ///// /////	++
Vincia	//	+
Elliot		+++++ +++

Figure 5.1. The Frequency Collection Data Sheet allows you to count and record occurrences of behavior via tallies, plusses, minuses, and so forth to have an accurate record to help tailor interventions.

Using simple tools like this can make your job easier and leave you feeling more fulfilled: Your energy and emphasis are on prosocial behaviors. Furthermore, the student misbehaving is not publicly embarrassed nor ostracized, and the other students do not see attention delivered for something problematic.

Improving the Level System

Another common strategy is the level system, in which teachers designate colors like green, yellow, and red for particular levels of a student's behavioral status. If you are a teacher who is having some success using the level system strategy that entails progressively moving a clip down from one color to the next (another form of public posting), consider more colors and start students in the middle. This allows students to also move up for exceptional behavior. When students start at the top and can only move down, it quickly takes away motivation and tends to create more misbehavior. It is important that if students move down, they are allowed to move back up for improvement. Leaving their clip down is like perpetually leaving them in the doghouse. Nobody wants that, and it's difficult to see how motivation can improve when there is nothing to earn. When kids have nothing to lose and no hope of moving their level up, they are likely to engage in misbehavior.

Avoiding Accidental Reinforcement Outside of Class

Removing students from class is a difficult proposition. Even the best classroom manager might consider removing the student from the classroom at times. Though they have the best intentions and do the best they can, many administrators and staff have not been provided proper training on effectively managing student removals, which may inadvertently reinforce (i.e., increase) the undesirable behavior they seek to eliminate. In these cases, consider whether what is being done outside of the class when the student is removed is more reinforcing than the student being in class. We discussed this more completely in Chapter 3.

Whether you are teaching in a primary or secondary school, students who are removed from your class for misbehavior should be brought to an environment that is inherently less reinforcing than the one from which they were removed. However, students who are removed for misbehavior are not being placed into a "black hole" where there is no reinforcement available. Nonetheless educators identify and control these potential reinforcers. The science of human behavior has proven that all behavior functions essentially to get something or get away from something. For students trying to escape nonpreferred tasks, teacher directions, and so forth, it is critical that they escape to an area that is less reinforcing to avoid the inadvertent reinforcement of escape-motivated behavior. For example, if it is hot inside, but hotter outside, we would not choose to go outside as a strategy for escaping the heat.

Some attempts at helping, such as attempting to talk a student through a problem once they are removed from the classroom, provide the student with more attention than they were receiving in the classroom. This is not to imply that counseling is bad. However, students who value adult attention might engage in misbehavior as a method of seeking out attention from adults. Barring a true crisis situation, if you've tried counseling a student and it's not working (e.g., the student is a frequent flier), try pre-teaching expectations and/or providing the counseling at a later time after the student is back on task, not in the environment where the student is sent following removal.

Remember, the goal is to avoid allowing the student to access desired attention for misbehavior and to "pay them" for engaging in desired behaviors. Talking with a student at a later time minimizes the delivery of reinforcing attention when students are removed. Limiting attention can be effective in reducing the likelihood of the problem. This is a powerful strategy, especially when paired with increased attention when the student is in class and back on task.

Effective Strategies for Correcting Behavior

Nonprogressive Consequences

A powerful strategy for effectively addressing misbehavior is to create a menu of potential nonprogressive consequences that align appropriate and function-based consequences to misbehavior and its magnitude. Nonprogressive consequences are characterized by being the same every time. For example, school staff might consider using time owed—for every second a student is out of their seat, they owe time away from a favorite activity such as using a certain swing during recess or, for older students, transitioning in the hallway with their peers. Time owed works well as an intervention for lower magnitude, higher frequency behavior such as calling out answers (e.g., 15 seconds time owed for each call out) when the expectation is that students will first raise their hand before responding.

There are numerous reactionary strategies teachers can use with misbehavior. Some small examples of other strategies to use include

- **Restitution** (cleaning the learning environment to its original state): Used if a student throws paper, knocks something off a desk, or demonstrates other low-intensity behavior that damages the environment. This includes restitution to educators and peers in some logical form (e.g., an apology) when warranted.
- **Overcorrection:** Used if the student continues to throw lots of paper or knock something off a desk. This might entail cleaning up all the paper on the floor, even the paper that they didn't throw.
- **Positive practice:** Another strategy for less intensive misbehavior, such as a student running in the hallway, which simply entails requiring them to walk back.

In other cases, teachers sometimes provide a misbehavior point or demerit for each occurrence of a misbehavior. This can be a powerful and effective response to high-frequency and lower magnitude misbehavior. When the student earns X number of points for the misbehavior, a consequence is applied such as completing a QUICK ACTion Plan ("ACT" in reference to Acceptance and Commitment Training; see Appendices 19–21) or perhaps 5 minutes owed from a favorite activity. The key to dealing with lower magnitude misbehaviors is to have consequences that are just annoying enough for the student to want to avoid them, and that the teacher feels comfortable delivering consistently and in a business-like manner. It does not require a detailed analysis or a significant change in course of action.

Table 5.1 provides a matrix of consequences that can be used in the classroom. As we've mentioned, overuse of any reduction procedures can backfire and result in more of the very misbehavior you are trying to eliminate. To reiterate, finding four opportunities to provide positive feedback for every one correction weights the balance in overwhelming favor of reinforcement. Administrators and staff should allow corrective feedback to serve as a prompt for themselves to look for opportunities to find the student being corrected, and all other students as well, engaging in prosocial, pro-academic actions—such as helping a peer, participating in group discussions, following directions, or completing assignments—and deliver positive feedback shortly thereafter.

Progressive Consequences

For continued lower or moderate-magnitude behaviors, or behavior you consider impulsive (e.g., a student calling out an answer because they are excited), you can also consider using progressive consequences. Much as when a driver receives increasing penalties for speeding (e.g., warning, fine, and loss of license), these consequences move from lower to higher magnitudes and should match the intensity of the misbehavior they intend to reduce. This can be tricky because punishment that is too weak may not work and can even desensitize the student to the punishment procedure. On the other hand, punishment that is too harsh can result in negative emotional and corresponding behavioral responses that might persist, as harsh punishment can negatively impact relationships.

Think about the driving analogy. Imagine being pulled over for driving just 5 miles per hour over the speed limit and immediately losing your license. This might seem excessive! However, driving 50 miles per hour over the limit could warrant such a severe consequence. Similarly, a $5 fine payable on the spot might not deter future speeding if the consequence feels trivial—some might see it as worth the risk.

The same principle applies in the classroom. When consequences are too lenient, students may feel the "cost" of misbehavior is acceptable. Conversely, when consequences are too severe for minor infractions, they may feel unfairly targeted. Educators should carefully match the consequence to the severity and frequency of the behavior. If misbehavior escalates—becoming more frequent and deliberate rather than impulsive—teachers should apply consequences consistently and without delay. For example, if a teacher warns a student about being removed from class but the behavior continues, the teacher must follow through with the consequence. Failing to act can teach students that rules are negotiable and only enforced after repeated warnings. Effective classroom management requires striking a balance between fairness, consistency, and reinforcement to create environments where expectations are clear, and appropriate behaviors are consistently reinforced.

Reminder on Corrections

Remember, necessary corrections should be stated briefly, calmly, and consistently. More importantly, remember to follow the reinforcement and encouragement procedures at a 4:1 rate. Misbehavior, and its correction, remind the teacher to find instances of desirable behaviors and attend to them. The fundamental premise of behavior management strategies in schools should be to strengthen relationships through structuring the environment and increasing positive interactions to reduce the likelihood of misbehavior. A reason for utilizing these strategies schoolwide is to develop the necessary repertoires to help all students, particularly those with problem behaviors, as well as to provide uniform expectations and methods for school staff. Adopting these strategies does not require educators to remember separate procedures. The strategies are practical, can address function, and continue to emphasize the paramount need to improve and maintain relationships through the use of positive reinforcement. Leaders, here is where you can build a school culture of caring and structure that fosters a positive learning environment for all.

Consequences Based on Frequency and Intensity

Table 5.1 provides a sample of potential consequences based on frequency and intensity. However, it's always important to get at the root of the misbehavior—its function. To aid you with this, we've included a modified version of the Student Performance Diagnostic Checklist in Appendix 18 (adapted from Carr et al., 2013b; Gavoni & Weatherly, 2024). This simple-to-use checklist will help you determine if the student's misbehavior is a "can't do" versus a "won't do" issue. This is important because if a student is being punished for a "can't do" issue, this won't solve the problem and is likely to create many more issues. Similarly, if you try to teach an expectation but the issue is a "won't do" and not a "can't do," you may inadvertently reinforce undesirable behavior. The tool is also a good self-assessment to ensure you set the stage for developing and maintaining desired behaviors related to academic tasks or classroom management expectations.

Table 5.1. Menu of Classroom Management Consequences Based on Intensity

Magnitude continuum	Behavior	Teacher response
New behavior, low intensity	**Intermittently cooperative** (e.g., following instructions, sharing, helping); engaging in simple off-task behavior	This is the time we need to teach skills and replacement behaviors that have been targeted to increase. Strategies include developing a good rapport, pivot praise, redirection, humor, reminder, pre-correction.
Low intensity, moderate frequency	**Uncooperative** (e.g., walking around the room, avoiding academic demands, breaking pencils)	Set limits and expectations. In doing so, state the behavior you want the student to do in a way that is Clear/easy to understand. Reasonable (match the behavior and ensure it's within their ability). Enforceable (idle threats don't work). Make sure it is within your ability to make it happen, and that you follow through with it.
Moderate intensity, moderate frequency	**Uncooperative** (e.g., walking around the room; choosing preferred activities/items; creating major disruptions; throwing items; using inappropriate language, tone, cadence, and volume; etc.)	Staff contacts QUICK Team (more on this later) or administration and places them on a standby if behavior is expected to escalate. Restate expectations and follow through with consequences for appropriate behaviors as well as the consequences for inappropriate behaviors.

Magnitude continuum	Behavior	Teacher response
High intensity	Crisis-level behavior (continuous physical aggression, continuous self-injurious behavior, and/or continuous high-magnitude disruption [Fleisig, 2004])	Staff contacts QUICK Team or administration. Refrain from any talking, comforting, and/or attempts to teach new skills. Attempt to get behavior under control in the environment where it occurred (if possible) without giving attention. Attention after a crisis should be minimal and low intensity. If not, the behavior may continue if the function is attention. Additional staff should not provide attention after a crisis. It is best to have one person lead the process and be the point of contact.

Beyond Punishment: Teaching Students What to Do

Even with the best classroom and behavior management, misbehavior may escalate. In some situations, educators or staff may need to request assistance from an administrator. In most cases, the administrator responds to the situation, asks a series of questions, provides a reprimand for the misbehavior, and then provides counseling regarding what the student "should have done." After the student is required to sit in a designated area, the student is typically returned to class with an obligatory, "Don't do that again!" Later that day, week, or month, a similar behavior occurs and the whole process occurs again: remove, reprimand, counsel, and return; remove, reprimand, counsel, and return; remove, reprimand, counsel, and return. It is commonly said the definition of insanity is repeating the same thing and expecting different results, yet this is what happens in school settings day after day. It's no wonder we've heard many teachers and school leaders comment that they want to pull their hair out! We don't blame them. We've been there.

Here is an important reminder: Punishment, in and of itself, is often insufficient for changing misbehavior. Punishment does not teach students what to do. A better rule for educators is any behavior resulting in a reprimand should end in the student being told what to do. If Murray ran out of class, the administrator might say, "That's not appropriate. Please sit in your seat and let the teacher know if you need something by raising your hand."

This brings up important issues in schools: Even when punishment follows problem behavior, children often do not get sufficient time to practice the necessary skills. We assume the child knows what to do if they are told what not to do. When students are told what to do, the direction is ambiguous: "Be good," or "Behave." Educators flourishing in challenging school environments with challenging behaviors know the importance of specificity. They do not question, "Why?" publicly and then demand an answer. The student running out of class needs to practice and receive reinforcement for remaining in their seat or class. They need more frequent prompts to raise their hand. They need to be shown when they can ask to leave or leave the class. They then need to demonstrate the appropriate behavior and receive reinforcement for doing so. Misbehavior, as we've mentioned, is a signal to educators that appropriate behavior needs to be prompted, modeled (taught), and given more attention (reinforcement).

Educators know how this works, but some may balk, as it takes time to produce the desired outcomes. This is a fair critique and concern. However, the time spent is more likely to establish the foundation students need to succeed and is more likely to replace problem behavior with more acceptable repertoires. Any time invested in practicing good, desirable in-school behaviors is time well spent and will equal more instructional time. In the end, investing in the expected behaviors eventually creates a culture in which teachers' and school leaders' jobs become a little easier and more focused on academic instruction as students routinely behave well and enjoy learning.

When combined with ample positive reinforcement, the interventions outlined in Table 5.2 can accelerate on-task and prosocial behavior. In the table, we provide you with a quick scenario to illustrate the use of the correction within the school setting. To make the corrections salient and easy to implement, we've also included very specific, step-by-step procedures in the appendices intended to guide you. Remember, for any misbehavior you try to reduce, it's important that you continue to look for opportunities to prompt and reinforce desired alternatives or incompatible behavior. In other words, "catch your students being good" as much as possible. In the end, you will get more of the behavior you want to see.

Time-Out and Its Variations

Time-out is a procedure often used to manage problem behavior. Many think of time-out as having a student removed from an area. This may or may not be time-out. Time-out is the temporary removal of access to reinforcers, wherever that happens. Readers have probably heard of the popular notion that the length of time-out is 1 minute per 1 year of age. Time-out, though, can be done without removal, and the number of minutes is fairly arbitrary. There are, in fact, several different ways to implement time-out: time-out, work-out, in-class time-out, out-of-class time-out, in-class work-out, and out-of-class work-out (see Table 5.2). While the particulars of various time-out procedures vary, correct implementation can reduce problem behavior with a procedure that, while imperfectly understood, is widely accepted as a correction to problem behavior.

Overcorrection and Its Variations

Overcorrection is a procedure that requires students to correct the impact of their misbehavior and practice appropriate behaviors. It is designed not only to address the immediate issue but also to teach and reinforce prosocial actions. There are three primary forms of overcorrection: restitution, restitutional overcorrection, and positive practice. Restitution involves restoring the environment or relationships affected by the misbehavior to their original state, such as picking up items that were thrown. Restitutional overcorrection goes further, requiring students to leave the situation better than they found it, like picking up additional items beyond the ones they disrupted. Positive practice focuses on rehearsing the desired behavior multiple times to establish a habit, such as writing a name on assignments repeatedly to prevent future omissions. These variations ensure that correction not only addresses the problem but also builds skills to prevent recurrence.

Response Cost and Its Variations

Response cost is a procedure that involves the removal of reinforcers following misbehavior to decrease its future occurrence. It can be implemented in several ways. Students may lose points on a point sheet or raffle tickets in a lottery system, or earn demerits that lead to larger consequences. For example, in a point sheet system, students start with a set number of points and lose one for each instance of misbehavior. Remaining points can be exchanged for rewards. Similarly, a response cost lottery involves students losing raffle tickets for misbehavior, with remaining tickets eligible for prize drawings. Demerits accumulate over time, leading to consequences like reduced privileges or parent contact. Another variation includes ignoring minor, nondisruptive behaviors—sometimes called junk behavior—to avoid reinforcing attention-seeking actions. While response cost strategies can be effective, they should be paired with reinforcement strategies to teach and maintain desired behaviors.

Behavior Contracts

Behavior contracts are written agreements between a teacher and student that outline expected behaviors and consequences. These contracts are particularly effective for students who are not responding to typical classroom management strategies and may be considered at risk. A behavior contract clearly defines expectations, goals, and the actions required to meet them. It also specifies consequences for meeting—or failing to meet—those expectations. For example, a teacher might review the contract with a student like Victoria (see Table 5.2) at the start of class, keep the contract visible on the desk as a reminder, and provide verbal feedback throughout the lesson. At the end of class, the teacher can review the student's progress, offering praise for meeting goals or discussing strategies for improvement if goals are missed. This structured approach helps reinforce accountability and supports positive behavioral change. See Appendix 14 for sample contracts and implementation procedures.

Action Plans

Action plans are structured interventions used to address moderate-intensity behaviors by guiding students through reflection and planning. They are particularly effective when implemented immediately following a behavioral incident. An action plan outlines the behavior, its impact, and steps the student can take to prevent recurrence. For example, if a student calls another student a jerk, the teacher can assign a QUICK ACTion Plan as a consequence and later discuss the plan with the student. This process allows the student to take responsibility, reflect on their actions, and develop strategies for improvement. See Appendices 19–21 for templates and procedures.

Table 5.2. Classroom Interventions

Time-out & variations		
Correction	**Works best when**	**Example**
Time-out: A period of time where the student loses access to reinforcers or the ability to earn reinforcers following misbehavior (Cooper et al., 2020).	Time-outs typically work best when the duration is shorter (e.g., 2 minutes as opposed to 20) and there is a "time-in." Essentially, the student "likes" their current task or activity.	Jionni enjoys recess. During recess, he is not following expectations. After Jionni is reminded of expectations, he continues to misbehave. As a result, he is required to sit out of recess for 2 minutes and then allowed to return.
Work-out: This uses the same principles as time-out, but reinforcement is withheld contingent upon completing a particular task.	Best utilized when the student's problem behavior is occurring so they can avoid or escape completing a task.	Anna is asked to complete her math worksheet. She refuses to begin the assignment. Anna needs to complete the math worksheet prior to joining peers outside for recess.
In-class time-out: The student is required to sit in an area that minimizes attention from peers, but where they can still be observed by the teacher. The student should have no access to items or activities. The student must follow the time-out expectations for a designated amount of time: • Remain in a designated spot. • Remain quiet. • Remain seated unless other-wise noted.	Best utilized when the problem behavior occurs so the student will gain attention from peers or adults. If the student leaves the area or purposely makes noise, the timer is reset for a specified amount of time. This is repeated until the student completes the in-class time-out as expected.	Ethan enjoys math but continues to talk out and disturb the other students trying to complete their assignments. Ethan is moved to a place within the classroom that is out of view of his peers. When the time-out is over, he returns to his seat. If Ethan refuses to go to time-out or becomes so disruptive that it prevents the continuation of classroom activities or instruction, then he may need to be removed from the classroom. See Appendix 6.
Out-of-class time-out: The student is removed to another location where they cannot disrupt other students. Follow the same procedure for in-class time-out. Once the student cooperates with time-out expectations, they are returned to the classroom, where they must complete the in-class time-out as originally directed. Once the student completes the in-class time-out, they may return to normal activities and the opportunity to earn reinforcement.	Used when problem behavior occurs to gain attention from peers or adults, but the attention cannot be removed, or the student may be too disruptive to the classroom environment (e.g., screaming, banging on desk, cursing). During these procedures, the staff involved in removing the student should minimize attention to the student.	Ethan's behaviors escalate in the classroom and the teacher can't teach due to the loud "pig" noises he is making. In addition, he is provoking peers by making faces at them. In-class time-out escalated the intensity of his disruptive behavior. Ethan is removed from class to complete an out-of-class time-out. When he returns to class, he completes his in-class time-out as described above and then returns to the task. See Appendix 7.

Time-out & variations		
Correction	**Works best when**	**Example**
In-class work-out: Reinforcement (of any kind) is withheld until the student cooperates with a given task. The student can remain in their seat or be directed to another location in the classroom (not near other students), depending on the function of the behavior. The student is directed to complete the task. State the expectation: "Raise your hand if you need help or when you are done."	Most effectively used for behaviors maintained by task/demand escape. Keeping the demand in place and requiring completion breaks the contingency between the problem behavior and the consequence.	Dani's behaviors escalated in the classroom, but the teacher can still teach. The other students are still learning. Once she completes her in-class work-out, reinforcement will again be available. See Appendix 6.
Out-of-class work-out: The student is removed to another location where they cannot disrupt other students. Follow the same procedure for in-class work-out, but use a different task than the one initiated in the classroom. Staff should have this prepared ahead of time. Once the student completes the out-of-class work-out, the student is returned to the classroom to complete the original task. Once the student completes the original task, they may return to normal activities and the opportunity to earn reinforcement.	Used for behaviors that are maintained by task/demand escape (negative reinforcement). Sending the work with the student and requiring completion will break the contingency between the problem behavior and the consequence. During these procedures, the staff involved in removing the student should minimize attention to the student.	Billy's behavior is repetitive and disruptive. After exhausting nonprogressive consequences, the teacher has the student removed. A review of the data indicates Billy's behavior occurs after a math task is presented. When Billy leaves the classroom, you send prepared work. Once the work is completed, Billy returns to the classroom and completes the original task. See Appendix 8.
Time owed: If a student refuses to comply when provided a directive, a time owed can be used as a "cost" for the student's misbehavior.	Use for behavior that disrupts classroom instruction time if the function is not escape.	Murray continues to call out. Each time he does, the teacher charges him 30 seconds from his recess time. For every second a student is out of their seat, they "owe" time by sitting away from peers during lunch.

Overcorrection & variations		
Correction	**Works best when**	**Example**
Restitution: If a student engages in misbehavior that causes "damage," a logical consequence is for the student to engage in behavior that rectifies the consequence of their misbehavior to return it to the original preexisting state (Cooper et al., 2020).	Use for behaviors that alter or cause damage to the environment and relationships.	Evelyn threw a milk container in the lunchroom. Staff directed her to pick it up. Evelyn yelled at a peer. Staff directed Evelyn to apologize. Evelyn still needs to pick up the milk container.
Restitutional overcorrection: If a student engages in misbehavior, they are required to correct the consequences of their misbehavior by restoring the situation to an improved state from before the event (MacKenzie-Keating & McDonald, 1990).	Use for behaviors that alter or cause "damage" to the environment and relationships and where restitution proved ineffective.	Evelyn threw a milk container in the lunchroom. Staff directed her to pick up it and other garbage from the floor. Back in class, Evelyn yelled at a peer. Staff directed Evelyn to apologize to the peer and other peers for disrupting their learning. Evelyn is still required to pick up the milk container and other garbage on the floor. See Appendix 9.
Positive practice: If a student breaks a rule about a behavior that can easily be practiced correctly, positive practice is appropriate (Carey & Bucher, 1981).	Works best for shorter durations and relies on the student engaging in/practicing the correct behavior to decrease the likelihood of breaking the rule in the future.	A student hands in a paper without a name. The teacher has the student write her name on the paper and, for the remainder of the week, has the student write her name on a piece of paper to reinforce this habit. See Appendix 10.

Response cost & variations		
Correction	**Works best when**	**Example**
Response cost point sheet: Student is provided X number of points on a point sheet at the beginning of the day and loses 1 point for each instance of a targeted misbehavior. The remaining points can be exchanged for identified reinforcers (Conyers et al., 2004).	Students know a rule but choose not to follow it, or may be impulsive or in the habit of behaving in a certain way under different conditions. Teachers who use this strategy should have a relatively good relationship with the student. For students who have been labeled "defiant" or do not have a good relationship with the classroom staff, this strategy can backfire, as it pairs the staff with something aversive.	A student learned to raise her hand when a teacher asks a question but calls out because she is excited to answer it. If the student calls out an average of 21 times a day, the teacher might give the student a point sheet each day with 21 points on it. On this sheet, the student can lose up to 3 points each class period. Every time the student calls out, she loses a point. Points left on the sheet can then be traded in at a designated time for access to predetermined rewards.
Response cost lottery: Student is provided X number of raffle tickets at the beginning of each day and loses one for each instance of targeted misbehavior. Raffle tickets go into a box and can be drawn for prizes at a designated time (Witt & Elliot, 1982).	A variation of the response cost strategy listed above and can be used with the same type of behavior, but with groups of students.	Many students in a class have difficulty remaining in their area during small group activities. Each student is provided X number of tickets at the beginning of each day for elementary, or each week for middle or high school. Each time a student leaves their area, the student loses a ticket. At the end of the day/week, the students write their names on their remaining tickets and put them in a container for a drawing at a specific time. Raffle tickets drawn can be traded in for specific items or activities. See Appendix 12.
Ignoring junk behavior: Teacher ignores minor, unwanted behaviors that may be annoying but are not dangerous or harmful to self, others, or the environment.	Effective for low-magnitude behavior. Typical "junk" behavior from students may be annoying but is not harmful to the student or others.	Examples of junk behavior are eye rolling, teeth sucking, mumbling, or a student talking under their breath. See Appendix 13.

Response cost & variations		
Correction	**Works best when**	**Example**
Demerits: Demerits represent negative points that, when accumulated, result in the loss of a privilege or in the imposition of a negative consequence.	Works great with the whole class, especially when the teacher has a good relationship with the students. Demerits can be used to soften a predetermined consequence that might otherwise be overly harsh for a single example of misbehavior but allows for consistent correction of that behavior.	To use demerits, teachers simply have a daily or weekly list with the students' names on it. Each time a student displays a targeted misbehavior, the teacher verbally corrects the behavior and then puts a mark next to the student's name. For example, a high school teacher might tell students that each time he has to speak to a student about talking out in class, the student will receive a demerit. If the student receives two demerits within 1 day, that equals a QUICK ACTion Plan (see Appendices 19–21). Four demerits within a day equals a call home to parents. For elementary school, it might be that each demerit equals 15 seconds off a daily favorite activity. Using demerits not only allows for consistency with the student, but it also reminds the other students of expectations.

Behavior contracts		
Correction	**Works best when**	**Example**
Behavior (contingency) contract: A behavior contract is a written contract between a student and teacher that pinpoints specific behaviors the student will engage in and the consequences that will be delivered by the teacher as a result (Strahun et al., 2013; Ruth, 1996).	Good to use with a student who is not responding to typical classroom management strategies and who may be identified as at risk. Contracts should clearly state the who, what, where, when, and how.	1. Teacher reviews goals and strategies at the start of the class with Victoria. 2. Teacher places the contract on the desk during the entire class. 3. Teacher taps the contract when Victoria needs a reminder of goals. 4. Teacher meets with Victoria at the end of class and asks a. Do you think you met this goal? b. Why or why not? 5. Teacher a. offers praise and encouragement if the goal is met. b. review strategies for goals not met. See sample behavior contract and procedure in Appendix 14.

Action Plans

Correction	Works best when	Example
QUICK ACTion Plan Matrix: The student completes the QUICK ACTion Plan so they can reflect on and be more mindful of their actions and the impact of their actions, and identify replacement behaviors to avoid future problems (Polk et al., 2016).	It can be provided in a single instance for moderate-intensity behavior.	A student calls another student a jerk. The teacher provides the student with a QUICK ACTion Plan as a consequence, then discusses the plan with them at a later time. See Appendices 19–21.

Key Points

- Using effective strategies for correcting behavior, combined with ample positive reinforcement, can accelerate on-task and prosocial behavior.
- Teaching replacement behaviors to students is often needed.
- "Old-school" strategies, such as publicly posting names, may be effective when correcting misbehavior in a classroom that is already operating effectively. The effectiveness of public posting or any corrective strategy is gauged by observing what occurs immediately after the consequence is delivered.
- A misbehavior recording sheet can be used instead of public posting. Using a misbehavior recording sheet allows you to record instances of misbehavior more discreetly. This recording sheet can simply be a piece of paper with students' names that allows you to keep a tally of both misbehavior and exceptional behavior.
- Level systems are another common behavior management strategy used in classrooms. These systems use colors to indicate a student's behavioral status. Remember to allow for upward movement, not just downward.
- Students removed from the classroom to an alternative setting should be sent to a less reinforcing environment. Be mindful of when talking/counseling takes place. Students removed from class for misbehavior may learn it is an efficient means of escaping class demands and gaining adult attention.
- Consider using nonprogressive consequences for continued lower or moderate-magnitude behaviors, or behavior that you consider impulsive.
- State the desired behavior and provide corrections briefly, calmly, and consistently. If your school has a behavior management system (e.g., SW-PBIS), follow it. Try to provide positive feedback to corrective feedback at a 4:1 rate.
- Overuse of corrective techniques is too common and can result in the reduction of effectiveness.
- Remember: Punishment, in and of itself, is often insufficient in changing problem behavior. Punishment does not teach students how they should behave.
- Investing in the behaviors you want to see eventually creates a culture in which teachers' and school leaders' jobs become a little easier and more focus can be placed on academic instruction, as students routinely behave well.

Reflect on It

- Behavior can feel personal. Are you the precipitating factor?
- What are some ways to remember it's not about you?
- What are some common classroom situations that cause misbehavior?
- What strategies listed above will help with some of the misbehavior in your classroom or school?
- Based on what you've learned, are you ready to develop or refine your own classroom management plan? If so, use the Effective Classroom Management Planning Guide located in Appendix 16 to help you.

CHAPTER 6

Collaborative Classroom Management Through the ACT Matrix

    At Hawkins Middle School, Ms. Ava Neu faces a daily battle against chaos in her seventh-grade classroom. Disruptions are rampant, and her initial enthusiasm for teaching wanes under the weight of constant conflict and disorder. The more she tries to control the class, the more it spins out of control.

    Ms. Neu, a passionate educator with years of experience, prides herself on connecting with students and fostering a positive learning environment. However, this particular group of seventh graders tests her patience and strategies. Every morning, she walks into her classroom with hope and trepidation, determined to make a difference, yet unsure how to regain control.

    Her attempts at enforcing rules are met with resistance. Students ignore her instructions, talk over her lessons, and engage in frequent side conversations. The noise level often escalates to the point where meaningful teaching becomes impossible. Despite her best efforts, the classroom atmosphere grows tense, and she notices its impact on her students' engagement and academic performance.

    Ms. Neu seeks advice from her colleagues, who offer various strategies—some suggest stricter discipline, while others recommend more engaging lesson plans and activities. She tries implementing reward systems, restructuring seating arrangements, and incorporating interactive activities, but nothing seems to have a lasting effect.

    On one particularly challenging day, Ms. Neu questions her career choice. She had always dreamed of being an inspiring teacher, but now she feels more like a disciplinarian. Her frustration peaks when, during a math lesson, a group of students starts a loud argument that disrupts the entire class. Feeling defeated, she ends the lesson early and asks the students to read silently while she retreats to her desk, contemplating her next steps.

Her turning point comes during a heartfelt discussion with Mr. Luis Gomez, a colleague known for his effective classroom management. Over shared concerns and school-brewed coffee, Mr. Gomez introduces Ms. Neu to the ACT (Acceptance and Commitment Training [or Therapy]) Matrix (Polk et al., 2016). He credits his use of the tool with transforming his classroom dynamics. He recommends building relationships and creating a classroom community where students feel valued and respected. Mr. Gomez also advises Ms. Neu to establish clear, consistent expectations and to involve students in developing classroom norms.

ACT is a mindfulness-based approach rooted in the science of human behavior (Chiesa & Malinowski, 2011). It focuses on helping people become better observers of their behavior, understand the impact of their behavior on the environment, and recognize the influence of the environment on their behavior. This includes becoming aware of both external factors and internal thoughts and feelings. ACT encourages individuals to commit to behaviors that align with their values, while acknowledging that not all thoughts and feelings are pleasant. The ACT Matrix is a tool to help people identify their values and sort through their covert behaviors or private events, thoughts, feelings, and bodily sensations that only they can observe, as well as the overt behaviors that everybody else can see them engaging in.

Ms. Neu is unsure that this approach would work. Given her students' current behavior, she isn't sure the students will be responsive. With encouragement from Mr. Gomez—and driven by desperation and hope—Ms. Neu implements this approach, inviting her students to become active stakeholders in their shared educational journey.

Starting With Shared Values

Our values serve as a personal guide in life, as they influence our decisions based on the life path we desire. They reflect our aspirations and what we aim to embody. When our values as a group align, we are more equipped to assess situations, solve problems, make decisions, and take actions that lead us in meaningful directions. To align with shared values, it's important to understand not only your values but also the values of others. For instance, if you prioritize student engagement and cooperation, as Ms. Neu does, you could promote collaborative learning and student interaction during educational tasks. Furthermore, allowing students to make choices about the activities they enjoy involves them and gives them options.

With renewed resolve, Ms. Neu holds a class meeting to discuss the issues and gather student input on improving the classroom environment.

Ms. Neu introduces her seventh-grade class to the ACT Matrix (Figure 6.1), setting the stage for a transformative day. With the classroom rearranged to foster an open-dialogue circle, she initiates a discussion different from the usual curriculum talk.

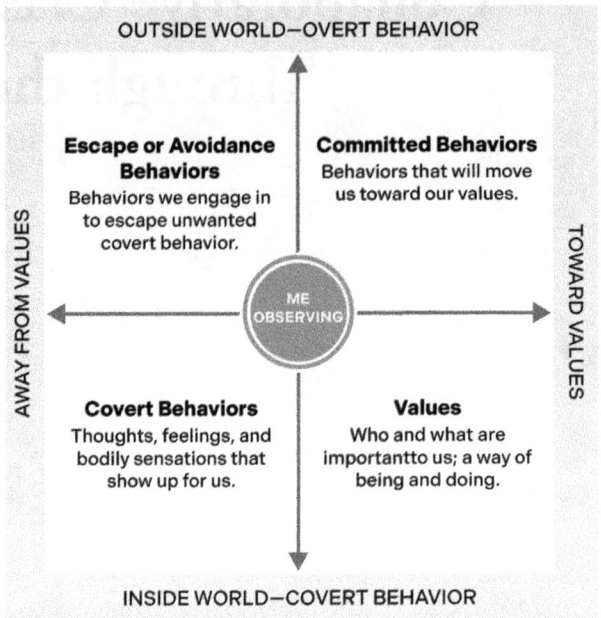

Figure 6.1. *The ACT Matrix as a self-observation tool, which involves noticing and being aware of one's behavior (adapted from the Prosocial ACT Matrix tool developed by Atkins et al. [2019]).*

"Today, we're not just discussing rules; we're exploring what matters to us deeply," Ms. Neu begins, her voice full of seriousness and excitement. "What kind of classroom environment do we want to create? What behaviors or actions do we believe will get us there?"

While initially curious and somewhat skeptical, the students gradually warm up to the conversation. Ms. Neu shares her values with the students and invites them to share theirs. During the discussion, she encourages her students to identify core values that could guide their classroom culture (Figure 6.1, lower right quadrant). Ms. Neu emphasizes the importance of these values not just as abstract ideals but as actionable principles that would inform their daily interactions.

The students propose various values, and after thoughtful discussion, they agree on three fundamental principles:

- **Respect:** Listening attentively when others speak, acknowledging diverse opinions, and treating each other courteously.

- **Teamwork:** Emphasizing collaboration over competition, encouraging group projects, and supporting each other's learning journeys.
- **Curiosity:** Maintaining an open mind, asking questions to deepen understanding, and exploring new ideas without fear of making mistakes.

To her surprise, Ms. Neu's students respond positively and offer insightful suggestions showing that they want a more respectful and productive classroom atmosphere. She also discovers that she and her students share values. These values form the foundation of their new classroom management plan, and Ms. Neu guides the students in envisioning how these values could manifest in their behavior and interactions.

Addressing Covert Behaviors

Covert behaviors are internal, and therefore unnoticed by others, but they profoundly influence one's actions. Only you can observe your thoughts, feelings, and bodily sensations. Sometimes, thoughts are negative talk, or self-deprecating things we say to ourselves. These are the crummy thoughts, feelings, and sensations that show up inside you when you walk into challenging or uncomfortable situations or environments. We have all experienced these feelings and don't like feeling them. When we experience negative thoughts and feelings, we often try to change our mindset or think positively. However, attempting to suppress or alter these feelings is comparable to holding a ball underwater. Eventually, those emotions will resurface.

Ms. Neu, a seasoned educator, has been having difficulty managing her seventh-grade class. She has been struggling with classroom management and is struggling to teach. We can imagine that Ms. Neu had many negative thoughts and feelings when arriving at work every day. She may have said things like "I think I need to quit," "These students are not listening or participating in the lesson," "Why am I even here?" or "I try so hard, and these students don't even care!" Ms. Neu has probably said those things—and many others like them.

Even after meeting with Mr. Gomez and being introduced to the ACT Matrix, she may have felt that it wouldn't work to help her improve her classroom culture. After reflecting on her worried and anxious thoughts, Ms. Neu considers her students and the environment in which they are trying to learn. It is an environment of chaos, unpredictability, and disengagement. Ms. Neu wants to understand what covert behaviors are showing up for her students.

Ms. Neu directs the students to reflect on their covert behaviors, or those behaviors preventing them from living up to their shared values (Figure 6.1, lower left quadrant). She explains what covert behaviors are and what thoughts and feelings she experienced coming to school every day. As Ms. Neu finishes speaking, several students raise their hands to join the conversation. The students openly share their feelings about how they feel when they come to class. Ms. Neu empathizes with the students' concerns about not knowing what to expect in class. They discuss feeling afraid to ask questions and express frustration with the interruptions in instruction. They also mention that some students' behaviors often disrupt fun activities in class, leading to group punishment. Some students add that they don't enjoy coming to class because it feels boring due to the disruptive behavior of some students, and they miss out on the fun activities.

During the discussion, Ms. Neu's students identify several internal or covert experiences:

- **Anxiety:** Fear of punishment or failure that might prevent them from participating or asking questions. The students say, "I don't even know what she wants us to do," "Every time someone asks a question, they get yelled at. I'm not asking anything!" and "I'm just going to put my head down so I don't get in trouble."
- **Boredom:** Feelings of disinterest or disengagement that could lead to distractions during lessons. The students say, "Ugh, this class is so boring," "I need to figure out how to get out of here; we're not doing anything anyway," "I'm going to the bathroom to see who's around," and "I'd rather be in the dean's office than in here."
- **Resentment:** Feelings of being treated unfairly or being overlooked could lead to passive-aggressive behavior toward peers or authority figures. The students say things like "Why is she yelling at me? I didn't even do anything!" "She always catches me talking, but the students who always talk, she calls on them to answer questions all the time, and they never get in trouble," and "I'm not listening to Ms. Neu, and she doesn't care what I do!"

Ms. Neu notes these on the ACT Matrix and begins to see how her behavior affects the students. She acknowledges to the students that she has not been a good observer of her behavior and hasn't realized its impact on them. Although it is hard to hear what her students are saying, Ms. Neu understands that discussing, recognizing, and acknowledging these covert behaviors is critical for dealing with them effectively.

Confronting Escape Behaviors

Consider the experience of distancing yourself from negative thoughts and sensations. No one enjoys feeling anxious or frustrated. Therefore, if you engage in certain behaviors and experience relief from those unpleasant thoughts and sensations, you effectively engage in escape behavior. While we all behave in ways that allow us to escape things that may be aversive, sometimes these behaviors move us away from what we value, and often they prevent us from reaching our goals. Though they provide us with immediate relief, such relief tends to be only temporary.

In Ms. Neu's case, she engages in behaviors such as ignoring misbehavior, retreating to her desk, and ending her lessons early. While these actions temporarily relieve uncomfortable feelings, they conflict with her core values. Ms. Neu's behavior does not align with her values, causing her to move away from them. Engaging in escape or avoidance behaviors can provide immediate relief and lead to a cycle where such behaviors worsen negative thoughts and feelings. This is exactly what has happened to Ms. Neu. Because she didn't recognize her behavior, her attempts to escape stress in the classroom led to increasing challenges associated with meeting the demands of her role as the classroom leader.

Ms. Neu guides the students in confronting their escape and avoidance behaviors. With a better understanding of their internal experiences, the class discusses escape behaviors—actions to avoid the discomfort caused by covert behaviors (Figure 6.1, upper left quadrant). Ms. Neu shares her escape and avoidance behaviors with the students. When she is done, she reminds the students they are in a safe space to share their experiences and learn from each other. Ms. Neu breaks the students into small groups and has them collectively discuss some behaviors they engage in to avoid classroom situations or escape the class. After several minutes, Ms. Neu brings the students back to share with the whole group.

The students identify and discuss several escape behaviors:

- **Zoning Out:** Disengaging by using their phone, daydreaming, ignoring activities, or being off task.
- **Disrupting Others:** Talking while others talk, telling inappropriate jokes, calling out, making noises, throwing materials, or getting out of their seat without permission.
- **Withdrawing:** Not participating in group activities or discussions, or misbehaving to be sent out of class. Not raising their hand to be called on, putting their head down, or falling asleep.

Ms. Neu emphasizes that certain behaviors, although they provide temporary relief, ultimately prevent the class from achieving their desired environment. She reminds her students of the shared values they have identified in the lower right quadrant. This prompts the students to start making connections. As they respond, the students begin to realize how their actions are contributing to the problematic classroom culture and begin to be more self-aware of the impact of their behavior.

Committing to Committed Behaviors

In the most critical phase of Ms. Neu's session with her students, it is important for her to identify specific behaviors that would align with their established values (Figure 6.1, upper right quadrant). As you work through the matrix, you should list behaviors that align with your values in the upper right quadrant. Consider the positive impact of having students in Ms. Neu's classroom cooperate and encourage each other. By acknowledging negative thoughts and feelings and choosing behaviors that align with your values, you can achieve your value-driven goals and experience a sense of satisfaction. Ms. Neu gives some examples of her committed actions and the behaviors that she would engage in to help support changes in their classroom culture and move them toward their shared values.

Ms. Neu commits to outlining expectations for classroom routines and procedures. She also tells the students that she will include them in developing the classroom management plan. She shares some ways she might incorporate fun activities into instructions, also gaining the students' input. Ms. Neu then asks the students to return to their small groups and brainstorm specific behaviors and actions that could help improve their classroom culture.

The students identify several committed behaviors:

- **Active Participation:** Engaging in class discussions and activities, asking questions, and coming prepared for class. Asking for help when needed.
- **Following Expectations:** Listening attentively to the teacher and following instructions. Being prepared for class with all necessary materials. Completing assignments on time and to the best of their ability.

- **Respectful Communication:** Speaking kindly; listening without interrupting; and addressing conflicts directly, respectfully, and privately.

The students and Ms. Neu commit to behaviors they feel capable of undertaking. This creates a sense of accountability and collective responsibility.

Implementation and Continuous Review

With the ACT Matrix framework established, Ms. Neu and her students plan a strategy to implement these behaviors. They set clear, achievable goals and develop metrics for evaluating their progress, such as tracking instances of active participation and measuring the decrease in disruptive incidents.

The class commits to revisiting the matrix weekly to discuss their progress and challenges in order to remain aligned with their values and to make necessary adjustments to their strategies.

Improved Classroom Culture

Ms. Neu and her students collaboratively developed a set of classroom norms that everyone agreed to follow. She also introduced regular class discussions to address ongoing concerns and celebrate successes. Over time, she notices a gradual improvement in student behavior and engagement. The classroom, once a source of daily stress, begins to transform into a place of mutual respect and learning.

Though challenges still arise, Ms. Neu feels more equipped to handle them. She realizes that fostering a positive classroom environment is an ongoing process that requires patience, flexibility, and collaboration. Her journey is far from over, but she is no longer fighting the battle alone. Together with her students, Ms. Neu is building the classroom community she has always envisioned.

Through this detailed application of the ACT Matrix, Ms. Neu's classroom transforms into a collaborative and engaged learning environment. The students become more respectful and proactive and develop key life skills in self-management and empathy. This journey highlights the power of involving students in shaping their educational experiences, proving that a values-driven approach to classroom management fosters significant and lasting change.

Key Points

- Students bring their personal learning histories, encompassing various events that influence their engagement with the classroom environment. Similarly, teachers bring their accumulated experiences, which significantly impact the classroom environment.
- Instead of avoiding inner thoughts and feelings, one acknowledges and accepts them for what they are—thoughts.
- Learning the skill of acceptance can help teachers and students articulate their feelings and emotions.
- Covert behaviors are internal experiences, such as thoughts and feelings, that only individuals can observe. They often involve getting caught up in our thoughts, letting them control our actions, and causing us to get stuck. These negative thoughts and feelings arise in difficult, challenging, or uncomfortable situations. Covert behavior is the negative self-talk we engage in about our behavior.
- Engaging in escape or avoidance behavior involves distancing oneself from negative thoughts and sensations, which provides immediate but temporary relief. However, these behaviors can move us away from our values and goals.
- Pinpointed committed behaviors are essential for cultivating a learning atmosphere where students feel included and empowered to participate. This quadrant focuses on specific behaviors that help the classroom move toward its shared values despite challenges and that foster a culture of respect, engagement, and mutual support.
- The ACT Matrix allows the classroom community to openly discuss thoughts and feelings, which leads to actions dedicated to achieving common goals of respect, engagement, and support. This process helps create a harmonious classroom environment and equips students with essential life skills.
- The ACT Matrix helps teachers and students identify shared values, recognize behaviors that impede learning, and promote a positive learning environment.
- The ACT Matrix is an adaptable tool that can be used in multiple ways with different types of groups. Review the ACT Matrix for Classrooms in Appendix 22 for a sample plan for incorporating the matrix into classroom instruction.

Reflect on It
- Identify and define your values. How can identifying personal values help students and the classroom leader cultivate a positive classroom environment?
- As the classroom leader, do you know what committed behaviors you want to see from your students? Before working through the ACT Matrix, identify some value goals for the class to guide your instruction.
- What might you, as the classroom leader, do more, less, or differently to support students' appropriate behavior in alignment with shared values?
- Consider how you can create a safe space for students to share. It can be challenging for students to be honest about their thoughts and feelings regarding their classroom experience. As the classroom leader, how can you make students comfortable sharing their thoughts and feelings?
- What would be some indicators that student behavior is moving in the right direction toward the classroom's shared values? How will you let students know that their behavior is moving in the right direction?

SECTION II:

School Leadership for Reducing Misbehavior

CHAPTER 7

Changing Student Misbehavior Requires Good Leadership

Until now, our discussion on misbehavior has largely centered around the teacher's role within the classroom environment. Now it's time to broaden our perspective to include the external factors linked to student behavior. For teachers reading this chapter—and we hope all of you are—you might feel that what happens outside the classroom is beyond your influence. This isn't entirely true. Often, a lack of awareness about how far-reaching your impact can be limits your involvement. If you possess expertise in behavioral management, sharing your knowledge with school administrators or the discipline team can significantly enhance their effectiveness and help them become part of the solution, rather than having them perpetuate the problem.

For school leaders, this chapter aims to explore misbehavior in relation to leadership roles and responsibilities, and to introduce systematic approaches that could prove transformative.

Effective student behavior management and academic achievement require collaboration. It's a misconception that the responsibility for educational success or challenges rests solely on teachers. Such a notion not only harms morale but also simplifies complex issues and obstructs efforts to improve learning and reduce misbehavior. In truth, education is delivered by a team, and effective teamwork necessitates strong leadership.

A fundamental objective of public education is to equip students with the necessary skills to succeed in college and their careers. Research has shown that an effective school environment significantly boosts the likelihood of student success (Marzano & Waters, 2009). However, studies have also identified several barriers to achieving these outcomes, including ineffective teacher preparation programs (Eckert, 2013; Organisation for Economic Co-operation and Development, 2023) and inadequate leadership (Marzano, Waters, & McNulty, 2005; Marzano & Waters, 2009; Grissom et al., 2021), which detrimentally impact student achievement. Echoing B. F. Skinner's sentiments in "The Shame of American Education" (1984), we believe that untaught students reflect unprepared teachers, who themselves are products of deficient preparatory programs that fail to incorporate behavioral science into their curricula.

The importance of leadership in education cannot be overstated. Leaders require tools that simplify their roles and foster optimal outcomes. If you are a classroom teacher, consider viewing yourself as an organizational leader, with your classroom as a small enterprise where your "employees" (students) work toward crucial "business" results (academic success). If you are in a school or district leadership position, or aspire to one, the following insights will be particularly relevant. No matter your official title, we address you as a leader because that is precisely what you are. Leading may not be easy, but it can be simplified through systematic approaches.

Many educators find themselves ill-equipped to handle the behavioral challenges of their students, a predicament exacerbated by insufficient training in behavior management, overstretched school resources, and overwhelming staff responsibilities. Preparing educators to better manage and prevent misbehavior is essential for resource optimization and workload management. This book outlines numerous strategies and practices to achieve these ends, yet knowledge alone may not suffice. Implementing these strategies effectively requires strong leadership. Fortunately, the principles of organizational behavior management (OBM) and behavioral science offer powerful tools for leadership that can significantly enhance operational dynamics in educational settings.

Achieving Results Through Behavioral Alignment

Imagine a midsize public school somewhere in the United States heartland. This school is known for its dedicated teachers but plagued by rising incidents of student misbehavior.

In one particular year, the school introduces a new principal, Mr. Thompson, who is eager to make his mark. Early in his tenure, a significant altercation in the cafeteria leads to a school board meeting, where the blame is placed squarely on the teachers for failing to effectively manage student behavior.

The meeting is charged with tension. Teachers feel scapegoated and demoralized, parents are concerned, and the administration is defensive. Mr. Thompson, feeling the pressure, initially considers focusing on teacher training and stricter disciplinary policies. However, he soon realizes that the issues are symptoms of a larger systemic problem rather than individual teacher failings.

This realization marks a turning point. Mr. Thompson understands that a broader approach is needed—one that encompasses not just the teachers but the entire ecosystem of the school. Just like designing instruction with the end objective in mind, he decides to adopt a systematic approach, starting by envisioning the desired student behaviors and working backward to determine what will enable these behaviors to flourish.

First, Mr. Thompson considers the ultimate goal: well-behaved students who are engaged and successful. He asks himself, "What student behavior will achieve the intended results?" This leads him to the next question: "What teacher behaviors are likely to create these desired student outcomes?" It becomes clear that teachers need more than just discipline strategies; they need support, resources, and a voice in school governance.

Reflecting further, Mr. Thompson ponders, "What do teachers and staff need from their leadership to help them demonstrate the necessary behavior?" This question opens up a dialogue about trust, respect, and professional development. It also leads to the crucial question of what Mr. Thompson himself needs: "What does leadership need from the district to promote the desired teacher and student behavior?" And finally, "What do districts need from the state so they can maximize potential?"

By addressing these questions, Mr. Thompson initiates a shift from a blame-focused culture to one of systemic evaluation and support. This approach does not just look at individual components, but it examines how they interconnect within the larger educational system. This narrative sets the stage for a transformative approach in the school, focusing on leadership at every level and showing that when it comes to reducing misbehavior and improving outcomes, systemic thinking and comprehensive leadership are indispensable.

Stop Blaming, Start Behaving

As Mr. Thompson recognized, blaming the teachers is useless. In fact, it's harmful. The behavior that needed to change first was his! When it comes to reducing misbehavior, an effective leader like Mr. Thompson should focus on evaluating the school's behavior management system and everyone involved. This can be accomplished systematically by planning strategically with the end in mind (Figure 7.1; Gavoni & Costa, 2023).

First Approach

This approach begins with determining the most important result, and then aligning behavior by beginning with the student and moving up the hierarchical ladder by asking the following questions:

1. What is the desired result?
2. What student behavior will achieve the intended results?
3. What teacher behaviors are likely to create the desired student outcomes?

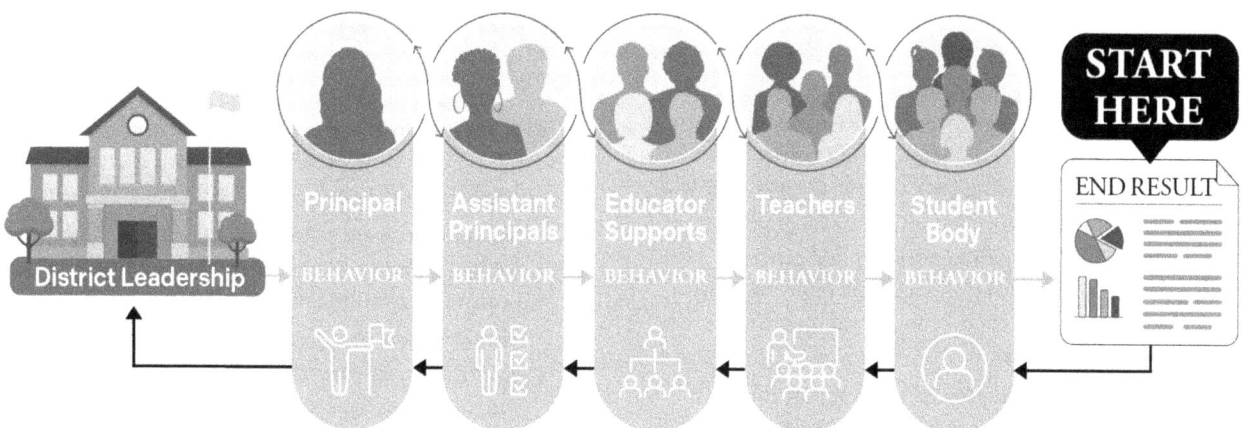

Figure 7.1. School leaders can systematically align behavior, beginning with the desired end result.

4. What do teachers and staff need from their leadership to help them demonstrate the necessary behavior?
5. What does leadership need from the district to promote the desired teacher and student behavior?

By employing this behavioral engineering logic, improving student behavior can be addressed through a systems approach that links the behavior of classroom leaders, school leaders, and district leaders. You see, it's all about leadership—at every level.

Check this out. According to Marzano et al. (2005), "A highly effective school leader can have a dramatic influence on the overall academic achievement of students" (p. 97). In one study, the researchers found a 0.25 correlation between the leadership behavior of the school's principal and the average academic achievement of the school. To make this clearer, a correlation of 0.25 means there is a noticeable, positive connection between how well the principal leads and how well the students do in school. For example, if a principal improves their leadership skills significantly, it could lead to better grades and test scores for the students. Furthermore, researchers found that principals who were one standard deviation above the average in terms of leadership skills could raise student achievement by as much as 34%. Folks, this is just the effect of one person—the school leader! As such, a primary focus of districts should be on creating a system that allows for effective recruiting, selecting, training, and coaching of school leaders; all processes that can be firmly supported by OBM.

Second Approach

Once critical behaviors are identified and aligned at each level within the school and district, the second approach should be to use performance diagnostics to determine why a student, classroom leader, or even school leader is not performing to a standard. Performance diagnostics allow for precise intervention, as this analysis informs if a performance issue is a "can't do" or a "won't do." Let's face it, not everybody needs training, and training can be costly in terms of money, time, and human resources. Some folks just need reminders, more efficient processes, or maybe just a little bit of coaching to get them in touch with valued outcomes (reinforcement) by engaging in the right behavior. We'll unpack a process that allows leaders to quickly self-assess and diagnose performance issues in the next chapter.

Third Approach

The third practical approach that should occur is for all district and school leaders to be trained to shape performance (behavior). Shaping performance is the process of reinforcing successive approximation toward a desired goal (Skinner, 1956). As part of this process, leaders should be taught to emphasize the use of positive reinforcement through effective feedback. District, school, and classroom leaders who understand and effectively use feedback to positively reinforce are much more likely to gain what Aubrey Daniels calls discretionary effort (Daniels & Daniels, 2004). This simply means educators and students go above and beyond ... even when the leader is not looking. This is in contrast with district, school, or classroom leaders who gain compliance at the expense of morale, retention, and student achievement as they rely heavily on threats of punishment and other coercive means. Since the shaping process uses positive reinforcement from a strength-based perspective (i.e., beginning where the performer is), it typically improves the climate and culture of schools. Both teachers and students are primarily recognized (receive reinforcement) for what they are doing right and then provided with feedback (teaching replacement behaviors/expectations) on how they can become even better.

Fourth Approach

The final practical approach is to measure leaders based on the improvement of the followers they directly supervise. In many districts, assistant superintendents or district leaders with a variety of other titles "supervise" a group of principals; however, many times they are not directly evaluated based on the performance and accomplishments of these principals. If eight principals under an assistant superintendent fail to achieve, the accountability often falls solely on the principals. Thinking back to strategic planning with the end in mind,

- The assistant superintendent should provide leadership coaching and learning opportunities to the principals and be measured by their accomplishments.
- Principals should provide these opportunities to teachers and be measured by their performance.
- Teachers should provide learning opportunities and be measured based on student performance.

Mr. Thompson in Action

Let's get back to Mr. Thompson to see how he applied his strategic approach to transforming the school's discipline system.

Recognizing the critical need for systemic change, Mr. Thompson embarks on implementing a behavioral engineering strategy, starting with the end in mind, to address and reduce student misbehavior. This methodical approach requires clear identification of desired outcomes at every level in order to ensure that all members of the school ecosystem are aligned and contributing positively.

Identifying Desired Outcomes and Behaviors

Mr. Thompson starts with the end goal: reducing suspensions and fostering a positive and engaging school environment. He poses critical questions to delineate the path forward:

- What is the desired result? Specifically, a reduction in student suspensions.
- What student behavior will achieve these results? Compliance with school rules, active engagement in learning, and effective conflict resolution among students.
- What teacher behaviors will foster these student outcomes? Development and consistent application of effective classroom management plans, positive reinforcement strategies, and corrective measures maintaining a 4:1 positive-to-negative interaction ratio.
- What do teachers need from their leadership to exhibit these behaviors? Clear guidelines; adequate resources; ongoing professional development; and supportive, constructive feedback.

Engaging Leadership at Every Level

Mr. Thompson understands that for this plan to be successful, it needs strong leadership at both the school and district levels. Thus, he ensures that

- School leaders are trained to observe, provide feedback, and support teachers using the same 4:1 positive interaction ratio.
- School leaders practice self-monitoring and reporting, evaluating their effectiveness in supporting teachers and enhancing the school's behavioral environment.
- District leadership provides necessary support to school leaders, including resources for professional development and tools for effective behavior management.

Systematic Implementation and Feedback

Mr. Thompson emphasizes the importance of continuous feedback and adjustments based on real-time data. This involves

- Performance diagnostics to understand the root causes of misbehavior or performance issues, distinguishing between "can't do" and "won't do" scenarios.
- Shaping behavior through successive approximations, encouraging and reinforcing small steps toward the desired behaviors at all levels—students, teachers, and leaders.
- Regular training and reinforcement for leaders to use positive feedback effectively, enhancing motivation and engagement across the board.

Evaluating Success and Sustaining Change

Finally, Mr. Thompson institutes a process for evaluating the effectiveness of the interventions:

- Measuring impact through specific metrics, such as reductions in suspension rates and improvements in student engagement and academic performance.
- Establishing feedback loops where teachers, staff, and students can share their experiences and the impact of the new strategies, fostering a culture of openness and continuous improvement.

By applying this comprehensive strategy, Mr. Thompson aims not only to reduce student suspensions but also to create a more supportive, effective educational environment. His leadership demonstrates the profound impact that thoughtful, systemic change can have on a school's culture and student success, proving that leadership at every level is crucial in shaping positive outcomes in education.

Measurement

As demonstrated in Mr. Thompson's approach, effective change in school environments begins at the top and must be systematically implemented at each level of the educational hierarchy. Leadership at both the district and school levels plays a pivotal role in shaping the behaviors and outcomes within their respective domains. A thorough assessment of leadership practices, using tools such as 360-degree surveys, interviews, and analysis of existing data, is crucial (Allen & Hartman, 2008; Northouse, 2007; Owens & Valesky, 2010). Additionally, incorporating measures of social validity at the classroom level, such as surveying students to gauge their perceptions of classroom leadership, can significantly enhance our understanding of the educational climate and culture, leading to measurable improvements in student achievement (Ferguson, 2012).

By establishing a robust system of measurement, leaders can provide targeted coaching and developmental opportunities to enhance performance across all tiers—from assistant superintendents to students. This structured approach not only aims to improve student behavior sustainably but also enriches the job satisfaction of educators by creating an environment that brings out the best in everyone involved.

An often overlooked aspect of shaping an effective educational environment is recognizing the influence that behavior—whether of students, assistants, teachers, or administrators—has on the behaviors of others. Supporting adults in a manner that leads to observable, positive changes in student behavior serves as a powerful, naturally occurring reinforcer. When the intervention is straightforward and paired with supportive leadership, it increases the likelihood that teachers and other school staff will continue to engage with and apply recommended strategies, even those that might require a greater effort.

However, it's important to acknowledge the challenges inherent in self-assessment and performance change. Like their students, adults may struggle to accurately observe their behaviors and understand the impact of their actions on the environment and vice versa. This underscores the need for leaders to employ an OBM approach, utilizing observation and precise measurement to align desired outcomes with specific behaviors. For instance, classroom behaviors such as on-task versus disruptive actions, and teacher behaviors including setting clear expectations, providing ample positive reinforcement, addressing misbehavior constructively, and engaging students academically, are all critical areas for focus.

Utilizing tools including the Student Performance Diagnostic Checklist, outlined in Appendix 18, can help pinpoint the root causes of behavioral or academic issues and guide targeted interventions. The classroom, much like a small organization, requires the teacher, as the leader, to continually assess and adapt strategies to optimize both individual and collective student performance.

In preparing for intervention, it is essential for educational leaders to collect baseline data to understand the current performance levels of students and teachers. This information forms the foundation for goal setting, planning interventions, and shaping progress through systematic feedback. Data collection tools focused on classroom ecology can reveal key insights, such as the frequency with which teachers acknowledge positive behaviors versus misbehavior.

A continuous emphasis on positive reinforcement remains central to this approach. By ensuring that adults within the school consistently acknowledge and praise students for appropriate behaviors and establish themselves as positive reinforcers, we create an environment where prosocial behaviors (i.e., behaviors that benefit others) are more likely to occur. When these positive behaviors align with essential educational outcomes, such as student achievement, the results can be transformative, creating a thriving educational ecosystem where every member can succeed.

Measuring Behavior Management Performance

Our experience has shown that teachers often receive more of the behaviors they pay most attention to. Unfortunately, misbehavior tends to be noticed more frequently than appropriate behavior, even when there is plenty of positive behavior deserving recognition. As previously discussed, a good rule of thumb for teacher-student interactions is to maintain a ratio of 4 positive interactions to every 1 correction, with some even advocating for an 8:1 ratio. This principle of emphasizing more positive than negative interactions should similarly guide school leaders in their dealings with teachers.

Defining what constitutes a positive versus a negative interaction is pivotal for both understanding and improving teacher performance. To achieve this clarity, we must remove judgment and subjectivity from our evaluations. The nature of an interaction should not be based on the perceived quality of the exchange between the teacher and the student but rather on what the student is doing at the time of the interaction. If a student is engaged in appropriate behavior when the teacher interacts with them, that should be considered a positive interaction. Conversely, if a student is engaged in inappropriate behavior and the teacher responds, that interaction should be marked as negative. This approach prevents the inadvertent reinforcement of undesirable behavior and ensures that feedback is objective and actionable.

Moreover, interactions can be further classified, for example, using a B if behavior-specific praise was used, or an R if a reprimand was given. The primary goal of collecting these data is not to critique or find fault with teachers but to identify strengths and areas for improvement that can lead to a measurable decrease in classroom disruptions and an increase in on-task behavior. Therefore, it's essential that teachers are involved in this process and understand that the data are used as a tool for positive reinforcement, not as a punitive measure.

Establishing trust with teachers before beginning to collect data is vital. Teachers should be assured that observations are not part of their formal evaluations and that any data collected will remain confidential. They need to feel confident that the purpose of data collection is to develop interventions that enhance outcomes for both them and their students.

Addressing behavioral issues can be challenging, and resistance from teachers is understandable. They often feel blamed for problems beyond their control. However, just as we would never accept a behavior specialist resigning to the notion that a student "will never change," we should not accept this mindset for teachers. In reality, teachers are learners too, and leaders must be equipped to support them effectively. If a teacher struggles with behavior management or classroom control, it's often due to skill deficits or motivational gaps.

As leaders, it's our role to foster an environment where teachers feel supported and valued, creating a positive feedback loop that enhances both teacher performance and student behavior. By applying the same principles we expect from teachers in their interactions with students, school leaders can significantly improve the educational experience for everyone involved. This sets the stage for exploring how we can address skill and motivation deficits among teachers, which we will delve into in the next chapter.

Key Points

- Many school personnel enter their districts unprepared to meet the behavioral needs of students.
- Preparing leaders and teachers to better prevent and manage misbehavior is a good way to maximize resources.
- Getting people to follow a good plan and develop good habits requires good leadership.
- School leaders should stop putting 100% of the focus on the teachers and refocus some of their energies on looking at the school's behavior management system and everybody involved via a behavioral engineering approach that begins with the end result.
- Identify critical behaviors within the school and district. Align these behaviors at each level.
- Use performance diagnostics (covered in the next chapter) to determine why a student, classroom leader, or even school leader is not performing to a standard.
- Leaders should be taught to emphasize the use of positive reinforcement through effective feedback.
- District, school, and classroom leaders who understand and correctly use effective feedback to positively reinforce are much more likely to gain discretionary effort (Daniels & Daniels, 2004) from educators and students, as evidenced by them going above and beyond, even when no one is looking.
- Improving student behavior in a way that is sustainable requires adjusting the environment so that it brings out the best in them. An added benefit is making the jobs of school and classroom leaders easier!
- People tend to be poor observers of their own behavior, the impact of their behavior on the environment, and the impact of the environment on their behavior.
- The classroom is like a small organization, complete with the teacher as the leader and systems, processes, tasks, and behaviors all aimed at producing an extremely important "business result," which is, ultimately, student achievement.

Reflect on It

- Using a systems approach and leadership grounded in principles of OBM, think about the following questions:
  - What student behavior will achieve the intended results?
  - What teacher behaviors are likely to create the desired student outcomes?
  - What do teachers and staff need from their leadership to help them demonstrate the necessary behavior?
  - What does leadership need from the district to promote the desired teacher and student behavior?
  - Why are some teachers resistant to change related to student behavior?
  - What are some ways to minimize resistance?
  - What are some ways to support teachers in improving their classroom management?

CHAPTER 8

Changing Student Misbehavior Requires Performance Diagnostics and Coaching

Effective school leaders prioritize boosting student achievement by nurturing teachers' capacity to consistently apply appropriate practices across various situations. This approach helps foster behaviors that are directly connected to positive outcomes, gradually turning these actions into ingrained habits. Wagner (2012) emphasizes that the objective for school leaders should be to design and implement strategies that expedite the formation and continuation of these positive habits within classrooms and schools.

Performance evaluations, often viewed as a necessary evil within educational settings, are commonly used to foster such habits. However, despite good intentions, these evaluations can be counterproductive and are frequently dreaded by both teachers and administrators. Instead of traditional evaluations, we advocate for the adoption of straightforward coaching strategies based on behavioral science. These strategies focus on enhancing teacher performance rather than merely assessing it, which we will explore in greater detail.

Consider a scenario where a school leader observes two new teachers who fail to employ effective questioning techniques, both scoring a 1 on a 0–4 evaluation scale, indicating that their skills are at a beginner level. What follows? Does the leader opt for additional training, or are other methods like direct modeling or focused coaching considered?

Suppose that these teachers recently attended a district-led professional development session on questioning techniques. It's critical to remember that attendance at a training session does not guarantee that the teachers are now proficient in these skills. Training can enhance knowledge, but transferring these skills into the classroom is another challenge altogether.

Research by Joyce and Showers (2002) suggests that training involving theoretical discussion leads to only a 10% increase in knowledge and a mere 5% increase in performance during the training. What's worse, the study found that 0% of the skills taught in these sessions were applied back in the classroom without further support (see Figure 8.1).

This stark discrepancy highlights the need for school leaders to critically assess the effectiveness of professional development before investing in it as the sole solution to performance issues. It's vital to consider whether other barriers might be preventing the effective application of new skills. Even with training, a nuanced approach that includes ongoing support and reinforcement is crucial for ensuring that new skills are not only learned but also consistently applied. Thus, the role of the school leader extends beyond sending teachers to training: It involves a comprehensive strategy that supports the actual application of learned skills in the classroom.

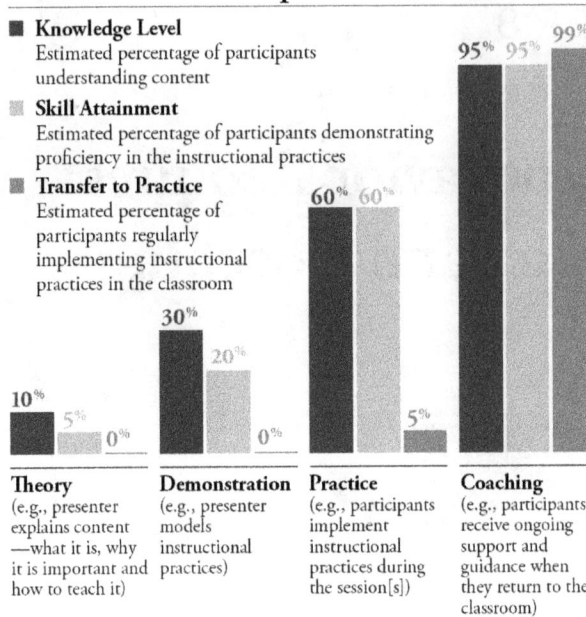

Figure 8.1. In the example here, we see data that show the outcomes related to coaching. Teachers showed a marked improvement in their knowledge, demonstration, and application of various training components following coaching within the classroom. Adapted from Joyce and Showers (2002).

Performance Diagnostic Checklist—"Can't Do" or "Won't Do"?

Training can indeed be costly and time-consuming, and it's not always the optimal solution to performance issues. This requires that leaders first comprehensively understand the reasons behind performance deficits before initiating any intervention. Typically, the root causes boil down to two simple explanations: Either the teachers can't do it due to lack of ability, or they won't do it due to lack of motivation. The strategies for addressing these issues vary significantly, necessitating a precise diagnosis.

Organizational behavior management (OBM) provides a valuable tool for discerning these root causes—the Performance Diagnostic Checklist (PDC), developed by Austin (2000; Carr et al., 2013a). This tool consists of a series of straightforward questions designed to pinpoint the underlying reasons for performance lapses. The PDC is utilized by OBM practitioners to gather data for a detailed performance analysis, yet its simplicity makes it accessible for use by school leaders as well. Employing the PDC involves only a brief questionnaire and requires only minimal time and effort but potentially yields substantial insights. The data collected can help identify specific issues affecting individual teachers, as well as common trends affecting groups, and can guide the development of targeted and effective interventions.

When teachers fail to meet performance expectations, too often the immediate reaction is to blame them. However, such an approach seldom resolves the underlying issues and instead creates a number of issues that typically hurt morale; performance; retention; and, ultimately, student achievement. Instead, the PDC approach focuses on identifying practical root causes related to factors such as antecedents and training, knowledge and skills, processes, and motivation. This method avoids placing blame and instead emphasizes adjusting the environment to better support teacher performance. This shift allows school leaders to focus on their crucial role in motivating and supporting teachers.

To facilitate this process, we have included a modified version of the Student PDC in Appendix 18, tailored for use as a self-assessment tool by educational leaders. We have also included a PDC for Coaching (Appendix 23). These help district, school, and classroom leaders evaluate their own performance as well as that of those they are supporting. Whether you are a district leader coaching a school principal, a principal coaching teachers, or a teacher guiding students, self-reflection is vital to ensure that the necessary support structures are in place.

The modified PDCs enable leaders to determine the root causes of performance issues more effectively, serving as a road map for identifying the most appropriate interventions. For example, if the issue is not about the lack of skill but rather the need for reminders, implementing a simple visual support system might be more effective than additional training. This could help reinforce the desired behavior until it becomes habitual.

Similarly, when a student underperforms, teachers need to look beyond presumptive skill or knowledge deficits. Sometimes, the issue may be related to motivation rather than capability. The PDC emphasizes the importance of tailored, assessment-driven interventions, underscoring a fundamental principle of effective behavioral science and practice. This structured approach ensures that interventions are not only appropriate but also implemented in a way that maximizes the likelihood of lasting positive change, enhancing both teacher performance and student achievement.

Can't Do

First, targeted professional development is crucial. Effective professional development should be sustained over time and include practical, hands-on components. One highly effective method is behavioral skills training (BST), which involves four main components: instruction, modeling, rehearsal, and feedback. BST has been shown to significantly improve teachers' implementation of new strategies by providing clear instructions, demonstrating the desired behaviors, allowing teachers to practice these behaviors, and offering immediate feedback (Darling-Hammond et al., 2017; Parsons & Rollyson, 2012). This method ensures that teachers not only understand the new strategies but also have ample opportunities to practice them in a supportive environment.

Second, the importance of ongoing support and coaching cannot be overstated. Darling-Hammond et al. (2017) found that continuous coaching and feedback significantly enhance the application of new teaching strategies in the classroom. This means that after initial training sessions, teachers should receive regular follow-up support to help them refine their skills and overcome any implementation challenges. Moreover, collaborative approaches to coaching, as highlighted by Weddle et al. (2023), promote teacher capacity by fostering student-centered discussions and mediating between teachers and school leaders to develop shared goals.

What's more, creating professional learning communities (PLCs) within schools provides a platform for teachers to collaborate, share experiences, and learn from each other. Research has shown that well-implemented PLCs significantly contribute to teacher professional development and improved student learning outcomes (Cheng & Zhao, 2023). PLCs foster a culture of continuous improvement and mutual support, which is essential for skill development.

Additionally, providing necessary resources and tools is vital for teachers to succeed. These include instructional guides, lesson plans, and classroom management tools tailored to the specific needs identified through the PDCs. Ensuring that teachers have access to these resources can help bridge the gap between knowing and doing.

In summary, addressing the "can't do" scenario involves a comprehensive approach that includes diagnosing skill deficits, providing targeted professional development, offering ongoing support and coaching, fostering collaborative learning through PLCs, and supplying necessary resources. By implementing these strategies, educational leaders can ensure that teachers are well-equipped with the skills they need to enhance their classroom practices, and ultimately, student achievement.

Won't Do

When tackling the issue of a "won't do" scenario, where teachers possess the necessary skills but fail to consistently implement them, it's important to understand the profound impact of effective coaching and feedback. According to Joyce and Showers (2002), while instructional strategies such as modeling and rehearsal with feedback during training sessions might yield a minimal return of about 5% in terms of actual application in the classroom, coaching as a follow-up can dramatically increase this to about 99% (Figure 8.1). This divide highlights the essential role of ongoing support in the form of coaching, which ensures that skills learned during training are effectively transferred to classroom practice.

The success of coaching hinges largely on the frequency and immediacy of the feedback provided, as well as the teacher's ability to see the positive impacts of their instructional behaviors on student outcomes. Without these elements, even well-trained teachers might not exhibit the desirable behaviors that lead to significant student achievement over the long term.

Feedback is a critical component in this process, encompassing not just corrective or constructive criticism but also reinforcing and even corrective feedback. Reinforcing feedback, in particular, is vital as it helps teachers align their behaviors with positive outcomes. For instance, when teachers can see that a specific teaching strategy directly leads to better student engagement or learning, they are more likely to feel motivated to continue using that strategy.

Corrective feedback, when used appropriately, is helpful and supportive. It involves providing immediate and clear indications of behaviors that need adjustment to improve effectiveness. For example, if a teacher consistently overlooks a key component of a teaching strategy, constructive feedback can highlight areas for improvement and suggest ways to enhance student learning (Guinness et al., 2020; Johnson et al., 2023).

This type of feedback should be seen as a positive and helpful tool aimed at stopping ineffective practices and encouraging growth. When coaches balance reinforcing feedback to motivate and corrective feedback to guide improvements, teachers receive a comprehensive understanding of their performance, which facilitates continuous improvement and better teaching outcomes.

Motivation, in this context, is defined not as a value judgment but as the likelihood that a professional will choose to engage in a specific action. Therefore, providing positive reinforcement can strengthen a teacher's inclination to employ certain skills by enhancing both their abilities and their motivation.

To improve motivation effectively, interventions can be simple yet impactful. For example, direct feedback, such as leaving appreciative notes on a teacher's desk, can make a significant difference. Notes might say something like, "I really appreciated how you incorporated choral responding today. It was great to see all your students actively engaged and on task during the math lesson," or "The way you implemented the 'Jot Thoughts' strategy we discussed really stood out. It fostered meaningful dialogue among the students and noticeably reduced misbehavior."

This type of feedback helps teachers see the tangible effects of their efforts and align their behaviors with meaningful changes in the classroom environment. By ensuring that teachers not only know how to perform certain actions but also see the positive outcomes resulting from these actions, school leaders can effectively foster a more motivated, skilled, and responsive teaching staff. This approach not only enhances the educational experience for students but also contributes to a more supportive and productive environment for teachers.

Antecedents

Incorporating feedback through the use of the PDC extends beyond mere correction—it targets critical antecedent strategies such as goal setting and prompting to initiate desired behaviors. By clearly specifying the skills that leaders want teachers to use, or by providing timely reminders before observations, leaders can increase the likelihood that teachers will implement these skills. This approach hinges on the teachers using specific behavior management techniques and observing the positive effects on student behavior, thereby reinforcing the likelihood of these techniques being used again.

For instance, if a teacher applies a particular classroom management strategy and sees an improvement in student behavior, this positive experience is likely to encourage repeated use of the strategy. Antecedent strategies such as goal setting and prompting can effectively initiate these beneficial behaviors. Such interventions can be implemented school-wide—during meetings and announcements, or even through emails.

It's important for school leaders to understand that while training, goal setting, and prompting are essential antecedent strategies, they are just the beginning. These strategies help start the behavioral change, but what truly sustains the change is the consequences (reinforcers) that follow. Therefore, while antecedents set the stage for behavior, the subsequent reinforcers ensure its maintenance and enhancement.

The role of educational leaders extends to adjusting both antecedents and consequences to shape and maintain teacher behavior. This involves creating opportunities for educators to practice the desired behaviors, receive constructive feedback, and experience positive reinforcement in their natural teaching environments. This cycle of practice and reinforcement helps develop lasting habits that lead to beneficial outcomes for both teachers and students (Gavoni & Weatherly, 2024).

Environmental factors play a significant role in shaping behaviors across all levels of a school system. By thoughtfully analyzing and arranging these environmental variables, leaders can avoid placing undue blame, focus on developing skills, and address motivational issues effectively.

When district, school, or classroom leaders encounter performance issues or fail to meet expectations, the PDC serves as an invaluable tool for diagnosing the root causes. This tool aids leaders in identifying the precise actions needed to enhance performance and achieve desired outcomes. These actions might include ensuring that teachers and students are equipped with the necessary tools, processes, knowledge, skills, and motivation.

Interestingly, the application of the PDC isn't limited to leaders. Teachers can also use it with their students to discern why certain behaviors or performances are lacking—whether it's a "can't do" or a "won't do" situation (Witt & Beck, 1999). Understanding the underlying reasons for performance gaps allows for targeted interventions, moving from diagnostic insights to effective coaching and improved outcomes. Thus, the PDC not only facilitates a deeper understanding of behavior and performance but also empowers leaders and teachers to implement strategic changes that enhance the educational environment.

From Evaluator to Coach

It's been our experience that performance appraisals are typically ineffective for improving performance and might even be detrimental to the progress of an organization. Midyear and annual evaluations are often based on an employee's most recent performance, on the relationship between the employee and the supervisor, or on the supervisor's concerns of retaliation from the employee (Daniels & Daniels, 2004). In other words, these appraisals are not a true reflection of employee performance. Unfortunately, in many organizations, including schools, rather than functioning to improve performance, appraisals more often function as written documentation to avoid union issues and help get rid of an employee without fear of retribution (Robbins et al., 2013).

Not only do they suck time and energy away from leadership and management, but performance appraisals tend to only be successful in creating fear and a culture of compliance. Skills are not fostered, and motivation is not maximized with coercion. If you are a leader who truly wants to improve performance and the related outcomes in your school and classrooms, consider shifting from appraisal processes that only serve to "judge" performance to coaching processes.

Most districts and schools need to significantly improve how they measure employee performance, both in method and frequency. District, school, and classroom leaders are aware of this need. However, it seems that state and federal leaders have not fully recognized or addressed this issue yet. Leaders at all levels in districts want to be effective, and not just check boxes out of compliance, as they know this does not lead to improved behavior, performance, or student achievement. Effective leadership requires regular, easy to implement, and appropriate measurement that allows employees to recognize small improvements occurring over time through a process called shaping. Like many behavior analysts, we use this process when supporting performance improvement of both adults and children. We don't wait until they finish performing before we give them feedback. To help them perform or behave their best, we function much like an athletic coach. The constant focus is on measuring and providing feedback, which offers information on where their performance is relative to a goal and what it takes to reach that goal.

Districts and schools would be more effective if they implemented measurement and feedback systems that allow for the recognition of small improvement and provide frequent opportunities to reinforce behaviors as educators move toward goals. The process of shaping is at the root of behavioral coaching. Leaders who use shaping through behavioral coaching are more likely to see returns on investment after training initiatives. This can include increased morale; initiative; retention; and ultimately, student achievement. Training is about teaching skills, while coaching is about supporting the transfer of those skills into the natural environment.

As we mentioned earlier, training without coaching does not stick. In Appendices 1–14 and 23–28, we provide several tools that allow you to measure and reinforce performance related to improving misbehavior.

Remember, even after training, in almost all cases, most people do not perform to a given standard. However, by using the process of shaping through behavioral coaching, leaders can learn to be more effective as they observe and reinforce small changes in real time with the goal of improving outcomes and creating sustainability. This process entails targeting small goals and just a few critical behaviors required to meet them (e.g., behavior-specific praise, increasing opportunities to respond, following QUICK Response procedures); collecting simple data as a feedback tool; and then providing strength-based feedback as a means of purposefully, precisely, and systematically improving performance. Data collection doesn't have to be difficult. One approach might simply be self-monitoring with a checklist and reporting to leadership (e.g., using shared cloud-based forms). Another approach might be recruiting peer feedback through systematic processes, such as classroom walk-throughs during which teachers observe and provide feedback on critical elements of classroom management. Observing and delivering feedback provides learning opportunities related to goals for both the giver and receiver of feedback. These goals might be performance related (see Appendices 29–31; e.g., achieving a 90% on the QUICK Response Fidelity Monitoring Form) or related to student behavior outcomes (e.g., reducing the frequency of codes, referrals, or suspensions by 30%).

Since the process is rooted in action as opposed to the judgment or inaction that characterizes most ineffective appraisal systems, behavioral coaching methods should be built into day-to-day routines, helping educational leaders and designees get into the habit of providing timely feedback. This isn't typical feedback. Instead, this is composed of feedback based on questioning strategies used to help the performer become a better observer of their own behavior and the impact of their behavior on the environment as it pertains to established goals. For example, if the classroom leader (teacher) were coaching a student, rather than reminding the student of the expectations, they might say, "Leo, I noticed that you were out of your seat. What are the expectations during this activity?" or "Leo, I noticed you were out of your seat. What consequences have we established for students who are out of their seats?"

A similar approach can be effectively used when a school leader is coaching a teacher, enhancing the coaching interaction by emphasizing self-reflection and accountability. Here's an example: Imagine a scenario where a school principal observes a teacher struggling to maintain classroom order, perhaps during a group activity where the noise level is counterproductive to learning. Instead of simply reminding the teacher of the school's expectations for classroom management, the principal might engage the teacher in a reflective conversation to deepen understanding and improve practices:

"Ms. Jackson, I noticed during the group activity session that the classroom became quite noisy, making it difficult for some students to focus. What are our school's expectations for noise levels during group work?"

Or, taking it a step further to connect consequences and responsibilities.

"Ms. Jackson, I observed that the noise level during group work exceeded what we've found conducive to learning. Can you remind me what strategies we've discussed in our trainings that could help manage this better? How do you think applying one of those strategies might change the outcome next time?"

These types of questions prompt the teacher to recall training and expectations themselves, fostering a sense of ownership and responsibility for their classroom environment. This method encourages teachers to reflect on their actions and the school-wide standards, empowering them to identify and commit to adjustments in their approach.

Behavioral questioning approaches like these can rapidly improve adult performance and student behavior, while fostering independence, preserving the rapport between teacher and student, and supporting the transfer of newly learned skills into school or classroom environments. When district leaders coach principals, principals or assistant principals coach teachers, and teachers coach students, performance and positive behavioral outcomes rapidly accelerate across schools.

So, if you genuinely want to improve educator performance and reduce misbehavior, knock out useless appraisal systems and focus on embedding good behavioral coaching processes into your school systems.

Parting Thoughts on Reducing Misbehavior Through Behavioral Coaching

District, school, and classroom leaders often invest considerable effort, with disappointing returns on investment. To enhance the outcomes of their hard work, a systematic approach focused on developing positive habits at all levels of the educational hierarchy is essential. These habits range from self-management and effective learning techniques in students to robust instructional and classroom management skills in teachers, and adept management, leadership, and coaching practices in school and district leaders.

For meaningful improvements in student behavior and overall school performance, it's crucial to have these systems aligned from the bottom up to ensure that the practices at every level support the development of these vital habits (Hall & Hord, 2011; Gavoni & Weatherly, 2024).

Why is this approach effective? It ensures that everyone—from students to superintendents—has a clear understanding of the behaviors they need to engage in and the positive results these behaviors will yield. Such clarity is foundational to effective coaching, which can then be employed to maintain these behaviors long enough to produce significant outcomes.

Effective coaching systems play a crucial role in this context. They not only support individuals in adopting and maintaining necessary behaviors but also ensure these behaviors become ingrained as habits. When these habits are rooted in the principles outlined throughout this book, they lead to environments where misbehavior is drastically reduced and learning is enhanced. This systematic alignment of behaviors and outcomes facilitates improved instruction and classroom management, which are critical for elevating the educational experience in any school or district.

Implementing such a system requires a commitment to ongoing coaching and feedback and ensures that each layer of the educational system is consistently moving toward well-defined goals. The success of this approach hinges on the ability of leaders at all levels to not only model these behaviors but also actively foster them in others, thus creating a culture where continuous improvement is the norm and where every member of the educational community is empowered to achieve their best.

Key Points

- One significant, false assumption about performance issues is that training is always the answer.
- Before deciding that training will be part of intervention, leaders should determine whether other factors serve as barriers to teacher performance.
- Training is costly and time consuming ... and it's not always the answer.
- When teachers fail to perform, people tend to point fingers at the teacher. Unnecessary blame rarely resolves problems.
- The PDC allows educational leaders to determine the root cause of performance issues to guide their intervention more effectively.
- Without coaching and feedback delivered frequently and immediately, or without the ability for the teacher to observe positive outcomes related to instructional behavior, desirable and long-lasting instructional behavior linked to student achievement will not occur.
- Reinforcing feedback helps the teacher align their behavior with positive outcomes.
- Providing reinforcement strengthens the teacher's behavior, bolsters skills, and enhances motivation.
- Midyear and annual performance appraisals are typically ineffective for improving performance and might even be detrimental to the progress of an organization.

Reflect on It

- How can a leader determine whether the teacher has a skill or motivation deficit?
  - What process can they engage in?
  - What are some tools they can use?
- What are some key habits of school and district leaders related to good management, leadership, and coaching that bring out the best in those they lead?
- How can you as a leader bring more reinforcing feedback into your routine?
- How can you as a leader help others contact positive outcomes? In short, how can you help your stakeholders behave well enough and long enough so that they produce outcomes they find valuable, like students behaving better, learning more, or perhaps feeling a sense of accomplishment?

CHAPTER 9

Suspending: The Good, the Bad, and the Ugly

Thus far, we've explored the importance of leadership and systematic approaches for bringing out the best in teachers. Now we will shift our focus to systematic approaches beyond the classroom. Specifically, we will address high-magnitude misbehavior and reducing suspensions through a behavioral approach. In Chapters 10 and 11, we will delve into procedures you can adopt in your schools, but first, let's take a closer look at the good and the bad of suspensions as a common administrator response to some challenging behaviors.

Suspensions can be downright detrimental. While there are instances where suspensions might be necessary and produce positive results, we are aware of abundant research demonstrating the harmful effects of suspensions (e.g., Noltemeyer et al., 2015). Suspension, particularly out-of-school suspension (OSS), should always be approached with caution. Suspensions result in less time for learning—students cannot be successfully engaged and learn if they are suspended at home. Employing this consequence may inadvertently deny the student free, appropriate public education. Sometimes, sending students home—especially those who don't want to be in school—can be akin to sending them from the aforementioned pit to paradise. This can reinforce the misbehavior and increase the likelihood of the misbehavior occurring in the future. When we scrutinize the situation closely, it becomes clear that there are many drawbacks to implementing suspensions.

However, isolating suspensions to examine under a microscope is problematic because it ignores other variables. We must step back and consider the broader perspective of what can make suspensions good or bad. Remember, when we aim to reduce suspensions, we measure the responses and behavior of adults, not necessarily the behavior of students. In other words, people suspend students for different reasons. Sometimes there is no rhyme or reason, just what an individual may judge as a "suspendable" offense. A suspension might also be based on biases formed by a student's prior history of disciplinary offenses, while taking into consideration the magnitude of the behavior that warranted a suspension.

Issues With a Focus on Reducing Suspensions

We must recognize that the decision to suspend a student is often influenced by subjective judgments and contextual factors. This means that suspensions can be inconsistent and may reflect biases or the specific circumstances surrounding an incident. A suspension can have both positive and negative effects on all parties involved.

Consider the following scenario.

Billy, a fifth grader, uses profanity toward his teacher. The principal, eager to keep Billy in the educational environment and move suspension data in the right direction, refrains from suspending him. Because the elementary school does not have internal suspension, the principal notifies Billy's parent and leaves Billy in the front office as a time-out to teach him a lesson about his misbehavior. Not wanting Billy to miss further instruction, the principal returns him to class after an hour.

Mission accomplished, right? The principal kept Billy in the instructional environment, avoided the pit to paradise issue, and kept the suspension data from worsening. The principal's boss, observing a decreasing trend in suspension data, praises the principal for his good work, thus reinforcing the principal's decision-making behavior.

Now, can the above scenario result in an intended impact? Under the right conditions, this might be a perfectly logical approach. However, overgeneralization of this process can be problematic. In struggling schools with high behavior problems and low morale, this scenario can be the straw that broke the camel's back. Focusing solely on reducing suspensions can be a significant mistake. Avoiding suspensions under some conditions can have a ripple effect that inadvertently harms every student in the school. This scenario may have had a positive effect on reducing suspensions but a negative effect on the future frequency of the misbehavior.

In the Classroom

Let's hear about some potential problems with failing to suspend a student from a classroom, as told by an administrator, who was also a behavior analyst, as they began implementing many of the procedures outlined in this book.

As an administrator tasked with turning around a high-poverty, failing elementary school, I once broke up a fight between a girl and a boy. After watching the video, it was clear the boy instigated the fight and threw the first few punches. Although the girl fought back to defend herself, the boy had reportedly been "messing" with her for weeks, according to the students we interviewed. As such, we did not think it was fair to give her the same 2-day suspension we gave the boy.

Consequently, we required her to serve 3 hours in the QUICK Room (see Chapter 11), essentially a time-out room where she was responsible for completing a variety of tasks, including a QUICK ACTion Plan. This plan required her to respond to questions such as what she might do differently, the potential consequences of fighting, more effective alternative behaviors, and the possible outcomes of those behaviors. This seemed like a reasonable consequence, and to many, it was. This was what we might call a teachable moment. Unfortunately, when consequences are meant as punishment, we often lose the opportunity to teach what to do next time, focusing instead on what not to do.

The next week, three more fights broke out in the same classroom. This was unusual. After interviewing different students, we discovered a pattern of responses. According to the students, failure to suspend the girl spread like wildfire in the classroom. The message other students took from the situation was, "If someone messes with you, you can fight back and you won't get suspended." For them, fighting back was a far better alternative when they believed they wouldn't get suspended. In many cases, it was like earning a badge of honor in the eyes of their peers. This made fighting back a reward and engaging in nonconfrontational behaviors that reduced the likelihood of fights far less valuable.

The lesson here is that while most students are not suspended, the threat of suspension (consequence) motivates many to avoid fighting. Behaviorally speaking, their alternative behaviors were under the contingencies of negative reinforcement (avoidance of the threat of being removed from school). In other words, they argued, asserted themselves, told off the teacher, or ignored each other instead of fighting to avoid being suspended, much like most people drive the speed limit to avoid getting a ticket. Once the threat of suspension was removed, their behavior changed.

Is it ideal for students to behave solely to avoid consequences? Of course not! Nobody wants to work, live, or engage in daily activities driven by fear of punishment. Under these conditions, people will do just enough to get by, and only comply when the person who delivers the punishment is present; and even then, it will only be effective in the short term. Think of the times you don't speed and the times you are more likely to speed. Who is present? The goal of the educational environment should be to teach and reinforce learning and prosocial skills, so students find more value in learning and helping others than they do in misbehaving or behaving to avoid punishment.

By avoiding suspension under certain conditions, a classroom or school can be set back. In this example, other students in the classroom decided a 3-hour time-out in the QUICK Room was worth the fight. Now broaden the scope of that phenomenon. When news spreads like wildfire through the classroom, it also has the potential to spread like wildfire throughout the entire school. The result is increased high-magnitude behavior; increased frustration on the part of staff; and decreased staff retention at the end of the year, which can strongly affect performance the following school year. The risks and benefits of suspension should constantly be assessed.

Issues at the Organizational Level

Discipline referrals do not simply occur because of a student's problem behavior; they occur at the end of a chain of student and staff interactions, which does not necessarily accurately reflect the frequency of high-intensity, "discipline referral–worthy" incidents (Gavoni et al., 2017). For example,

1. While a teacher is giving a lesson, a student interrupts by shouting out.
2. The teacher reminds the student to raise their hand next time.
3. The student shouts out again.
4. The teacher scolds the student for interrupting.
5. In response, the student shouts, "This class is dumb."
6. Similar incidents continue, with increasing frequency and severity.
7. The teacher requests help.
8. The student is escorted out of the classroom.
9. The teacher fills out a disciplinary referral.
10. The administrator determines the punishment (e.g., suspension).

For various reasons, this chain may be broken, resulting in unreliable discipline referral data. One reason is that teachers are busy, and writing referrals takes time and effort. Once the disruptive behavior is removed, writing a discipline referral can become aversive to teachers because it becomes just one more task they must do. Beyond this issue, discipline referrals have limitations as a data source. For instance, they often include possible bias on the part of educators and administrators, over-reporting of minority students, staff tolerance of behavior, and inconsistent documentation across staff and school districts.

Explicit and implicit bias, as highlighted at the beginning of this book, can impact the likelihood of a student being suspended by particular staff, under particular conditions, for particular behaviors. In some cases, a student might be sent home for the day, yet this is not recorded as a suspension. Suspension data, like discipline referral data, can become skewed even when suspension-worthy behavior increases. Again, we measure staff responses to student misbehavior in terms of documenting discipline referrals and suspensions, not necessarily student misbehavior. Ineffective and inconsistent data entry will result in the underestimation of the rate of high-magnitude behavior and suspensions.

Rules and Consequences

Rules: Prescriptive Rather Than Proscriptive

Rules in schools are often established to maintain a safe and orderly learning environment. One of the golden rules when fostering behavior improvement is telling folks what to do (e.g., walk) as opposed to what not to do (e.g., stop running). This prescriptive approach is not isolated to student misbehavior. This relates to staff performance as well. It wouldn't make sense to tell a teacher, "Stop telling students to stop running." It would make much more sense to tell them, "If you see a student running, ask them to walk." It's a more positive approach, and meanwhile, you incorporate a replacement behavior, giving the student an opportunity to access reinforcement.

The same concept applies to schools. Instead of telling schools to stop suspending (proscriptive), a more productive approach would focus on supporting them, integrating systems that lead to increased prosocial skills, a cooperative climate, and a collaborative culture. The outcome will subsequently result in increased achievement, increased teacher retention, and reduced suspensions.

Telling students what they should or shouldn't do and giving school staff professional development (which is basically telling them what they should and shouldn't do regarding behavior management) are standard practices for preventing misbehavior. Unfortunately, teachers and students aren't always educated on the all-important "knowing" what to do. How are teachers and students expected to understand the process of correctly reinforcing a positive impact on behavior if not given the proper training? If this expectation were accurate, educators could simply tell students their rules, and they would all behave accordingly. Similarly, school leaders could establish performance expectations and staff would perform to established standards. If only it were that easy.

Consequences for Rules

The reason students and staff follow or don't follow rules is because consequences have the largest impact on behavior. In other words, what happens immediately after behavior occurs is what leads to the biggest increase, decrease, or change in that behavior. Recall that a consequence, in behavioral terms, is something that occurs as a result of a given behavior.

Let's look at an example at the staff level: A teacher is told to perform a new skill. If this skill results in reduced effort, improved student behavior, and saved time (i.e., reinforcement), then most likely the teacher will perform the skill again. These meaningful consequences have a greater impact on the teacher's behavior than simply being told to use the skill. If the teacher used the skill and the opposite occurred (increased effort, increased student misbehavior, increased time [i.e., punishment]), there is a good chance the teacher will stop performing this skill and regress back to previous habits. Adults are not immune to the laws of behavior, so establishing rules and having those rules be followed is impacted by consequences.

Young children and students with severe disabilities can learn to behave consistently with a rule even if they can't state the rule back to the adult. This is highlighted by evidence that their behavior can be shaped by contingencies of reinforcement and punishment. In other words, even if they cannot tell someone what a given rule is, they recognize that this behavior gets this, and that behavior gets that, or doing this avoids getting that other thing (i.e., punishment). So certain consequences exert influence over certain behaviors. Some of these consequences (i.e., reinforcement) serve to make a behavior more likely to occur, and some of these consequences (i.e., punishment) reduce the future occurrence of a behavior. In both cases, the degree to which these consequences occur immediately and reliably as a result of either rule-following or rule-breaking holds a sustainable influence over a given behavior.

Some students may and some students may not be responsive to rule statements on their own. The latter group's behavior is mostly influenced by experiencing consequences directly. This does not mean educators should abandon establishing school-wide or classroom rules. They should discuss rules often. However, analyzing whether students are rule followers can help develop more salient plans for the students whose learning does not appear to be impacted by rules. The fact is some students (and adults, for that matter) must experience the good and not-so-good consequences for behavior to change. Those are the gamblers among us; they don't believe it until they experience it.

Suspension as a Consequence

Suspensions often do not meet the criteria of an effective consequence to reduce (punish) problem behavior (i.e., rule breaking). In the end, suspensions are an outcome that often results from misbehavior occurring, a teacher or staff member recognizing and reporting the behavior, and then a designated staff member (typically, an administrator) sending a student home as a consequence. Suspension is often implemented at the end of the school day for the next school day or further delayed. It is typically not immediate enough to reduce the problem behavior of students who frequently misbehave. Suspension comes from a general list of behaviors and prior steps. In too many cases, it is not function based. There are surely cases meriting suspension, but schools are better served when looking at how suspension impacts behavior for students.

Building a Culture Based on Desired Behavior

Inevitably, there are ways to increase prosocial behaviors and decrease rule-breaking behaviors. The focus should be on building a culture (i.e., shared behaviors) in which people are skilled at reinforcing desired behavior, not on reducing suspensions. Focusing on this type of culture will have positive effects across the entire school and increase student achievement and staff retention, while ultimately reducing suspensions.

Regardless of the student's ability to follow rules, rather than waiting for suspensions to occur, it is more effective to teach all staff key behaviors (i.e., reinforce prosocial skills, strengthen relationships, correct early-stage misbehaviors) and then systematically observe and reinforce both student and staff behavior. Over time, these behaviors will become habits as both students and staff observe the positive outcomes of their behaviors (i.e., reduced misbehaviors, increased student achievements). This is a proactive approach rather than telling schools they need to stop suspending. Behavior drives organizational change. Fewer misbehaviors leads to fewer suspensions.

Taking Momentum Into Account

Imagine the driver of a car low on gas climbing a hill. They are almost to the peak of the hill and know that if they make it to the top, they can coast down the hill to the nearest gas station. Suddenly, the car runs out of gas and the driver discovers they have no brakes! Knowing emergency action must be taken, they apply the emergency brake. They know the emergency brake will not move them forward, but it will stop any backward momentum until somebody comes along to help them push the car to the top.

In turnaround schools or schools moving in the wrong direction, velocity and momentum must be considered. When things are going down the wrong side of the hill, momentum must be stopped and moved in the right direction (Gavoni & Costa, 2023). Leaders must look for quick wins to strengthen relationships and build a culture of trust—for example, starting each school day with teachers and staff giving high-fives or fist bumps at the school entrance. This simple gesture requires minimal effort but sets a positive tone for the day and builds rapport between students and staff.

Research is clear about the impact of discipline issues on educators. If educators perceive they are not supported (and perception is reality), the whole school may continue rolling downhill. Effective leaders can come into a school and visibly reduce misbehavior with effective systems, and momentum can move behavior in a better direction and lead to desired results. Time is often not on the side of those trying to help reduce misbehavior. Momentum favors misbehavior. It is effortful, challenging, and necessary to halt the momentum of misbehavior, but it must be a priority to build the culture the school needs.

Summary

Adults should question their behavior and why they suspend students. The systems of how and why a student is suspended must be clear and not left up to individuals, who may be biased and subjective. Suspensions can reinforce the behavior of the individual doing the suspending. Educators must be careful not to let their biases of that student's past problem behavior determine "suspendable" offenses.

When implementing a plan to reduce suspensions, there's the good, the bad, and the ugly. The risks and benefits of suspensions must constantly be assessed to determine effectiveness. Focusing on just reducing suspensions without implementing systems embedding the teaching of prosocial behavior, creating a cooperative climate, and creating a collaborative culture among staff may result in unintended consequences.

For leaders, building a culture of trust is imperative in building and strengthening relationships with teachers and staff. Research shows that there is a significant negative impact of discipline problems on educators. Educators want to be supported in tackling discipline issues. Being proactive by putting effective classroom and school-wide management plans in place and establishing a system of reinforcement will have a positive impact on creating a supportive school climate and culture.

Key Points

- When looking to reduce suspensions, it is important to measure the response and behavior of adults, not necessarily the behavior of the students.
- Suspension can be reinforcing; educators need to consider the function to determine whether suspension is effective for changing student behavior.
- Suspension often does not meet the basic criteria of an effective procedure to reduce (punish) problem behavior, as it usually occurs at the end of the day and is not immediate.
- Suspension is derived from a general list of behaviors and prior steps and is not function based. It may allow the student to escape a full day (or more) of academic demands.
- While suspending students is often counterproductive to learning, refraining from suspending a student under certain conditions can be detrimental to other students.
- The systems of how and why a student is suspended must be clear and not left to individuals, who can potentially be biased and subjective. Suspensions can be reinforcing to the individual administering the suspension.
- Be prescriptive rather than proscriptive. When teaching appropriate behavior, tell students what to do (e.g., walk) instead of what not to do (e.g., stop running).
- The risks and benefits of suspensions must constantly be assessed to determine effectiveness.
- Sometimes momentum must be stopped to move behavior in a better direction.

Reflect on It

- What are some drawbacks of suspending students?
- What behaviors are considered suspendable offenses?
- Does your school have alternatives to OSS? What are some benefits of these alternatives?
- What strategies can be used to increase prosocial behaviors and decrease rule-breaking behaviors in the classroom? What about school-wide?
- What are some key behaviors that all teachers and staff should engage in?

CHAPTER 10

The QUICK Response

The Necessity for QUICK Responders: A Cautionary Tale

Consider a typical school day at Midland Elementary. In Dr. Patel's third-grade classroom, usually a place of eager learning and enthusiastic participation, the scene turns chaotic. It all starts when Miguel, a student with a history of behavioral issues, begins exhibiting aggressive behaviors, escalating from verbal outbursts to throwing books and flipping chairs.

Dr. Patel, despite her best efforts to employ the classroom management strategies she has learned, finds herself overwhelmed. She calls for help, and soon enough, the assistant principal, Ms. Nguyen, and the school counselor, Mr. Adebayo, rush in to assist. However, rather than diffusing the situation, their arrival inadvertently escalates it. Miguel, sensing the heightened attention, intensifies his outbursts, and this leads to a complete breakdown of order in the classroom.

As Miguel is escorted out, his peers watch in a mix of fear and confusion, the lesson for the day abandoned. Ms. Nguyen and Mr. Adebayo, unsure of the best course of action, place Miguel in the front office—a bustling, overstimulating environment. Miguel continues to act out, and the office staff, untrained in crisis intervention, struggle to manage him effectively. In the end, Miguel's behavior is not only reinforced by the attention and the unintended reward of escaping the classroom, but his behavior also creates a significant disruption for the entire school.

This scenario highlights several critical missteps that an effective QUICK Responder would avoid. The lack of a structured plan, the inadequate training in crisis intervention, and the failure to manage the environmental variables all contributed to a situation that spiraled out of control. Miguel's behavior, instead of being mitigated, was reinforced, and the classroom environment suffered as a result.

Severe problem behavior poses a significant challenge for educators, even when they are employing the effective classroom management strategies outlined in this book. Factors such as learning history, communication barriers, and current environmental variables can precipitate and escalate misbehavior. Severe circumstances may encompass continuous aggression or self-injurious acts, sustained disruption or property damage, elopement (leaving an assigned area unsupervised), or medical emergencies. When such circumstances arise, teachers often need immediate assistance, necessitating schools to identify team members capable of providing timely and effective support.

Unfortunately, as we've seen in our pit to paradise scenarios, when students are removed from class, administrators and responding staff may unintentionally reinforce the behavior that led to their removal. This unintended reinforcement not only disrupts learning but also complicates staff responsibilities. The root cause often lies in inadequate training on managing student removals and restoring instructional control to teachers—a critical oversight in teacher and educational leadership preparation programs.

Enter the concept of the QUICK Responder model, which features a dedicated group of trained responders equipped with systematic strategies for managing such incidents. The QUICK Responder model approach is not about adding new personnel but rather about empowering existing staff with the necessary tools and training to respond promptly and effectively. Their goal is to intervene in a manner that preserves the student's dignity, minimizes reinforcement of misbehavior, and restores instructional control to the teacher.

The remainder of this chapter will detail how to implement the QUICK Responder model effectively to ensure that your school is prepared to handle behavioral incidents with professionalism and care. Through this approach, we can safeguard the learning environment; support our educators; and most importantly, guide our students toward positive behavioral outcomes.

Introduction of the QUICK Team

You might be thinking, "Another team? We don't have the personnel!" The good news is the QUICK Team doesn't require additional personnel. It comprises those already responding to misbehavior incidents. At least one administrator should be involved, to ensure consistency. The aim isn't to create a new team but to equip this existing group with systematic strategies for effectively managing calls for assistance and student removals, thereby reducing misbehavior.[1] The QUICK Team may include the following individuals:

- dean
- behavior interventionist
- guidance counselor
- front desk clerk (usually serves as dispatcher)
- maintenance personnel
- school nurse or health care designee
- security personnel

Given the need for swift responses, we refer to this team as the QUICK Team. Their purpose is to promptly respond in a manner that facilitates student intervention while preserving dignity and minimizing inadvertent reinforcement of misbehavior. Table 10.1 presents the rationale and guiding principles for the QUICK Team Members, organized under the QUICK acronym:

Table 10.1. QUICK Team Guiding Principles

	QUICK Team
Questioning	Uncover the ABCs (Antecedent, Behavior, Consequence) of the incident from staff. Determine the function of the student's behavior. Avoid confrontational questions like "Why do you keep doing this!?" Understand triggers (antecedents) and immediate consequences, including staff and student reactions.
Unconditional Positive Regard	Aim to maintain nonjudgmental relationships with students and stakeholders. Acknowledge that misbehavior is frustrating. Communicate to minimize frustration and prevent escalation, avoiding challenges to students.

---

1 Please note: For dangerous behaviors such as fighting or elopement, conducting a functional behavior assessment and developing a behavior intervention plan is crucial. Additionally, responding staff should receive formal crisis prevention and intervention training to intervene effectively in such situations.

QUICK Team	
Intermittent Reinforcement	Understand the reasons behind a student's misbehavior, especially if it involves avoiding tasks or directives.
	Avoid inadvertently reinforcing escape behaviors by not allowing the student to shirk responsibilities.
	Be mindful of your own reactions to ensure they do not unintentionally reinforce misbehavior.
	Focus on immediate problem-solving rather than extensive counseling right after a behavioral incident.
	Reserve longer counseling sessions for when the student is back in their regular educational setting to prevent reinforcing misbehavior.
Constructive	Use questioning to facilitate problem-solving rather than providing direct counseling.
	Guide students to identify their behavior, antecedents, potential consequences, and alternative actions.
	Help students develop self-awareness of their behavior's impact on the environment and vice versa.
	Avoid "why" questions to prevent coming across as judgmental and escalating behavior.
	Provide constructive feedback, not criticism, especially when a student is struggling.
	Refer to Appendices 19–21 for action plans that can aid in guiding students through this questioning process.
Keep It Brief	Recognize that positive attention from adults can significantly influence behavior.
	Keep interactions brief and use a neutral tone to avoid inadvertently reinforcing misbehavior with additional attention.
	Provide abundant positive attention when students follow school rules.

Calling for Assistance

In situations requiring support, educators and staff should utilize radios, intercom systems, or phones to request assistance from the QUICK Team using a standardized code system. These codes enable the QUICK Team to differentiate responses and collect data based on the student's behavior. It is advisable for school districts to adopt a uniform code system to minimize confusion among staff serving multiple schools. These codes should distinguish the urgency and severity of the behavior. While schools can customize their own codes, here are recommended codes to initiate your system:

Code A: Continuous Aggression, Self-Injury, and/or High-Intensity Property Destruction. This indicates an immediate danger to the student or others.

Code O: Out of Assigned Area (OOAA). This is used when a student intentionally leaves their assigned area or elopes and cannot be located.

Code B: Continuous High-Magnitude Disruption and/or Low-Intensity Property Destruction. This signals severe and ongoing disruption or potentially hazardous behavior.

Code Medical: Used in cases of medical emergencies requiring immediate assistance.

Schools can adapt and expand on this system to fit their specific context, whether through color-coded, numerical, or descriptive terms (e.g., Code Yellow, Code 1, Behavior Code).

Implementation Guidelines

Upon establishing a QUICK Team and implementing a code system, it is crucial for all faculty and staff to understand that calling a code should be a last resort. Codes are reserved for emergencies or situations where normal classroom management strategies have proven ineffective. Codes should never be used as a threat in classroom management practices (e.g., "Johnny, stop or I'll call a code"). Ideally, one designated person should act as the dispatcher and be responsible for logging all code activations. Typically, this involves the teacher using the intercom to alert front desk personnel, who then coordinate assistance from available staff. The dispatcher must confirm that a QUICK Team Member is responding to each code and maintain a record of all activations, including time, location, involved student, and responding staff (Figure 10.1). These data are essential for analysis and refinement of intervention strategies as needed.

Date	Teacher	Grade	Time	Dispatcher	Responder	Student Name	Code A	Code O	Code B	Code Med
3/29/24	Ms. Jain	4	9:38	Mr. Jones	Ms. Goodwin	Johnny Attention-seeker			X	
3/29/24	Mr. Dagwood	2	12:15	Mr. Jones	Mr. O'Donnell	Jane Escaper		X		
4/1/24	Ms. Goldberg	5	11:04	Mr. Jones	Ms. Goodwin	Sabrina Twofists	X			
4/1/24	Mr. Johnson	4	2:17	Mr. Jones	Ms. Goodwin	Jionni Uncoordinated				X

Figure 10.1. This sheet highlights how data may be recorded. Here, we can clearly see data that are helpful in identifying individual concerns. We are able to identify who is reporting, responding, and involved in the code; code type; and time of the code, among other information.

Given occasional doubts about the reliability of discipline referrals when students are removed (Childs et al., 2015), meticulous data collection is vital for the QUICK Team to evaluate the necessity of removal and determine the behavior's function. Schools implementing School-Wide Positive Behavioral Interventions and Supports (SW-PBIS) must submit a discipline referral for each student removal (Gavoni et al., 2017), underscoring the importance of proper documentation. Except for medical emergencies, every code activation should result in a logged discipline referral.

When the QUICK Team responds, it is crucial for the referring teacher or staff member to provide the responding team member (the QUICK Responder) with antecedent-behavior-consequence (ABC) data. These data are pivotal in identifying environmental factors contributing to misbehavior, as they detail events preceding the incident, the nature of the behavior itself, and the consequences that ensued. To facilitate efficient data collection, we offer a straightforward ABC Code Form in Figure 10.2, which can also be found in a full-page format in Appendix 15 for easy access.

QUICK Team Code Responses

While behavioral circumstances can be diverse, here are some simple and differentiated strategies to guide QUICK Responders when responding to various codes.

Code A: Continuous Aggression, Self-Injury, and/or High-Intensity Property Destruction

- If a student hurts themselves or others, or engages in potentially costly or dangerous property destruction, staff call for assistance (e.g., using the intercom) and say, "Code A on Johnny S. in Ms. Smith's class, room 401." The dispatcher uses the radio to communicate to the QUICK Responder, stating, "Code A in room 401, Ms. Smith's class."
- A QUICK Responder verbally acknowledges to the dispatcher they will respond to the code A, repeat the location of the code, and respond immediately. For example, "Ms. Goodwin copies that and is responding immediately to room 401."
- Under conditions involving dangerous behavior, at least two available QUICK Responders should acknowledge the code and respond immediately at a brisk pace.
- All other QUICK Team Members with two-way communication or with knowledge of the code should remain on call in their own area, ready to assist if necessary.
- The QUICK Responders should attempt verbal de-escalation techniques or use district-approved emergency procedures they are trained in, if warranted.
- Upon reaching the problem area, and at the appropriate time after the student is de-escalated, the referring staff should privately (i.e., not in front of the student) provide a brief description of what happened and hand the Responder the ABC Code Form. It is important this information be shared quickly and privately to maintain calmness and confidentiality and avoid escalating the student's behavior.
- If the staff member who called the code does not have the ABC Code Form completed, they should quietly and calmly inform the QUICK Responder of the events (i.e., antecedents and consequences) surrounding the behavior incident. The QUICK Responder should return later to pick up a copy of the ABC Code Form to file as data.

ABC Code Form				
Student Name:		**Teacher Name:**		**Time:**
Briefly describe behavior:				
Circle Code A O B				
"Before" Conditions			"After" Conditions	
Curriculum	**Delivery**	**Antecedents**	**Teacher Responses**	**Peer Reaction**
☐ English Language Arts ☐ Math ☐ Social Studies ☐ Science ☐ Music ☐ PE ☐ Media ☐ Technology ☐ Math/Science Resource ☐ Other:	☐ Independent center ☐ Independent practice ☐ Small group center ☐ Small group teacher ☐ Whole group ☐ Other:	☐ Attention given to others ☐ Difficult task/activity ☐ Demand/request ☐ Challenge or teasing by other students ☐ Corrective feedback ☐ **Not** engaged in activity ☐ **Not** receiving attention ☐ Object/activity removed ☐ Specific peer interaction ☐ Transition ☐ Given consequence ☐ Did not receive point ☐ Other:	☐ Change of seating ☐ Choice given ☐ Clarification ☐ "First-then" ☐ Pivot praise ☐ Planned ignoring ☐ Proximity control ☐ Redirection ☐ Demerit ☐ Time owed ☐ Other: **Progressive Consequences** ☐ 1st <u>warning</u> ☐ 2nd ____ ☐ 3rd ____ ☐ 4th ____ ☐ 5th ____	☐ Disapproval ☐ Encourage ☐ Ignore ☐ Laugh ☐ Praise ☐ Provoke ☐ Reprimand ☐ Retaliate ☐ Warn **Possible Motivation** ☐ Escape adult demand ☐ Escape peer attention ☐ Escape task/activity ☐ Obtain teacher attention ☐ Obtain student attention ☐ Access preferred item/activity

Figure 10.2. This form is used to collect data on the before and after conditions of the code calls.

- The referring staff should complete an office discipline referral (if this is policy).
- Removal of the student may be necessary if the code of conduct warrants it, or if there is immediate potential for continued aggression or loss of physical control.
- If the student is removed, bring them to the designated area (e.g., QUICK Room) to gather information and determine the appropriate consequence.
- If the behavior warrants an out-of-school suspension, administrators should consider the QUICK Room as an alternative to OSS.

Code O: Out of Assigned Area (OOAA)

- Staff calling the code O should provide any helpful identifying information available, such as the student's attire and the direction the student headed. For example, "Code O on Johnny S., last seen headed east off the basketball court wearing a black shirt with blue jeans and white sneakers."

- A QUICK Responder or support staff verbally acknowledges over two-way communication that they will respond to the OOAA student. This does not include students who walked out of class but are within line of sight and are not actively eloping.
- The other QUICK Responder(s) and/or available support staff will promptly proceed to the designated area.
- Once the student is found, notify the dispatcher that the student was located.
- Only one of the responding staff will verbally redirect the student back to the assigned area.
- If the student is uncooperative, responding staff may call for additional support and should monitor the student to assist with maintaining a safe environment. When the student is calm, provide them with limited choices and remind them of the consequence of each choice. For example, "Johnny, if you return to your area, we can problem-solve. However, if you remain out of your assigned area, you are going to owe time in the designated area (e.g., the QUICK Room) and your parents will be notified of your behavior."
- If the student leaves campus, the QUICK Responder will notify an administrator immediately and follow existing school policies. See Appendix 32 for elopement reporting tips.
- If there is an active Code O and the student returns to their assigned area, the referring staff member must report this immediately to the dispatcher, who should then inform all QUICK Team Members.
- If after 5 minutes the referring staff member does not report the student "back in assigned area" (and the student has not been located), the dispatcher calls the classroom to confirm with the staff that the student continues to remain OOAA, and then notifies administration and all responding staff of the student's status. For example, the dispatcher can say, "There is still an outstanding Code O on Johnny S. He was last seen headed …"
- Once the student is located, bring them to the designated area (e.g., QUICK Room) to gather information and determine the appropriate consequence.
- If the behavior warrants an out-of-school suspension, administrators should consider the QUICK Room as an alternative to suspension.

In the event a student remains missing after a Code O is called, it is recommended school administration follow district policy, which likely includes immediately notifying the parent or guardian. Under conditions that a student is deemed unsafe (e.g., an elementary student or a student with severe disabilities), school professionals should enact whatever district safety protocols are necessary.

For students who demonstrate repeated episodes of elopement, aggression, or other dangerous behaviors, schools should convene their support team and complete a functional behavior assessment to determine function-based interventions.

Code B: Continuous High-Magnitude Disruption and/or Low-Intensity Property Destruction

- A QUICK Team Member verbally acknowledges over the radio that they will respond to the Code B and then responds as quickly as possible.
- Upon the QUICK Responder reaching the problem area, the referring staff member should privately (i.e., not in front of the student) provide a brief description of what happened and hand the QUICK Responder the ABC Code Form. It is important to share this information quickly and privately to maintain calmness and confidentiality and avoid escalating the student's behavior.
- If the staff member who called the code does not have the ABC Code Form, they should quietly and calmly inform the QUICK Responder of the events (i.e., antecedents and consequences) surrounding the behavior incident. The QUICK Responder should return later to pick up a copy of the ABC Code Form to file as data.
- If the student is removed, bring them to the designated area (e.g., QUICK Room) to gather information and determine the appropriate consequence.
- If the behavior warrants an out-of-school suspension, administrators should consider the QUICK Room as an alternative to suspension.

Code Medical: Medical Emergencies Requiring Immediate Assistance

- Members of the QUICK Team should promptly call 911 and radio "Code Medical." During this time the QUICK Responder should also follow any specific protocols the school has set in place and bring any necessary emergency medical supplies.
- When designated medical personnel attend to the student, other QUICK Team members should help manage the surrounding environments. This includes, but isn't limited to, keeping other students out of the way and calm, and maintaining space and privacy for emergency procedures.

- The QUICK Responder documents any necessary incidents and participates in a debriefing.

Recommended Procedures When Assisting the Student to Remain in Class

As previously stated, our position is that codes should only be utilized as a last resort for behavior that is no longer manageable within the classroom or common area setting. However, there are instances where substitute or inexperienced staff may call a code for behaviors of low intensity and frequency, such as chewing gum or wearing a hoodie or hat, which may not warrant such actions. In these cases, QUICK Team Members can employ the following strategies to support the student in remaining in the classroom:

- Make a collaborative decision between the teacher and the QUICK Responder to remove the student, or not, based on the perceived function of the behavior, the severity of the disruption to the rest of the classroom, the ability of the classroom staff, or the amount of time required to effectively intervene.
- If a decision cannot be reached, contact an administrator to guide the problem-solving and decision-making process.
- If staff suspect the behavior is escape-maintained (i.e., student wants to leave class), every effort should be made to keep the student in class. If staff suspect the student is attempting to escape to avoid doing an assignment, the QUICK Responder should prompt the teacher to use the work-out protocols highlighted in Chapter 5 and included in Appendix 8. If this effort is not successful and the student is removed from class, QUICK Team Members might consider using the out-of-class work-out protocol.
- If it is decided that the student will remain in the classroom, the QUICK Responder should stay until the potential for high-magnitude disruption is diminished or classroom functioning has been returned to normal. Note: QUICK Responders may assist the student with problem-solving to help them stay in class. There will be times when, even after a code has been called, the student does not need to be removed from class. (Additional resources can be found in Appendix 33 to assist the student in becoming fluent in problem-solving.)
- The QUICK Responder may enter the class and work one-on-one with the student in order to help them remain within the classroom. Note: It is important to monitor for patterns to ensure the student does not misbehave to access a particular staff member's attention or one-on-one support. If this is the case, that staff member's attention should be withheld following misbehavior but delivered as a reward for desirable behavior. This may mean having a designated QUICK Team Member responding to codes on a particular student.
- The staff may briefly problem-solve with the student in a separate area in the room where it is safer, and attention and disruption can be minimized. Staff should not try to problem-solve with the student until they are calm.

Revisiting the Scenario: Effective QUICK Responders in Action

Let's revisit that typical school day at Midland Elementary, this time with the QUICK Team model in place.

In Dr. Patel's third-grade classroom, Miguel, a student with a history of behavioral issues, begins exhibiting aggressive behaviors, which escalate from verbal outbursts to throwing books and flipping chairs. However, this time, Dr. Patel remains calm and quickly follows the established protocol by calling for the QUICK Team using the designated code system.

Within moments, the assistant principal, Ms. Nguyen, and the school counselor, Mr. Adebayo, both trained QUICK Responders, arrive. Instead of escalating the situation, they approach Miguel with calm and controlled demeanors. Ms. Nguyen uses verbal de-escalation techniques, speaking to Miguel in a calm, nonconfrontational tone, and maintaining a safe distance. Mr. Adebayo discreetly gathers information from Dr. Patel about the antecedents and consequences of Miguel's behavior using the ABC Code Form.

Ms. Nguyen and Mr. Adebayo then work together to guide Miguel out of the classroom to a pre-designated, low-stimulation QUICK Room, designed specifically to minimize reinforcement of misbehavior. This room is a quiet, neutral environment, free from the bustling distractions of the front office.

In the QUICK Room, Mr. Adebayo continues to engage with Miguel using the principles of unconditional positive regard. He listens to Miguel's concerns without judgment and helps him calm down. Meanwhile, Ms. Nguyen records detailed observations on the ABC Code Form to ensure accurate data collection for future analysis.

Once Miguel is calm, Mr. Adebayo facilitates a brief problem-solving session, asking constructive questions to help Miguel understand the impact of his behavior and explore alternative actions he could take next time. This conversation is kept brief to avoid inadvertently reinforcing the behavior with too much attention.

Ms. Nguyen and Mr. Adebayo then engage in planning restitution with Miguel, who agrees on the need to apologize to Dr. Patel and to pick up the books and flip the desks back to their original positions. Before re-entering the classroom, they prompt Miguel through a question strategy on what to do: "Miguel, do you remember what you agreed to do when you go back in?" Miguel responds quietly, "Yeah, first apologize to Dr. Patel. Then, pick up the book I threw and flip the desks back to show responsibility and respect."

Upon entering the classroom, Miguel walks up to Dr. Patel and says, "I'm sorry for my behavior." Dr. Patel acknowledges his apology with a nod and a smile, and then instructs, "Thank you, Miguel. Please pick up the books and flip the desks back."

Miguel follows her instructions, quietly picking up the books and flipping the desks back into their original positions. The classroom environment has remained relatively stable during his absence, thanks to the QUICK Responders' swift and effective intervention. Dr. Patel resumes her lesson with minimal disruption, and her students quickly refocus on their work.

This example illustrates the power of the QUICK Team model. By implementing the QUICK Team model, the staff handled the situation with professionalism and care. Miguel's behavior was addressed promptly and effectively without reinforcing his misbehavior, preserving the dignity of all involved. The learning environment remained intact, and Dr. Patel retained instructional control over her classroom.

Through systematic strategies and trained responders, schools can manage behavioral incidents effectively to ensure a positive and productive learning environment for all students.

Summary

These procedures serve as guidance for QUICK Team Members. Decision-making should ultimately be grounded in common sense and informed by the basic behavioral science principles discussed earlier. It cannot be overstated: Hypothesizing the function of a student's behavior is crucial when intervening. While some motivations may be obvious (e.g., a student expressing a desire to go home), other situations may require deeper assessments to accurately understand the root cause of misbehavior.

In Appendix 29, we provide a checklist designed to assist in shaping and maintaining the fidelity of the recommended procedures for the QUICK Team. This form ensures that all staff involved adhere to procedures correctly and enables ongoing monitoring of the effectiveness of the procedures.

Key Points

- High-magnitude, challenging behaviors may include one or more of the following: continuous aggression or self-injurious behavior, continuous high-magnitude disruption or property destruction, elopement (i.e., student OOAA and unsupervised), or a student medical emergency.
- Schools with high-frequency misbehavior and student removal should develop a coding system and identify team members who can effectively provide reasonably immediate responses to codes.
- When removing students from the classroom, schools need to consider location details and staffing of a designated area based on their current resources. We recommend using the principles we outlined for the QUICK Room.
- The front office is typically a no-no as a removal location because this is often a high-traffic area that provides all types of stimulation and reinforcement to students that can inadvertently increase misbehavior within the classroom.
- **QUICK** stands for
  - **Q**uestioning
  - **U**nconditional Positive Regard
  - **I**ntermittent Reinforcement
  - **C**onstructive
  - **K**eep It Brief
- The purpose of a QUICK Team is to provide strategies for staff to effectively respond to calls for assistance and student removal from the classroom or common areas.
- Under conditions in which support is needed, educators and staff should use a radio, intercom system, or even a phone to call for assistance from the QUICK Team via an established code system.
- Codes allow the QUICK Team to differentiate between responses and collect data based on the student's behavior.
- The QUICK Team is generally made up of staff who already respond to calls for assistance.

Reflect on It

- Reflect on your current removal procedures:
  - Are they effective?
  - How do you know?
  - Do you have a coding system?
- What type of training is needed for school teams to remove students effectively and safely from the classroom?
- When students return to the classroom after removal, what behaviors should the QUICK Team Members engage in? The teacher? The student?
- How do you know the student successfully transitioned back into the classroom? What are some indicators?
- If your school does not have a coding procedure or QUICK Team, how can you approach your school administrator with this information as a suggestion?

CHAPTER 11

The QUICK Room: An Alternative to In-School and Out-of-School Suspensions or Out-of-Class Time-Outs

In the staff room at Lincoln Middle School, a sense of defeat hangs heavily in the air as teachers and staff gather, their conversations a mix of concern and exasperation. The topic at hand was all too common: Jayden, a spirited eighth grader, had recently exploded with profanity at his teacher during class, a severe disruption that halted the day's lesson and left a palpable tension in its wake. Yet, instead of a meaningful intervention, the response had been woefully inadequate—a mere talking-to and then a swift return to the classroom, as if nothing had happened.

This approach was becoming a troubling pattern, one that not only fails to address the behavior but also seems to condone it. Each time a student like Jayden is sent back to class with such minimal consequence, it sends a dangerous message to the entire student body: Severe disruptions might be met with minor repercussions.

This perception threatens to normalize disrespect and disruptiveness, subtly eroding the boundaries of acceptable behavior. The implications for the school culture are immediate and significant. Other students, observing these lenient responses, could interpret them as a green light for similar behavior and begin testing limits with the confidence that the consequences would be light.

For the faculty, this cycle was demoralizing; it undercut their authority and sapped their morale, as they felt increasingly powerless to manage their classrooms effectively. Moreover, traditional models of suspension were proving ineffective, especially for repeat offenders like Jayden, whom staff ruefully referred to as frequent fliers. For these students, suspension was akin to sending them from the pit to paradise—giving them an unexpected break from school that carried little to no deterrent effect. Faced with this reality and the pressing need to reduce suspensions and disproportionality, well-meaning school leaders often found themselves without viable alternatives. This lack of options led to students being sent back to class, a decision that could have far-reaching and negative impacts on the school environment.

The Alternative: The QUICK Room

It was clear that something needed to change. This critical need spurred the creation of the QUICK Room—a response designed not just to punish but to correct and educate until the prevention strategies being built into the school culture could take over. This new setting was intended to provide real consequences and structured learning opportunities that directly addressed disruptive behaviors. By engaging students in meaningful tasks and holding them accountable within a controlled environment, the QUICK Room offered a robust alternative to the ineffective cycle of "talk and return," and aimed to restore the integrity of classroom management and uphold a culture of respect and responsibility across the school.

A well-run QUICK Room provides an effective alternative to sending students home, as it allows for constant supervision and access to curriculum, compared to out-of-school suspension (OSS). In addition, the QUICK Room provides a more structured alternative to traditional in-school suspension (ISS) programs, detentions, and out-of-class time-outs by addressing student behavioral and academic needs, while avoiding reinforcing certain behaviors maintained by escape or attention.

For years, we struggled to serve the needs of schools with high-frequency misbehavior. In these schools, suspension and disproportionality were constant issues until we created the first iteration of the QUICK Room as an alternative. Once we combined elements of the QUICK Room with the positive strategies discussed in earlier chapters, schools experienced 30%–90% reductions in suspensions, partly because misbehavior decreased. Since then, we've developed various iterations of the QUICK Room, complete with easy-to-follow procedures and software that provides real-time graphic feedback. We'd like to share the key elements of the QUICK Room so that you, too, can experience significant reductions in misbehavior. When we developed the first iteration of the QUICK Room, we didn't have any fancy software—just kitchen timers, pencils, and paper.

Creating an Effective QUICK Room Environment

To establish an effective intervention room following our QUICK model, you need a relatively small classroom or area with limited distractions, and an adult to monitor that area. The fewer stimuli present, the better. In the QUICK Room, rules should be displayed prominently for initial review during a student's intake following classroom removal. These rules can then be revisited if behavior correction is needed.

For the purpose of data collection and identifying patterns of student misbehavior, you need a descriptive sign-in sheet containing the student's name, time in and out, grade, and teacher's name. Another purpose of the sign-in sheet is to ensure that the student follows directions upon arrival. For example, when a student is removed from the classroom by the school code system, they are escorted to the QUICK Room and prompted to sign in. If the student signs in, they are more likely to follow the supervising adult's directions and be ready to continue.

Students must be under instructional control to enter the QUICK Room and begin earning their exit, a critical part of the process. Duration spent in the QUICK Room is initially determined by school policy; however, reductions in duration are possible based on meeting behavioral expectations of the QUICK Room. We recommend this approach, as decreasing time in a nonpreferred area can serve as a powerful incentive for students to engage in required tasks (such as completing one of the action plans in Appendices 19–21 along with any work provided by the teacher) presented in the QUICK Room. Timers are essential for providing the student with a visual reminder of their progress (more on timers later).

QUICK Room Monitor

In the QUICK Room, it is important to have a staff member who has in-depth training in the principles of behavior science for preventing and managing misbehavior as outlined throughout this book. This staff member is more likely to be successful when supervised by an administrator who uses the coaching strategies outlined in Chapters 7–9 and is invested in reducing both ISS and OSS. Appendix 29 includes a QUICK Response Fidelity Monitoring Form to guide and support the employee in running an effective QUICK Room. The form is used for self-monitoring and allows the monitor to review and confirm they are using the correct procedures. It can (and should) also be an interobserver agreement tool when the administrator or designee conducts a quick (no pun intended) drop-in to observe for themselves, check off what they see, and compare to what the monitor checked on their sheet. This is an important process and should occur a couple of times daily in the early stages of the QUICK Room to make sure this new initiative launches correctly. The process can then fade from once daily, to once weekly, and then bi-weekly to ensure the procedures of the QUICK Room are maintained.

As we mentioned, while in the QUICK Room, the staff monitor observes students for performance and duration. Performance is measured by how well students follow the expectations presented to them. The monitor should provide feedback with a simple point sheet scored in intervals. For example, every 10 minutes, the student earns a point for following expectations or zero points for refusing to follow them. Timers and point sheets, critical to the process, allow students to better anticipate reinforcement or the extension of their duration, based on their behavior. We provide an example of a daily and an hourly point sheet in Appendix 34. Under these conditions, we assume that leaving the QUICK Room and returning to the assigned class provides more access to positive reinforcement in the form of peer interactions, learning, good grades, attending preferred classes or recreational activities, and so forth.

While in the QUICK Room, we strongly recommend the monitor provide an incentive in the form of a discount in time for good behavior. In other words, if the student follows expectations and completes required tasks, they earn a reduction in the assigned duration (e.g., 25%). If the student remains on task, the timer continues to count down until they serve the required duration. For example, if they were assigned 1 hour and they remained on task for 45 minutes, they could earn a release from the QUICK Room 15 minutes early. If they earned 2 days (i.e., 12 hours) as an alternative to a 2-day OSS, they could earn 3 hours off, assuming that the school day is 6 hours long.

In contrast, if the student refuses to attend to a task or is disruptive, the monitor could use the option of pausing the timer (i.e., a work-out) until they begin following expectations, and then the timer can be resumed, not reset! Remember, we can't force students to do something, but we can withhold access to reinforcement until they comply. In this case, the reinforcement is leaving the QUICK Room, as when it's implemented correctly, it's a place they should not want to be. The visual timer and point sheet not only influence the student to get back on task as they observe their timer paused, but they also encourage other students to remain on task as they observe the consistent consequences of refusing to follow expectations (e.g., like the impact seeing another driver pulled over for speeding has on your driving).

In the QUICK Room, staff should provide the student with grade- and skill-level work they can complete independently without staff support. This is important because no school wants the QUICK Room to be an opportunity for the student to receive individualized attention and one-on-one tutoring with built-in rapport-building as the result of misbehavior! While one-on-one tutoring and building rapport are great interventions, they should be used as preventative measures, not as consequences to misbehavior—a big mistake we've witnessed in many schools. Doing this in the QUICK Room only increases the likelihood a student will misbehave to escape needed and appropriate instruction.

Misbehavior in the QUICK Room

Even when you follow all the procedures, misbehavior will still happen. And it will likely occur in the QUICK Room. Keep in mind that misbehavior resulted in the student being assigned to the QUICK Room. The secret sauce to the QUICK Room is the consistent adherence to the principles of behavior, as guided by the procedures we've outlined. For frequent fliers, it is important that interventions are specific to the function of the misbehavior. Remember, for some students, being sent to the QUICK Room *might be* reinforcing for one reason or another. This must be assessed based on each student's response to the QUICK Room.

Using the function of behavior as a guide, the QUICK Room can be used strategically. For example, for attention-maintained behavior, significantly reducing or withholding access to social reinforcement is a powerful intervention. In this case, potentially withholding a student's opportunity to participate in eating lunch with other students in the cafeteria might be powerful enough to keep the student on task. For escape from classwork, implementing a contingency of leaving the QUICK Room based on completing classwork similar to the work that provoked the misbehavior might be another function-based intervention.

It's important that a student who misbehaves to escape work (assuming it's not a "can't do" issue) is transitioned to the QUICK Room with the work following them. This can be as simple as the teacher handing the QUICK Responder a worksheet the student refused to complete, or perhaps a book with the instruction to write a chapter summary. This breaks the contingency of misbehavior and escaping work. Having a structured alternative like the QUICK Room in place makes it more effortful for the student to engage in misbehavior.

Implementing the QUICK Room

If you plan to implement your own QUICK Room, we recommend you have a good school-wide behavior management system in place. If you do not have good antecedent strategies in place that serve to teach and positively reinforce behavior, and you rely solely on the QUICK Room as your behavior intervention strategy, it is almost certain to backfire. As part of an effective school-wide system, consider establishing the following:

- A designated and quiet area that is safe and where a student can safely transition with a staff monitor.
- A designated team (the QUICK Team) trained in the principles outlined in this book to pick up student and transport them to the QUICK Room.
- Team members trained in student de-escalation and transportation.
- For patterns of dangerous behaviors, team members should be trained in a variety of crisis management programs. See our example in Appendix 35.

- A designated monitor trained in the principles outlined in this book to manage student behavior in the QUICK Room.
- The duration reduction that can be earned by students based on following expectations. We recommend 20%–25%. See point sheet examples in Appendix 34.
- A sequence of progressive consequences for continued misbehavior in the QUICK Room that includes stopping the timer.
- The number of minutes the timer will be paused for misbehavior prior to moving to the next step in the sequence of progressive consequences.
- A procedure for transitioning the student back to the classroom.
- If the student returns to the same class, a procedure for transferring instructional control back to the teacher.
- Here are some general procedures we've used in schools that you may find helpful if you decide to develop your own QUICK Room.
  - Initiate a Code Call: When a behavior incident occurs, a teacher or staff member calls a specific code to initiate the QUICK Room process.
  - Respond and Assess: A designated QUICK Responder assesses the situation. If removal is warranted, the Responder will transition the student from the area.
  - Escort to the QUICK Room: The QUICK Responder escorts the student to the QUICK Room. The student must be calm, nondisruptive, and responsive to instruction before entering the room.
  - Sign in and Check Readiness: Upon arrival, the staff member prompts the student to sign in. This moment is critical for ensuring that the student is ready to adhere to the QUICK Room monitor's directives while the escorting Responder is still present.
  - Distribute Point Sheet: Provide the student with a point sheet (see Appendix 34 for examples) where behaviors are measured and reinforced at set intervals.
  - Set Expectations: Give the student a visual timer and start the time immediately if they are on task. Clearly explain the expectations and consequences as listed on the point sheet (e.g., remain quiet, no sleeping or putting their head down).
  - Assign Task: Provide the student with tasks, which could include an action plan (refer to Appendices 19–21 for examples), academic tasks, or a combination thereof that the student can complete independently. This is not a time for one-on-one tutoring. If the student was removed for refusing to complete an assignment and the teacher did not send work with them, draw from a preprepared bank of assignments that align with current educational standards.

Behavior Monitoring and Reinforcement

For short intervals (e.g., 1 hour), mark behaviors at 10-minute intervals.

For longer durations or as an alternative to suspension, use 1-hour intervals or shorter, depending on the need for more frequent reinforcement.

If the student meets expectations, remind them that following the rules is how they earn their way out of the QUICK Room.

If the student fails to meet expectations, implement the progressive consequences as outlined on the point sheet.

Transition Back to Class

Once the tasks are complete and the timer ends, the QUICK Team facilitates the student's return to their classroom. If the student is returning to the original class, the teacher should do the following:

- Briefly welcome the student back.
- Implement any necessary restitution (e.g., if the student left a mess, they should clean it up upon return).
- Reengage the student with their tasks, especially if they were removed while refusing to work. For instance, if the student had previously refused to complete specific math problems, the teacher should direct them back to those problems, or adjust as needed if the class has moved on.

Applying the QUICK Room to Our Example

Let's revisit Jayden and observe the changes following the implementation of the QUICK Room intervention at Lincoln Middle School.

Initiation and Response

During a challenging math class, Jayden's frustration escalates, leading to a verbal outburst toward his teacher. Recognizing the need for immediate intervention, the teacher calls the designated code for the QUICK Room. A QUICK Responder arrives swiftly to assess the situation. Finding the criteria for the code met, they escort Jayden out of the classroom, ensuring he is calm and ready to transition into the QUICK Room environment.

In the QUICK Room

Upon arrival at the QUICK Room, Jayden is asked to sign in, which marks the formal start of his session. The supervising staff ensure he understands the expectations and is ready to engage with the process. They provide him with a point sheet and explain that his behavior will be monitored and rewarded in intervals. Jayden is given a visual timer and a set of academic tasks. The tasks are ones that align with his current curriculum but had previously been a point of contention due to his refusal to engage.

Behavioral Adjustment and Monitoring

As Jayden works on the tasks, the QUICK Room monitor closely observes his compliance with the room's rules—staying on task, remaining quiet, and keeping his head up. Jayden marks his behaviors on the point sheet in 10-minute intervals—these marks give him immediate feedback. Positive behavior is reinforced subtly through acknowledgment and the potential to earn a reduction in time spent in the QUICK Room.

Transition Back to Class

After completing the assigned tasks and adhering to the QUICK Room expectations, Jayden has completed his session. The QUICK Responder facilitates his transition back to class. His teacher, prepared ahead of time, welcomes him back warmly and redirects him to a task he had resisted before his removal. She also has him correct a minor disruption he had caused earlier, such as picking up papers he had thrown during his outburst.

Long-Term Impact

This structured intervention has a noticeable effect on Jayden. The immediate consequences and clear expectations provided in the QUICK Room help him understand the link between his behavior and its outcomes. This positive trajectory is further enhanced by the collaborative efforts of Jayden's teachers, who focus on modifying assignments to better suit his learning needs and positively reinforcing his efforts whenever he asks for help. This comprehensive approach, combining the structured environment of the QUICK Room with proactive classroom strategies, leads to a marked improvement in Jayden's behavior.

The synergy between the QUICK Room's structured intervention and the classroom's supportive atmosphere cultivated a significant behavioral change in Jayden. Over time, he demonstrated increased engagement in his lessons, a reduction in disruptive behavior, and a more positive attitude toward schoolwork and his teachers. This holistic strategy not only supported Jayden's immediate needs but also contributed to a more positive and respectful classroom dynamic, benefiting all students involved.

This intervention illustrates the power of a well-structured behavior management system like the QUICK Room, not just in transforming individual behaviors but also in fostering a more respectful and productive school environment.

Final Thoughts on the QUICK Room

When considering the removal of a student from class for any reason, it's important to ensure that the alternative environment, such as the QUICK Room, does not become more reinforcing than the classroom itself. Creating a space that students prefer over their regular classroom can inadvertently encourage misbehavior. For instance, the quiet of the QUICK Room or the absence of peer distractions might appeal to students who find certain subjects or teachers aversive, leading them to act out just to be sent there. This creates a counterproductive cycle that must be addressed as soon as such patterns emerge.

While in the QUICK Room, it is imperative that students remain engaged with their assigned tasks and not use the time to socialize or relax. The QUICK Room is not a place for rest, socializing, or recreation. Allowing it to become a fun or desirable destination undermines its purpose and can lead to an increase in misbehavior rather than a reduction. Students should understand that the QUICK Room is a consequence of certain behaviors, and it is structured to encourage a return to regular class activities through compliance with set expectations. The most effective aspect of this approach is the contrast it provides: The regular classroom environment (time-in) should be more reinforcing than the QUICK Room (time-out).

It's also important to highlight that any alternative placement be tailored to the individual needs arising from a student's specific misbehavior. Utilizing data to identify patterns and determine function-based interventions is key. Behavior science does not support a one-size-fits-all approach; both reinforcers and punishers are highly individualized. This requires careful consideration and thoughtful design when developing interventions like the QUICK Room to ensure they are effective and appropriate for each student.

Key Points

- The traditional suspension model has limited success.
- Consider creating a QUICK Room as an alternative to suspensions and out-of-class time-outs.
- The QUICK Room allows for constant supervision and access to curriculum for students, compared to OSS.
- The QUICK Room is a reactive behavior intervention that results in a student's removal from the classroom to an area where they must work with reduced privileges and attention.
- Select a QUICK Room monitor who has been provided with behavioral training, in case misbehavior occurs.
- It's important to avoid inadvertently creating a QUICK Room that is more reinforcing than the classroom.
- Ensure the transition from the QUICK Room to the classroom is facilitated effectively and instructional control is transitioned back to the teacher.

Reflect on It

- Why is it important to create an environment less reinforcing than the classroom?
- If you currently do not have a room where students can be placed as an alternative to suspension, what are the first steps you can take to move in this direction?
- What do you need to consider if problem behavior occurs while the student is in the QUICK Room?
- What key components does the QUICK Room need to be effective?

CHAPTER 12

Crisis Management Versus Hands-Off Policies

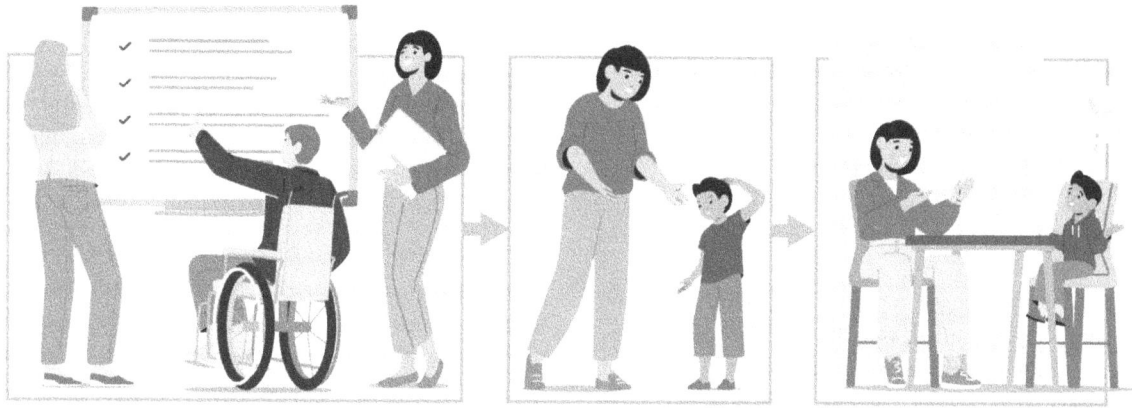

Nobody wants to see "holds" or restraints happen. The very idea of having to put hands on a student is unnerving; and it should be. When overused or used incorrectly, restraints compromise both the safety and dignity of a student. As a result, compassionate educators, advocates, and even state policymakers, disturbed by these safety issues, opt for the fix of implementing a hands-off policy. On the surface, it might seem great to avoid restraint and the associated risks. It's often not long, though, before frustrations grow as other issues arise. These include, but are not limited to, decreased learning for the student and peers and increased danger due to intensifying disruptive and dangerous behaviors. Unfortunately, this can compromise the academic, behavioral, educational, and general well-being of all.

The fact is, everybody in education dreams of a positive climate and culture, one characterized by an eagerness to learn, coupled with safe, prosocial behavior. However, there are numerous risks to this dream, as the safety of students and educators is compromised by those schools and districts that dismiss the prudent use of restraint for a student in crisis.

With the right crisis management system in place, educational dreams can be realized and positive prosocial school cultures created. It starts with a system of staff trained to competence in evidence-based prevention and de-escalation strategies, a system with precise criteria for restraints to prevent the misuse, overuse, or underuse of them. A system can be developed in which students are consistently offered choices based on behavior, even during restraint. Finally, a system can be designed to seamlessly reintegrate the student back into the educational setting following an incident.

Having a hands-off policy for restraints when there is imminent danger would be like a parent who allows their child to run into the middle of a busy road because they didn't want to hold them to prevent harm. Parents would never let this happen; neither should educators. If the school isn't hands-off when a child runs toward a busy intersection, then why are they hands-off when a teacher or peer is attacked? Why are they hands-off when self-injury occurs? The health and safety of all should be the primary consideration of the school policy.

How About Setting Limits?

As the noted behavior analyst and crisis management expert Dr. Merrill Winston reminds us in his book, *Adventures in Special Education and Applied Behavior Analysis* (2016), all parents set limits for their children. All parents. When children are older and have good language skills, these limits are usually set verbally. For very young children, however, verbal control often fails. As Dr. Winston proselytizes, if rules were sufficient to change behavior, there would never be a need to reinforce, extinguish, or punish behavior. Consequently, in dangerous situations, physical control is not only warranted but absolutely necessary for safety. Whether it's termed physical control, holding, or something else, no matter how mild, all procedures involving limiting mobility are forms of restraint. The problem is that when older, stronger, more experienced students engage in dangerous behavior, physical management becomes more challenging and dangerous for all.

Still, all would agree that older, stronger children must be kept safe themselves and from harming others. It is hard to imagine any educator would permit a student to continue banging their head against a glass window due to a hands-off policy. We must treat all students, with and without special needs, equally and equitably. This is their fundamental human right—afford them the respect they deserve, preserve their dignity, and maintain their safety. Fair, established limits are a way to inform what is tolerated, accepted, and accommodated.

The Risks of Not Restraining

When children engage in problem behavior, we do not want them to be handcuffed, as in the 2019 case of a 6-year-old Florida girl who was arrested at school for kicking and punching staff members; 3 years later she was diagnosed with post-traumatic stress disorder (Watkins, 2022). While striking staff is certainly unacceptable, how might things have turned out differently if the staff had been trained in effective crisis management? Oh, and let's not forget to mention the potential for students who engage in behaviors like the 6-year-old to be overmedicated, tased, pepper sprayed, or expelled from school, all as a result of avoiding physical restraint. There are far too many examples of reactive methods, which do not change behavior but do violate a student's rights and create an appearance of impropriety.

At the same time, we should not allow a student to destroy a classroom because we don't want the responsibility that comes with the use of restraint. The fear of restraint is a growing issue in education. It is true: Restraint can be used irresponsibly. But implementing hands-off policies can also be irresponsible and to the student's detriment. We must not eliminate the use of restraints, but we must ensure there is a crisis management system in place focusing on preventing crises in the first place. We must set limits gently, nonviolently, and nonpunitively. Yet we must set limits. To allow anyone to do anything they want, unchecked, sets them up for failure as a contributing member of their school, community, and society (Winston, 2016).

In our recent independent poll, 92% of respondents believed that restraints by trained practitioners were a better option than hands-off policies (Professional Crisis Management Association, 2022). Very likely, the 8% of respondents who voted for a hands-off policy either directly experienced poor restraints or heard they are harmful. Their views are understandable and cannot be dismissed. But let's not throw the proverbial baby out with the bathwater. Nobody we know "likes" using restraint. All the professionals we know wish to minimize its use. Failure to employ judicious, effective, and humane short-term restraint, though, can result in a lifetime of restriction or even trauma such as that experienced by the 6-year-old girl in Florida in 2019.

Ponder, if you will, allowing a student to destroy a classroom after the removal of their peers. This may immediately solve the issue of other students not being harmed. Allowing a student to demolish a classroom, not setting limits, and clearing a room, at face value, appears to adhere to being humane and hands-off. However, it is anything but—the student's behavior may be reinforced and be more likely to happen again and may become even more problematic. We cannot kick the can down the road. This is not someone else's problem. It is ours.

For example, consider a student who engages in dangerous behaviors because she seeks teacher attention (remember function). If everyone else is removed from the room, the student wins the "attention lottery" as she is now alone with the teacher. The student likely receives lots of reinforcement (i.e., teacher attention) for the very behaviors the teacher is trying to reduce. The teacher giving her attention to the student reinforces the student's behavior, increasing the likelihood the student will engage in the problem behaviors again in that classroom and perhaps in other school environments. The problem can generalize, intensify, and become a repeating cycle of events. And what about the student's peers who were removed from the classroom and the negative impact of the disruption on their learning?

We are not suggesting a room clear is never warranted. It might make sense under certain conditions. For instance, if the student has a medical condition that makes restraint dangerous to their physical well-being or perhaps if the dangerous behaviors function for peer attention, the prudent course of action is to clear the room. The question still exists: "Are we safer down the road following a room clear?" If the answer is, "No," "Not really," or, "Uncertain," other measures should be considered.

We've observed a number of schools and districts where we have previously worked and consulted that went hands-off. This policy change has resulted in teachers and administrators being forced to call the police and has sometimes ended with the student being restrained by law enforcement, involuntarily committed to a mental health facility, and/or receiving an increase to their dosage of psychotropic medication to "treat" their behavior. Whatever the necessary and available steps, it becomes a problem for the students as their behaviors worsen, they become unable to function in society, and the locus of control shifts to outside sources (the police, medical restraint).

What's the Right Way?

Well, first off, you must *always* follow the policies established by your state and school district. The recommendations and suggestions in this book are just that—recommendations and suggestions. But from our perspective, we should accommodate individuals who require accommodations. We should create a positive climate and culture powered by the science of human behavior to minimize or even eliminate the need for restraints. We should train crisis management practitioners to fluency, where the staff can quickly and accurately engage in the appropriate actions: in prevention, de-escalation, and restraints that are humane and preserve the safety and dignity of the student. We should increase the provision of educational and clinical oversight to maintain a positive learning environment, while we also guarantee the proper use of restraint.

But let's not go overboard and create a fictional world where we inadvertently teach that all behavior is allowable. We should not rely on law enforcement for interventions we can implement ourselves with the proper training. Believe us, law enforcement and school resource officers do not want to be involved in these situations any more than we do!

Now let's look at what you should consider in relation to crisis management procedures and training.

Crisis Management

Within any crisis management system, physical holding is just one part of that system and should never be used to "punish" bad behavior. A complete crisis management system should be implemented to

- prevent
- set limits
- de-escalate
- increase safety for all through transportation (i.e., an escort involving adult assistance and, perhaps, hands on in some manner) or restraints when behavior becomes dangerous to the student or others
- reintegrate students back into the classroom

Crisis management systems should also be used to prevent and respond to intense, high-frequency, and severe problem behaviors (e.g., destroying property) that have the potential to be strengthened as the result of reinforcement.

Many schools work with increasingly dangerous behaviors including physical aggression and self-injury. In an earnest attempt to address these mounting issues, they seek training in crisis management but end up with training in programs that primarily focus on techniques such as de-escalation and restraint.

While these are both critical components to managing crises, they do not represent a complete crisis management system. In fact, de-escalation and restraint must compose just the smallest part of the system. As a result of the narrow focus on de-escalation and restraint, dangerous behaviors occur again, and again, **and again**. This leads to frustration, low morale, injury, litigation, and staff and faculty turnover. It negatively impacts relationships between the educators and the learners and ultimately impedes the education of the individual and other students.

Educators, staff, parents, and guardians desire a crisis management system that doesn't just put a Band-Aid on the situation but that leads to a reduction in the frequency and severity of dangerous behaviors and associated issues. However, if they are in perpetual crisis, they will never see the forest for the trees. The goal should be to maintain relationships in a way that helps, not hurts, the educational or treatment processes. Every school that struggles with the behaviors outlined in this chapter needs to have QUICK Team Members trained in a complete crisis management system to respond in precisely the right way at precisely the right time.

What Is a Complete Crisis Management System?

Imagine taking a young child to the pediatrician for issues associated with being overweight, and the doctor makes diet and exercise prescriptions not backed by rigorous research. The doctor also fails to educate the parents on the importance of healthy eating habits and incorporating movement into the child's daily routine. Therefore, the parents fail to create a home environment that provides regular opportunities for healthy eating and exercise. This is what it is like for schools without a complete crisis management system.

A complete crisis management system, grounded in behavior science, is critical to reduce dangerous behavior. It is vital to understand behavior science because systems are made up of several processes; processes are made up of procedures; and procedures are ultimately made up of behaviors. A complete crisis management system must have procedures to address all the components associated with a cycle of crisis:

- those that prevent crisis behaviors
- those that respond to precrisis behaviors
- those that manage crisis behaviors
- those that address what to do after the crisis to reintegrate the student back into their regular setting

Unfortunately, most schools are not equipped with systems or behavioral science because they overemphasize de-escalation as crisis intervention. Too little attention is given to prevention and seamless reintegration of the student back into the educational environment.

Crisis Management Procedures

If your school experiences dangerous behavior and you seek training in crisis management, here are some criteria you should consider in regard to the procedures, in addition to what we've already mentioned. Use this as a checklist:

- ☐ Are there substantial procedures that teach how to create an environment that prevents escalating behavior? These should include procedures to build and maintain relationships, strengthen behavior, and respond to low-intensity misbehavior in ways that are not coercive. A complete system does not begin at de-escalation and focus on restraint; rather, it aims to prevent escalation of behavior.

- ☐ Are there precise behavioral criteria for when to restrain? Be careful of verbiage like "dangerous" or "unsafe" behavior. Precise description prevents the overuse and misuse of restraint.

- ☐ Do the restraint procedures use shaping and fading (i.e., the systematic application and reduction of physical prompts) to respond relatively immediately to the student's behavior? This is critical, as applying and fading physical procedures within just a few seconds provides feedback to the student that they will be systematically released as soon as they start to calm. Beware of crisis management curricula that do not include precise criteria for release (i.e., shaping, fading, and procedures that specify times).

- ☐ Do the physical procedures employ natural body positioning, with no pressure on joints? Every time a restraint occurs, there is the danger of injury to the student and staff. Because of the nature of restraints, if the student is in an awkward position (i.e., being bent over at the waist or restrained with their arms in an unnatural direction), there is an increased risk of injury and pain. If the student experiences pain during a restraint, it can quickly increase problem behaviors. This poses a greater risk of injury for all. Think about it. If somebody restrained you and it hurt, you would likely fight back. And if they hurt you, it would also likely damage your relationship with them. It is for these reasons that physical procedures employing natural body positioning with no pressure on the joints to avoid pain should be the only ones considered.

- ☐ Do the physical procedures avoid positional asphyxia? Positional asphyxia, also known as postural asphyxia, occurs when someone's position prevents them from getting enough oxygen. This can be from the position of the student's body or the position of the staff member's body in relation to the student. Some research suggests restraint that involves bending the restrained person or placing body weight on them has a greater effect on their breathing than face-down positions alone (Vilke, 2020).

- ☐ When implementing prone or supine restraint, do the procedures call for the use of a mat to ensure students are not restrained on the floor? Much like the point about body position and pressure on joints, restraining a student on a hard surface increases the risk of injury for all, can damage relationships, and might be considered inhumane.

- ☐ Has the crisis management system been medically evaluated to ensure safety for both the students and the practitioners?

Crisis Management Training

Now let's look at the actual training procedures. Even if there is a solid crisis management system in place, it's important that it be trained to fluency. Again, consider using this as a checklist.

- ☐ Does the training incorporate repetitive practice of physical procedures and require participants to demonstrate fluency of those procedures? The goal shouldn't just be that staff receive a card or certificate as proof of crisis management instruction. The goal should be for trainees to be able to respond accurately and automatically over time with long-term maintenance of the needed skills (Binder, 1996). This requires high repetition of the procedures during instruction. In short, staff must return to the school following training and be able to quickly apply the correct procedure at the correct time. As such, beware of crisis management training that only requires a practitioner to perform a procedure a couple of times correctly during the training. These types of training approaches likely result in staff who are not confident and able to do the right thing at the right time.

- ☐ Does the training have competency-based assessments? When we say competency-based, we mean real assessments that likely result in not all people passing the course all the time! For example, not everybody is able to implement transportation or restraint procedures. The worst thing that can happen is for a staff member who is unable to effectively perform physical procedures to become involved in a crisis that requires restraint. This is a recipe for disaster for the student, the school, and the individual staff member's own well-being.

☐ Is annual recertification required? Part of ensuring competency is regular practice of learned procedures to avoid procedural drift. In short, procedural drift occurs when there is a mismatch between how the crisis management system was designed and how it is applied. Crisis management systems that require less than annual recertifications drastically increase the likelihood of procedural drift. Even if you train in a crisis management system that requires annual certification, we highly recommend regular practice of the skills, with competency measured on a regular basis within the school setting.

Final Thoughts on Crisis Management

The goal of training educators in crisis management should never be about gaining student compliance but about keeping students, educators, and staff safe in a way that maintains relationships. In addition, the goal of having educators and staff trained in crisis management should never be to simply check a policy box that indicates people are trained. If you lead or work within an educational setting with students who engage in dangerous behavior, and hands-off policies are being instituted, please consider the points we made about the potential risks involved. If you currently have a crisis management system or you are thinking about bringing one into your school or district, consider the criteria above when evaluating your current system or choosing a crisis management training for your QUICK Team Members. You'll want your team trained in a complete crisis management system, one grounded in the same behavior science that is being highlighted across this book.

Key Points

- Crisis management should never be about gaining compliance or punishing students for their behavior.
- Crisis management should be used to increase safety and maintain relationships.
- Hands-off policies can have unintended consequences such as increased medication, mechanical restraint, and law enforcement involvement.
- Using prevention strategies to establish a safe, caring, and engaging learning environment is key.
- A complete crisis management system includes prevention, de-escalation, physical intervention, and reintegration, not just de-escalation and physical restraint procedures.
- Crisis management systems should be grounded in behavior science and include shaping and fading procedures.
- Crisis management systems should have precise criteria for restraint to reduce the likelihood it will be overused.
- Crisis management systems should use body positioning that does not produce pain or allow for positional asphyxia.
- Crisis management systems should be medically evaluated.
- Crisis management practitioners should be trained to fluency.
- Crisis management training should require competency-based assessments and regular recertification.

Reflect on It

- Are key staff (e.g., the QUICK Team) at your school trained in crisis management?
- Does the system you are using meet the criteria laid out above?
- If staff were trained, how do you know they are implementing the procedure with fidelity?

CHAPTER 13

Transforming School Culture: Principal Lack and the ACT Matrix

Hawkins Middle School, led by Principal Brian Lack, has encountered significant challenges in maintaining a positive school culture and staff morale. Despite Principal Lack's dedication and care for his team's well-being and effectiveness, several underlying issues have compounded, leading to a distressed educational environment. About 50% of Hawkins Middle School teachers work outside their areas of expertise, creating significant gaps in knowledge delivery and subject competency. Even among those qualified in their subject areas, only a few have received formal training in classroom management, which is essential for creating an environment conducive to learning. Many teachers are finding it challenging to manage their classrooms effectively and express frustration, feeling ill-equipped to meet the diverse needs of their students.

The faculty tend to blame external factors such as students' backgrounds and parental involvement for their challenges, leading to a sense of helplessness and resignation. This has resulted in a significant decline in morale. Teachers doubt their ability to influence and manage student behavior, which is critical for their confidence and professional satisfaction. Typical statements include "These kids just have too many needs," or "Their parents are the problem." These attitudes reflect the staff's growing frustration and demoralization. The cumulative effect of these issues has been detrimental to the school's overall environment. The lack of qualified staff and effective classroom management has led to a chaotic learning atmosphere, making it difficult for students to achieve academic success. Moreover, teachers' pervasive sense of doubt and frustration further exacerbates the problem, creating a vicious cycle of low morale and poor student outcomes.

Principal Lack is acutely aware of these issues and is deeply concerned about the well-being of his faculty and staff—and Hawkins Middle School's education quality. However, he feels overwhelmed and unsure how to address these complex problems. His efforts to support his staff have not yielded the desired results, and he is now at a crossroads, needing to find effective strategies to turn the situation around.

One afternoon, Principal Lack is walking through the seventh-grade wing of the building. The scene in Ms. Neu's class makes him pause. He witnesses a classroom that isn't as chaotic as it typically is. The seventh graders are on task and actively participating in cooperative learning group activities. Thinking about it, Ms. Neu's class has many students who are frequently being removed from the classroom at the teacher's request for various infractions. Principal Lack decides to take a closer look. Upon entering the classroom, he observes the students working collaboratively in small groups, with each person assigned a specific role for their project.

The students communicate respectfully, actively listen to one another, and share their thoughts and ideas for the project. When the group work is over, Ms. Neu signals the end by using a chime and instructs the students to start wrapping up their conversations, informing them that they have approximately 1 minute left to finalize their work. The students diligently put the finishing touches on their posters, and when the minute is up, Ms. Neu signals for their attention. Principal Lack cannot believe what he is witnessing. This is the same classroom that he frequently visited due to behavior challenges.

This year, Ms. Neu, a seasoned teacher, had been struggling with classroom leadership. Principal Lack decides to stay a bit longer. Ms. Neu notices Principal Lack standing in the back of the classroom. She smiles at him and continues with her lesson. She uses a random picker to select students to be called on, and almost all students are engaged while their classmates are presenting their posters to the group. Ms. Neu praises the students for their correct answers and provides positive support when students need to be redirected back to the task. When the lesson is finished, Ms. Neu reminds the students they need to pack up and prepare for dismissal. The students straighten the desks, put away the markers and the other materials they used for their activity, and pack their backpacks. When the bell rings, Ms. Neu stands at the door and releases the students row by row. She thanks them for a great class and says she'll see them tomorrow. Principal Lack cannot believe the remarkable change in the students' and Ms. Neu's behavior. He has to know how this significant change in her classroom happened.

Ms. Neu laughs and tells Principal Lack, "It's a miracle, right?" Principal Lack, puzzled, asks her how she achieved well-behaved and engaged students. Ms. Neu explains that Mr. Gomez had introduced her to the ACT Matrix (Polk et al., 2016) and recommended using it to build relationships with her students. She acknowledges that she needed to create a safe and respectful environment, establish clear expectations, and involve students in developing classroom norms. Ms. Neu shows Principal Lack the ACT Matrix. She explains how she and the students identified and used shared values, such as respect, teamwork, and curiosity, as the foundation of their new classroom management plan. Principal Lack is inspired to implement this approach school-wide after seeing the positive impact in Ms. Neu's classroom, and he aims to create a collaborative and supportive atmosphere among the adults in the building.

Initial Observation and Inspiration

Encouraged by Ms. Neu's success, Principal Lack introduces the ACT Matrix at a faculty level, aiming to enhance the school culture by aligning it with shared values and committed actions. He recognizes that just as students need a supportive learning environment, educators need a workplace where their values are respected and their challenges are collectively addressed.

Facilitating Faculty Involvement

On the following professional development day, Principal Lack begins with a presentation illustrating how Ms. Neu used the ACT Matrix (Figure 13.1) to transform her classroom dynamics. He emphasizes the potential for similar positive changes within the faculty and staff and decides to work through the entire ACT Matrix with the faculty and staff. Principal Lack announces, "Today, we're not just discussing policies; we're shaping the future of our school together." This sets a tone of collective effort and mutual respect. "What kind of school environment do we want to create? What behaviors or actions do we believe will get us there?"

Just like Ms. Neu's students were when presented with this option, the faculty are skeptical and need to feel that they are in a safe space to have this critical discussion. Principal Lack divides them into cooperative learning groups by grade and subject and begins the conversation by sharing his values with the faculty and inviting them to share theirs. He encourages the faculty to identify core values that could guide their school culture (Figure 13.1, lower right quadrant). Principal Lack reminds the faculty of the importance of these values—not just as abstract ideals but as actionable principles that will inform their daily interactions. The faculty begin discussing what is important to them as educators and why they entered the profession. They talk about their ideal work environment and identify their sources of motivation. The faculty delve deep into the discussion to identify their core values. When Principal Lack brings them back together, he discovers that many faculty members share the same values.

CHAPTER 13 | TRANSFORMING SCHOOL CULTURE: PRINCIPAL LACK AND THE ACT MATRIX

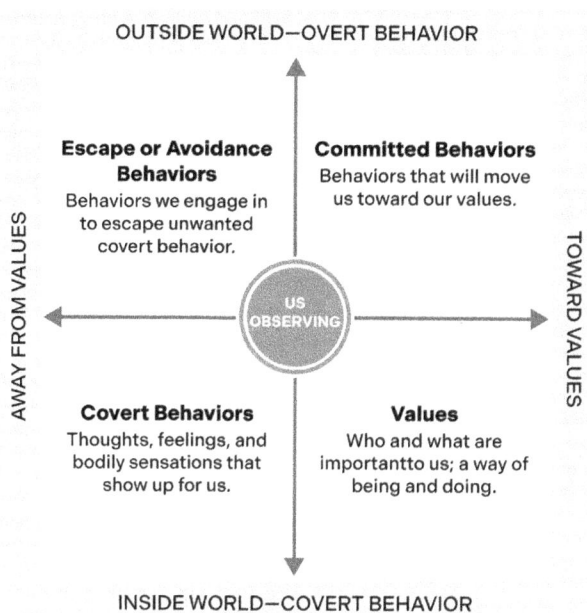

Figure 13.1. The ACT Matrix, the group observation tool, which involves noticing and being aware of a group's behavior and the impact on the environment. (Adapted from the Prosocial ACT Matrix tool developed by Atkins et al. [2019].)

In the following steps, Principal Lack facilitates a group discussion to identify and affirm the shared values essential to their professional community.

Identifying Shared Values

In Chapter 6, we discussed the concept of values. Values act as a personal guide, influence our decisions, and reflect our aspirations. They shape our way of being and doing. When our values are aligned, we are better equipped to assess situations, solve problems, make decisions, and take actions that lead us in meaningful directions.

Starting in the bottom right side of the matrix (Figure 13.1, lower right quadrant). Principal Lack invites the faculty and staff to consider the values of being an educator. As he calls on the educators to share their responses, they begin to identify shared values. Principal Lack encourages staff to consider principles that guide their interactions with students, particularly in challenging situations. As the faculty and staff share their thoughts, a theme explicitly related to behavior management begins to emerge. They agree on several values:

- **Compassion:** Understanding students' backgrounds and challenges and responding with empathy.
- **Fairness:** Ensuring that all students are treated equally and that disciplinary measures are applied consistently.
- **Respect:** Maintaining respect for each student's dignity in all interactions, even during disciplinary actions.

These values are recognized as essential for creating a supportive and effective learning environment where students felt valued and understood.

Addressing Covert Behaviors

Next, Principal Lack instructs the faculty to examine their covert behaviors that deviate from their shared values. Initially, Principal Lack shares some of his thoughts and feelings as the person responsible for all the students, faculty, and staff.

- He is facing numerous challenges with student behavior and faculty and staff conduct.
- He is worried about the well-being of his educators.
- Despite attempting various strategies, he feels overwhelmed and uncertain about how to address the complex issues.

After disclosing his covert behaviors, Principal Lack guides the staff to contemplate their hidden behaviors—those internal thoughts and feelings that could lead to ineffective or harmful behavior management practices (Figure 13.1, lower left quadrant). Staff members openly discuss the emotions that commonly surface when dealing with disciplinary challenges.

Frustration: Feeling overwhelmed by repeated behavioral challenges. Some faculty say

- "I don't even know how they want us to teach these students; they are so bad!"
- "Every time I call for someone to remove a student, they bring them back 10 minutes later—they didn't even discipline them!"
- "I'm not calling for help anymore—it rarely comes, and when it does, the kids return worse!"

Impatience: Reacting quickly to problems without taking the time to understand the root causes. The faculty say

- "These kids don't come to school prepared."
- "Don't the parents discipline them?"

- "Why are they sleeping all the time? That's so disrespectful. They must get out of my class if they want to sleep!"

Powerlessness: The faculty are struggling to effectively manage behavior using constructive strategies. The faculty say

- "I'm so tired of dealing with all these bad kids."
- "I have the worst class."
- "They need to do something quickly, or I'm not returning!"
- "I don't know what I'm doing."
- "I don't know how to teach these kids."
- "I don't care if they learn or not. It's not my problem!"

Principal Lack acknowledges these covert behaviors and realizes they could lead to less-effective management tactics. He records these behaviors on the smart whiteboard matrix. He begins the work of understanding the impact of the challenges faced by the teachers on the school environment. He also recognizes areas where he needs to offer his faculty more, less, or different support. Furthermore, he considers how the struggles of the faculty might be affecting the staff. He realizes the importance of addressing these issues effectively despite how difficult it was to hear his faculty's concerns.

Confronting Escape Behaviors

Remember, while we all behave in ways that allow us to escape things that may be aversive, sometimes these behaviors move us away from what we value, and often they prevent us from reaching our goals. Though they provide us with immediate relief, that relief tends to be only temporary.

It is time to engage the educators for one of the more challenging reflections of this exercise. Principal Lack shares his avoidance behaviors with the faculty. He gives examples of how he has engaged in behaviors such as retreating to his office; shutting the door; and relying heavily on his administration, particularly the assistant principal, to deal with the behavior challenges. He explains how it felt good to avoid those uncomfortable feelings but he knew he wasn't living according to his core values. He was not a good observer of his behavior and wanted to escape the stress and the challenges associated with meeting the demands of his role as the school leader.

The faculty and staff discussion then focuses on identifying their escape behaviors—visible actions taken in response to the discomfort caused by challenging student behaviors (Figure 13.1, upper left quadrant). At first, the educators are reluctant to say out loud those behaviors they engage in to avoid the challenging situations they encounter and to escape those awful feelings that show up for them. Principal Lack's honesty and authenticity about his escape and avoidance behaviors encourage the staff to share their problem behaviors that are misaligned with their values. He helps the staff recognize and assess how these behaviors contradict their stated values, essentially moving them away from those identified shared values.

Examples of escape and avoidance behaviors include

- **Harsh Disciplining:** Using punitive measures disproportionately could undermine student trust and respect.
- **Avoidance:** Ignoring problematic behaviors until they escalate allows for avoiding immediate confrontation but potentially worsens the situation.
- **Overreliance on Authority:** Using positional power to force compliance could stifle understanding and respect between staff and students.

The faculty examine how these behaviors contradict their commitment to compassion, fairness, and respect and discuss the negative impacts these actions could have on the school culture.

Committing to Committed Behaviors

The most impactful part of the session involved defining committed behaviors that aligned with their values (Figure 13.1, upper right quadrant). To complete the matrix, as we outlined above, Principal Lack facilitated a brainstorming session where staff developed concrete, actionable behaviors to replace ineffective escape behaviors:

- **Professional Development:** During the discussions, it is realized that many faculty members need to be trained in effective classroom management practices. Principal Lack commits to ensuring that all teachers are trained in classroom management. Teachers agree to attend training as needed but commit to selecting meaningful professional development topics and activities within their grade group and professional learning communities.

- **Consistent Application of Rules:** The need to ensure that all students and faculty know the rules and expectations and that consequences are applied fairly and consistently becomes clear. In addition, faculty members agree that students must be taught the expectations and given feedback.
- **Focus on Positive Reinforcement:** The group agrees on the need to recognize and reinforce positive behaviors more frequently in order to encourage relationship-building with students.

These committed behaviors were identified to directly counteract the escape behaviors and offer the faculty and staff a choice to move toward values. While it took some time to identify the committed behaviors, the educators found commonalities in behaviors that foster a culture of collaboration, positive accountability, fairness, and respect. By acknowledging negative thoughts and feelings and choosing behaviors that align with shared values, staff can achieve their value-driven goals and experience a sense of satisfaction.

Implementation and Continuous Review

To monitor the effectiveness of these new strategies, the staff agree on specific metrics such as reductions in disciplinary referrals, improvements in student satisfaction surveys, and feedback from the student council. Principal Lack schedules regular meetings to evaluate progress based on these metrics, discuss challenges, and adjust strategies as needed.

This structured approach to behavior management through the ACT Matrix allows the faculty and staff at Hawkins Middle School to more effectively align their actions with their core values, which creates a more positive, respectful, and supportive school environment. This process improves behavior management outcomes and strengthens the school culture, demonstrating the transformative power of collective commitment and action in educational settings.

Key Points
• Faculty and staff bring their accumulated experiences, which significantly impact the classroom and school environment. • Instead of avoiding inner thoughts and feelings, one acknowledges and accepts them for what they are—thoughts. • Learning the skill of acceptance can help faculty and staff articulate their feelings and emotions. • Covert behaviors are internal experiences, such as thoughts and feelings, that only individuals can observe. They often involve getting caught up in our thoughts, letting these thoughts control our actions, and causing us to get stuck. These negative thoughts and feelings arise in difficult, challenging, or uncomfortable situations. Covert behavior is the negative self-talk we engage in about our behavior. • Engaging in escape or avoidance behavior involves distancing ourselves from negative thoughts and sensations, providing immediate but temporary relief. However, these behaviors can move us away from our values and goals. • Pinpointed committed behaviors are essential for cultivating a learning atmosphere where the faculty and staff feel included and empowered to participate. The upper right quadrant of the ACT Matrix focuses on behaviors that help the school move toward its shared values despite challenges, fostering a culture of respect, engagement, and mutual support. • The ACT Matrix allows the school community to openly discuss thoughts and feelings, which can lead to actions dedicated to achieving common goals of respect, engagement, and support. This process helps create a harmonious school environment with a culture of positive accountability. • The ACT Matrix helps educators work together to identify shared values, recognize behaviors that negatively impact the school environment, and promote a positive learning environment. • The ACT Matrix is an adaptable tool that can be used in multiple ways with different types of groups. Review the ACT Matrix for Groups and Teams in Appendix 36 for a sample plan to use the ACT Matrix with school groups and teams.

Reflect on It

- Identify and define your values as a school leader. How can identifying personal values help faculty and staff cultivate a positive school environment?
- As the school leader, do you know what committed behaviors you want to see from your educators? Before working through the ACT Matrix, identify some valued goals for the school to guide your ACT Matrix facilitation.
- How does faculty and staff learning history influence their current behavior?
- What might you, as a school leader, do more, less, or differently to support your faculty and staff in engaging in behavior aligned with shared values?
- How can you create a psychologically safe environment? Faculty and staff might hesitate to share their true thoughts and feelings when using the ACT Matrix. As a school leader, how can you tell if your school has a culture that encourages authenticity in sharing how things are going?
- What knowledge and skills are needed to support faculty and staff in aligning with the school's values? What resources or support will aid in implementing the plan?
- What would be some indicators that faculty and staff behavior is moving in the right direction toward the school's shared values? How will you let faculty and staff know that their behavior is moving in the right direction?

APPENDICES

Appendix 1:	Categorized Interventions for Behavior: Defining and Categorizing Misbehavior	111
Appendix 2:	Student Refusal/Offering Choices	113
Appendix 3:	Teacher Proximity: Off-Task Behavior	115
Appendix 4:	Verbal Redirection: Failing to Follow an Expectation	117
Appendix 5:	Setting Limits: Failure to Follow Directives	119
Appendix 6:	In-Class Time-Out: From Positive Reinforcement	121
Appendix 7:	Time-Out/Removal From Class	123
Appendix 8:	Work-Out Out of Class	125
Appendix 9:	Restitutional Overcorrection: Damage to the Environment	127
Appendix 10:	Overcorrection/Positive Practice	129
Appendix 11:	Response Cost: Failing to Follow Expectations	131
Appendix 12:	Response Cost Lottery: Off-Task or Inattentive Behavior	133
Appendix 13:	Junk Behavior: Attention-Seeking Behavior—Ignoring Junk Behavior	135
Appendix 14:	Behavior Contracts	137
Appendix 15:	ABC Recording	139
Appendix 16:	Effective Classroom Management Planning Guide	141
Appendix 17:	Emotional Regulation for Students: Training and Coaching	149
Appendix 18:	Student Performance Diagnostic Checklist	151
Appendix 19:	QUICK ACTion Plan A	153
Appendix 20:	QUICK ACTion Plan B	155
Appendix 21:	QUICK ACTion Plan C	157
Appendix 22:	ACT Matrix for Classrooms	159
Appendix 23:	Performance Diagnostic Checklist for Coaching	163
Appendix 24:	Reducing Tardiness—Managing Late Arrivals	165
Appendix 25:	Reducing Stealing Behavior With the "Green Dot" Procedure	167
Appendix 26:	Reducing Tattling—Managing Reporting Behavior	169
Appendix 27:	Reducing Vocal Disruptions Procedure	171
Appendix 28:	School-Wide Tardiness Reduction Procedure	173
Appendix 29:	QUICK Response Fidelity Monitoring Form	177
Appendix 30:	QUICK Room Fidelity Monitoring and Self-Assessment Guide	179
Appendix 31:	QUICK Response Social Validity Questionnaire	181
Appendix 32:	Elopement Reporting Tips	183
Appendix 33:	Problem-Solving for Students	185
Appendix 34:	QUICK Room Point Sheets	187
Appendix 35:	Crisis Plan for Escalating Behavior	189
Appendix 36:	ACT Matrix for Groups and Teams	191

Appendix 1: Categorized Interventions for Behavior

Defining and Categorizing Misbehavior

Group 1	Group 2		Group 3
The first group is for low-magnitude or low-intensity misbehavior that, while annoying, does not continuously disrupt the flow of instruction. Behaviors like pencil tapping, talking out of turn, being out of seat, or other low-intensity or impulsive misbehavior.	The second group is for moderate-intensity misbehavior. Behaviors like task refusal, yelling out, and running around the classroom. These disrupt the student and the classroom environment but are not dangerous. These misbehaviors continue after the rule or expectation was taught, and the student has not responded to consequences for mild misbehavior.		The third group is for high-intensity behaviors commonly addressed in the school code of conduct. Behaviors like physically dangerous acts, threats, running out of class or building, and open defiance.
Mild misbehavior	**Moderate misbehavior**	**Continuous misbehavior**	**High-magnitude and high-intensity misbehavior**

• Tapping pencil
• Calling out
• Out of seat without permission
• Not following conversation level expectations
• Head on desk/sleeping
• Running/jumping
• Using materials inappropriately
• Talking to peers
	• Out of seat
	• Talking out of turn
	• Off task
	• Dress code violation
	• Inappropriate vocalizations
	• Language (low-intensity cursing)
	• Misuse of property (not honoring someone's space, feelings, or belongings)
	• Disruption (low-intensity, but inappropriate)
	• Physical contact (non-serious, but inappropriate)
	• Student is slow to follow directions or needs several reminders
	• Tardiness
		• Refusing to follow directions
		• Pounding on a desk
		• Telling jokes
		• Screaming
		• Being disrespectful
		• Lying/cheating
		• Teasing/taunting
		• Disrespect
		• Chronic tardiness
			• Physically dangerous behavior
			• Insubordination
			  ◦ Student uses profanity toward teacher
			• Threats
			  ◦ Student threatens to damage materials
			  ◦ Student threatens violence
			  ◦ Student threatens to bring a weapon
			• Abusive or inappropriate language
			• Alcohol
			• Drugs
			• Arson
			• Bomb threat/false alarm
			• Severe dress code violation
			• Forgery/theft
			• Harassment or teasing
			• Taunting/threats
			• Lying/cheating
			• Property damage
			• Sexual or pornographic materials or behavior
			• Truancy

Source: McKevitt and Braaksma (2008).

Strategies and Intervention for Correcting Misbehavior

Group 1	Group 2		Group 3
Mild misbehavior	Moderate misbehavior	Continuous misbehavior	High-magnitude and high-intensity misbehavior
Classroom-managed prompting and redirection *Consider using these informational/corrective responses at the beginning of the school year or with mild misbehavior.*	**Classroom-managed consequences** *These error correction strategies will be more effective if students are taught the rules and classroom expectations.*	**Progressive consequences** *Consider using these for low-frequency, higher magnitude misbehavior. Essentially, the penalty for misbehavior is progressively increased for repeated instances as in the example below.*	**Office discipline process** *A word of caution: Out-of-school suspension (OSS) is common for these behaviors. For "frequent flyers," OSS may reward behavior. Try alternatives like lunch/after-school detention or internal school suspension if OSS was used but has not curbed misbehavior.*

• Pre-correction
• Clarification
• Proximity control
• Gentle verbal reprimand
• Signal interference
• Family contact
• Humor
• Planned ignoring
• Pivot praise to those students behaving appropriately and responsibly
• Restitution
	• Time owed
	• Time out
	  ○ From favorite object
	  ○ From small group
	  ○ At desk
	  ○ In another location (consider the QUICK Room; see Chapter 11)
	• Restitution
	• Positive practice
	• Response cost—loss of points
	• Response cost—lottery
	• Detention
	• Action plan (see Appendices 19–21)
	• Demerits
		• 1st: 2 minutes off of recess
		• 2nd: 5 minutes off of recess
		• 3rd: 10 minutes off of recess
		• 4th: no recess (possible action plan)
		• 5th: parent contact
		• 6th: referral
			• Parent contact
			• Referral
			• Early intervention
			• Planned discussion
			• Targeted behavioral intervention
			• Behavior contract

Source: Modified from the consequence-level system found in McKevitt and Braaksma (2008).

References

McKevitt, B. C., & Braaksma, A. D. (2008). Best practices in developing a Positive Behavior Support system at the school level. In A. Thomas & J. Grimes *Best practices in school psychology V: Vol. 3* (pp. 735–747). National Association of School Psychologists.

Appendix 2: Student Refusal/Offering Choices

Defining the Behavior: This strategy relates to students who refuse to begin tasks or participate in teacher-selected or directed activities.

Common Function of the Behavior: Escapes from teacher demands; gets attention from the teacher. For these students, the activity or task is not necessarily (inherently) aversive; rather, the teacher presentation of the directive and the manner it is delivered is perceived as aversive.

Works Best When: When a teacher is already intervening early for mild to moderate behaviors, providing choices of activities, and maintaining a minimum of a 4:1 positive to negative ratio. Teachers who provide choices to students during learning activities usually experience less problematic behavior (Kern et al., 2002). Please note that when this foundation is not in place, the use of time-out, detention, or any response that results in removal of the task, instruction, or materials will likely serve to reinforce the refusal behavior.

Examples of the Behavioral Context:

- Student responds "no" to a directive to sit in a specific seat during an assembly.
- Student ignores or engages in behaviors or activities other than those selected by the teacher during a classroom activity.

Procedural Definitions:

- **Choice**—a procedure whereby a student is provided options to structure their academic tasks or activities.
- **Work-out**—withholding access to reinforcement until a task or activity is completed.

Procedure:

1. Create a menu of options from which students can select related to different learning tasks and activities throughout the day.
2. Offer the student a choice between at least two options versus providing a directive. Some examples include
   - Choice of two different learning activities (e.g., write an essay or present to the class).
   - Choice to work with a peer or alone.
   - Choice to stand or sit.
   - Choice of what materials to use.
   - Choice of where to work, at desk or table.
3. If the student chooses, praise the student for the choice.
4. If the student refuses to select, present the options again and allow time to choose.
5. If the student continues to refuse, consider a corrective consequence like a work-out (see Appendix 8).

References

Chandler, L. K., & Dahlquist, C. M. (2006). *Functional assessment: Strategies to prevent and remediate challenging behavior in school settings.* Merrill Prentice Hall.

Kern, L., Bambara, L., & Fogt., J. (2002). Class-wide curricular modifications to improve the behavior of students with emotional or behavioral disorders. *Behavioral Disorders, 27*(4), 317–326. https://doi.org/10.1177/019874290202700408j137

Appendix 3: Teacher Proximity

Off-Task Behavior

Defining the Behavior: Any behavior not aligned with established school/classroom expectations.

Common Function(s) of the Behavior: Peer/adult attention; access to other, more reinforcing materials; or escape from a non-preferred task.

Works Best When: In general, the amount of time a teacher moves around the classroom is directly correlated with both an increase in on-task behavior and a decrease in disruptions. Works best when the student or students have the skills to complete a task; the students know the established classroom management plan, which the teacher implements consistently; and the teacher regularly uses a 4:1 ratio of reinforcement to correction to shape established expectations.

Examples of the Behavioral Context:

- Student whispers to a peer during an independent assignment.
- Student doodles or draws pictures on a sheet of paper instead of attending to the teacher during whole group instruction in class.

Procedural Definitions:

- **Proximity control**—defined as teacher's proximity of 1 to 3 feet from a student.

Procedure:

1. The teacher establishes a classroom setting in which student desk placement allows enough room for the teacher to circulate among the students.
2. The teacher establishes a pattern of circulating such that proximity can be used with all students.
3. When students are on task, provide intermittent praise.
4. When a student is off task, use proximity control to prompt the student to task.
5. When the student attends to task, thank them and move on.
6. If the student continues to remain off task, consider using the Ignoring Junk Behavior procedure (see Appendix 13).
7. For continued off-task behavior, consider a function-based consequence like time owed (see Appendix 11), in which a student loses time away from a favorite object or activity.
8. For students who refuse to attend to a task or activity, the teacher uses the Setting Limits procedure (see Appendix 5) such that the teacher reminds the target student of the consequence of their choice of either attending to task or continuing to remain off task.

References

Gunter, P. L., Shores, R. E., Jack, S. L., Rasmussen, S. K., & Flowers, J. (1995). On the move using teacher/student proximity to improve students' behavior. *TEACHING Exceptional Children, 28*(1), 12–14. https://doi.org/10.1177/004005999502800103

Appendix 4: Verbal Redirection

Failing to Follow an Expectation

About the Procedure: Verbal redirection is a means for the teacher to redirect a student's misbehavior via stating the expectation. The teacher tells the student that the behavior is not acceptable and then provides a statement of the expectation. This procedure can be used for a student, a group of students, or the entire class.

Common Function of the Behavior: This procedure is appropriate for behavior that serves multiple functions including escape, attention, access to tangibles, or sensory.

Works Best When: When students have already learned the expectations and the behavior is new and mild to low-moderate. To make this procedure as effective as possible and to maintain a positive relationship with the student, it's important the teacher does not lecture the student and does not present directives in a judgmental, threatening, or condescending tone of voice. A neutral-to-firm tone of voice is best.

Examples of the Behavioral Context:

- A student yells an answer out during class
- A student leaves their seat in the cafeteria without permission
- A group of students talks too loudly during an assembly

Procedural Definitions:

- Differentiated praise—Behavior-specific praise intended to recognize a student for complying with redirection but has less value than the typical praise delivered
- Proximity—approximately 1–3 feet from the student

Procedure:

Using proximity, call the student's name; maintain eye contact; and speak in a clear, neutral tone of voice.

1. If the student fails to respond, use a slightly firmer, but not threatening, voice.
2. Tell the student to stop the inappropriate behavior and suggest an appropriate behavior they can engage in instead. For example, "Johnny, please stop calling out. If you need assistance, remember you must raise your hand and wait to be called."
3. Ask the student to demonstrate it or describe how they will behave in the future.
4. If the behavior continues, state to the student why the behavior is inappropriate and that if the behavior continues, they will receive a consequence. Be specific. For example, "Johnny, when you call out, you disrupt my instruction and the learning of other students. If you call out again, you will be required to complete an Action Plan (see Appendices 19–21) during your choice activity time.
5. If the student follows the directive, provide quiet differentiated praise.
6. If the student refuses to follow the directive, apply the corrective consequence.

Appendix 5: Setting Limits

Failure to Follow Directives

About the Procedure: This procedure, which reminds the student of the potential consequences of appropriate behavior versus potential consequences of inappropriate behavior, prompts the student to make a "good choice" based on the potential outcomes of their behavior.

Common Function of the Behavior: This procedure is appropriate for behavior that serves multiple functions including escape, attention, access to tangibles, or sensory.

Works Best When: It is not delivered as a threat, but rather as a choice and a "helpful reminder" of the potential outcomes of following versus not following expectations. It should not be delivered as a bribe (e.g., "if you sit down and finish your work, I'll give you a piece of candy"). Setting limits is most effective when delivered in a calm and collected manner and in a way that the student feels the reminder is intended to help, not punish them. When possible, use past appropriate choices to point out successful outcomes, to formulate choices, or to point out strengths. For example: "Last week when you raised your hand for help, you received help and were able to go to the playground during recess." When a limit is set, it's important the student experiences the stated consequences. Setting limits is typically delivered after other prompts for appropriate behavior have failed.

Examples of the Behavioral Context:
- After the teacher asks the student to sit down during class, they continue to leave their seat during lunch.
- The teacher taught the student to raise their hand instead of calling out during class, but the student continues to call out, even after a teacher prompt to raise their hand.

Procedural Definitions: None

Procedure:

Make sure that the limits being set are simple/clear, enforceable, and reasonable.

1. Give the student choices, usually two. (Keep it Simple/Clear)
2. Begin with the positive consequences of the appropriate choice, and end with the corrective consequences of the inappropriate choice. For example: "Johnny, if you sit down and finish your work, you will be able to play on the playground during recess; however, if you don't, you will not be able to play on the playground until your work is finished. I hope you make a good choice. (Reasonable)
3. Tell the student if they don't choose, then you will choose an option.
4. Give choices only when you can and will allow the student to experience the consequences of those choices. (Enforceable)
5. If the student makes the appropriate choice, praise them and allow for the positive consequence to occur. ("Great job, Johnny, thanks for sitting down and completing your work; you can go to the playground with your friends during recess.")
6. If the student makes the inappropriate choice, provide the corrective consequence stated when limits were set.

Appendix 6: In-Class Time-Out

From Positive Reinforcement

About the Procedure: The student must sit in an area that minimizes attention from peers but where they can still be observed by the teacher. The student should have no access to items or activities.

Common Function(s) of the Behavior: Attention seeking. This is not for students who attempt to avoid work tasks or classroom activities. Removal from aversive activities reinforces the problem behavior. Use the time-out procedure when problem behavior occurs to gain attention from peers or adults (i.e., behaviors that disrupt the learning of other students), and not behavior that occurs as a result of a demand.

Works Best When: Time-outs typically work best when the behavior accesses attention or the student is trying to access tangibles or activities; essentially, when the student likes the current task or activity. Time-out is a punishment procedure.

Examples of the Behavioral Context:
- Low to moderate disruptive behavior.
- The student refuses classroom or school-wide expectations.

Procedural Definitions: None

Procedure:
1. Place the student away from attention from staff or students (no other items or activities).
2. The teacher tells the student the reason for the time-out and the expectations while in time-out. The teacher sets a timer for a specified amount of time or indicates when the student may participate in the reinforcing activity or earn back the reinforcing tangible or item. The student must follow the time-out expectations. An example of time-out expectations:
    - Stay in designated spot.
    - Remain quiet.
    - Remain in assigned spot for a specified amount of time.
3. If the student leaves the area or purposely makes noise, reset the timer for a specified time.
4. Repeat this procedure until the student completes the in-class time-out as expected.
5. If the student refuses to go to time-out or becomes so disruptive that it prevents the continuation of class activities or instruction, then remove the student from class.
6. Follow the school-based protocol for calling for assistance.

Appendix 7: Time-Out/Removal From Class

About the Procedure: Remove the student from the class to a setting where they cannot gain access to positive reinforcement.

Common Function(s) of the Behavior: Attention seeking and access to tangibles/activities. This is not for students who attempt to avoid work tasks or class activities. Removal from aversive activities reinforces the problem behavior.

Works Best When: Time-out from the class typically works best when the behavior accesses attention and not when the student engages in problem behavior to escape a lesson or classwork. Time-out from class should only be used briefly (10–20 minutes). Time-out is a punishment procedure and should be a last resort after other antecedent strategies do not succeed.

Examples of the Context: Low to moderate disruptive behavior. The student refuses class expectations.

Procedural Definitions: Use the time-out procedure when the problem behavior occurs to gain attention from peers or adults (i.e., behaviors that disrupt the learning of other students), and not behavior that occurs because of a demand placed on the student. If a student's behavior is escape motivated and the behavior is so disruptive as to necessitate student removal from the classroom, ensure the student completes work missed during the time-out.

Procedure:

1. Place the student away from staff or students (no other items or activities available), with limited attention.
2. The teacher tells the student why they received the time-out and what the expectations are during time-out.
3. Remove the student to another location where they cannot disrupt others.
4. The staff/administrator who removed the student sets a timer for a specified time or indicates when the student may go back to class contingent upon following the time-out expectations. An example of time-out expectations:
   - Stay in designated spot.
   - Remain quiet.
   - Remain for the specified amount of time.
5. Once the student completes the time-out expectations, they return to class, where they must complete the in-class time-out as originally directed.
6. During these procedures, staff involved should not attempt to counsel the student about their behavior, reprimand, or talk to the student for any reason, except to calmly repeat the original direction.
7. Once the student completes the in-class timeout, they may return to normal activities and earn reinforcement.

Appendix 8: Work-Out Out of Class

About the Procedure: Withhold or withdraw reinforcement until the student cooperates with the original task or directive. Use this procedure when the student's problem behavior occurs to avoid or escape completing a task. Do not remove the demand, and withhold reinforcement until the student cooperates by completing the task or directive. Remove the student to another location outside of the class where they cannot disrupt other students.

Common Function(s) of the Behavior: Escape from task demands or avoidance of less-preferred academic task or assignments.

Works Best When: Use for behaviors maintained by task/demand escape (negative reinforcement). Send the work with the student and require completion to break the contingency between the problem behavior and the consequence. During these procedures, the staff involved in student removal should minimize attention to the student.

Examples of the Behavior and Context:

- A student's behaviors escalated in the class, and the teacher cannot teach. Learning is impacted by the student's misbehavior.
- Billy's behavior is repetitive and disruptive. After you exhaust progressive consequences, call for student removal. Using data, you found it occurs after presentation of math tasks. When the student leaves the classroom, you send prepared work. Once Billy completes the work, he returns to the class and completes the original task.

Procedure:

1. Remove the student from the class to another location.
2. Give the student a different task to complete than the one initiated in class (staff removing the student should have work ready for the student to complete ahead of time).
3. Staff direct the student to complete the task and the state the expectation: "If you need help, or when you are done, raise your hand."
4. During this procedure, staff involved should not attempt to counsel the student about their behavior, reprimand, or talk to the student, unless the student appropriately requests assistance to complete the task. In this case, staff should only provide verbal directions needed to complete the task.
5. Return the student to class once they complete the task assigned.
6. When the student returns to class, the teacher should welcome them back, without mention of the misbehavior, and instruct them to complete the original assignment.
7. Once the student completes the original task, they may return to normal activities and the opportunity to earn reinforcement.

Appendix 9: Restitutional Overcorrection

Damage to the Environment

About the Procedure: With this procedure, the student repairs the environment. The student must return the environment to the previous condition (before they engaged in the problem behavior) and make it even better. The student may need to repair items they broke, clean objects/environments they soiled, or apologize to others for their behavior toward them (Borich & Tombari, 1997).

Common Function(s) of the Behavior: Attention from others, escape, or avoidance of low-preference academic activities. Use the procedure when the problem behavior results in disruption and/or destruction of property and may also serve other functions like access to individualized attention or escape from academic activities.

Works Best When: For moderate to higher intensity problem behavior, and when the student is calm. The student restores the damage (including a relationship) they produced, possibly paired with other corrective consequences like time-out or an action plan. Look for opportunities to prompt and reinforce appropriate behavior in the future. Consider all of the inadvertent attention that may inappropriately reinforce the student's misbehavior. Be mindful of your body language and other students watching the scene. When you implement these procedures, arrange the environment to minimize this effect. Refrain from eye contact, unnecessary physical contact, counseling, or conversation with the student.

Examples of the Behavior:
- A student uses marking pens to write their name on a desktop. The student must clean their name from the desktop (e.g., perhaps with a spray designed to remove ink) and any other words written in ink on that surface. The teacher might even require the student to clean all the other desks in the classroom.
- If a student hits a peer, the student must apologize to the peer who was hit; perhaps in writing and orally, and by doing a favor for the peer. The student may need to also apologize to all the students in the class and assure them that the behavior will not happen again.
- A student throws a peer's milk carton on the floor during lunch. The student must wipe up the milk on the floor and any other liquid or garbage on the cafeteria floor.

Procedural Definitions:

Paraverbals—pitch, speed, or tone of voice. Essentially, how something is communicated.

Procedure:
1. If the student showed anger when they misbehaved, consider using the Emotional Regulation for Students procedure (see Appendix 17).
2. Using neutral paraverbals and facial expressions, ask the student if they know the expectation they violated and what they should do instead.
    - If the student does not know it, state the expectation and have the student restate it to you.
    - If the student cannot or does not explain what they should do instead, use the Problem-Solving for Students procedure (see Appendix 33).
3. Provide a verbal prompt related to what the student must restore and what else they need to do to make the environment better: "Johnny, pick up the paper, place it in the trash, and pick up all of the other trash in the classroom."
4. When the student completes the work, use neutral paraverbals and facial expressions to thank the student.
5. If the student refuses, restate the directive.
6. If they continue to refuse, use the Setting Limits procedure (see Appendix 5).
7. Apply any additional function-based consequences.

References

Borich, G. D., & Tombari, M. L. (1997). *Educational psychology: A contemporary approach* (2nd ed.). Addison Wesley Longman.

Kerr, M. M., & Nelson, C. M. (1989). *Strategies for managing behavior problems in the classroom* (2nd ed.). Merrill.

Appendix 10: Overcorrection/Positive Practice

About the Procedure: With this procedure, the student repeatedly practices the correct behavior for the situation after committing an infraction (Borich & Tombari, 1997).

Common Function(s) of the Behavior: This behavior commonly serves multiple functions including escape, attention, and access to tangibles.

Works Best When: Positive practice works best with shorter durations and relies on the student's cooperation to engage in the correct behavior that allows them to avoid problematic situations in the future. The overcorrection activity should be relevant to the problem behavior. Be sure the activity is long and repetitive enough to have an impact on the student.

Examples of the Behavior/ Context:

- Student interrupts class (calls out without raising their hand). The teacher directs the student to raise their hand, get called on, and speak, repeating this cycle 10 times.
- Student runs down the hall. The teacher directs the student to walk appropriately up and down the hall three times before they can go to their destination.

Procedural Definitions:

Paraverbals—pitch, tone, and speed of voice. Essentially, how something is said.

Procedure:

1. If the student showed anger when they misbehaved, consider using the Emotional Regulation for Students procedure (see Appendix 17).
2. Using neutral paraverbals and facial expressions, ask the student if they know the expectation they violated and what they should do instead.
    - If they do not know it, state the expectation and have the student restate it to you.
    - If the student does not know what they should do instead, use the Problem-Solving for Students procedure (see Appendix 33).
3. Provide a verbal prompt for a response related to the correct behavior in which the student needs to engage.
4. Have the student perform the correct behavior multiple times.
5. When the student cooperates, using neutral paraverbals and facial expressions, thank the student.
6. If the student refuses, restate the directive.
7. If they continue to refuse, use the Setting Limits procedure (see Appendix 5).
8. Apply any additional function-based consequences.

References

Borich, G. D., & Tombari, M. L. (1997). *Educational psychology: A contemporary approach* (2nd ed.). Addison Wesley Longman.

Appendix 11: Response Cost

Failing to Follow Expectations

About the Procedure: Much like a fine or a penalty, with response cost, the teacher takes away points, tokens, possessions, or privileges in planned, incremental steps following the occurrence of misbehavior. Simply put, each instance of misbehavior "costs" (i.e., loss of reinforcers) the student something they currently value.

Common Function of the Behavior: This procedure is appropriate for behavior that serves multiple functions including escape, attention, access to tangibles, or sensory.

Works Best When: A replacement behavior is targeted and reinforced at a rate greater (e.g., a ratio of 4:1) than the student receiving a "charge" for misbehavior like inappropriate language, calling out, or making noises or gestures. When considering the "charges," the fine must be consistent and reasonable, but enough that it reduces the misbehavior. As such, if there is no decrease in the misbehavior after the consistent charges for each instance of misbehavior, consider increasing the cost for each occurrence.

Examples of the Behavioral Context:

- A student yells an answer out during class.
- A student leaves their seat to go to the bathroom without permission during lunch.
- A student cusses after getting an answer incorrect during class.
- A student makes duck noises while they transition in the hallway.

Procedural Definitions: None

Procedure:

Explain to the student that the targeted inappropriate behavior is not allowed in the classroom.

1. Give examples of appropriate and inappropriate behavior and describe the impact of the behavior.
2. Tell the student that each instance of the targeted behavior will result in a fine or charge. Variations include
   - Time owed—for example, for every second a student is out of their seat, charge a second away from their favorite reinforcer.
   - A demerit—for each instance of misbehavior, the student receives a demerit. When the student receives X number of demerits, they receive a designated consequence. For example, complete an Action Plan (see Appendices 19–21) and receive a phone call home to parents.
   - Loss of points—for example, give the student X number of points at the beginning of each day that can be cashed in at the end of the day. Each instance of misbehavior costs the student a point.
3. Monitor student behavior and use a simple clipboard and piece of paper to keep track of each instance of misbehavior, or the duration of misbehavior in the case of the time owed variation.
4. For each instance of misbehavior, immediately inform them of the fine incurred, and charge them when appropriate (e.g., if time owed is the consequence, ensure the designated reinforcer is withheld for allotted time owed).

References

Conyers, C., Miltenberger, R., Maki, A., Barenz, R., Jurgens, M., Sailer, A., Haugen, M., & Kopp, B. (2004). A comparison of response cost and differential reinforcement of other behavior to reduce disruptive behavior in a preschool classroom. *Journal of Applied Behavior Analysis*, *37*(3), 411–415. https://doi.org/10.1901/jaba.2004.37-411

Iwata, B. A., & Bailey, J. S. (1974). Reward versus cost token systems: An analysis of the effects on students and teachers. *Journal of Applied Behavior Analysis*, *7*(4), 567–576. https://doi.org/10.1901/jaba.1974.7-567

Appendix 12: Response Cost Lottery

Off-Task or Inattentive Behavior

Defining the Behavior: Any behavior that interferes with task completion.

Common Function of the Behavior: This behavior typically serves multiple functions including escape, attention, access to tangibles, or sensory.

Works Best When: For low-magnitude behavior such as off-task or inattentive behavior during activities, as it incorporates rewards for cooperation and self-management. You can easily modify this procedure to work for the entire class.

Examples of the Behavioral Context:

- A student doodles during an assignment in class.
- A student stares out the window in class during an assignment.
- A student fiddles with a pencil in class during an assignment.
- A student talks to a peer in class while the teacher delivers instruction.

Procedural Definitions:

Baseline—the frequency of behavior prior to the intervention. Baseline provides a comparison point by which to judge the success of your intervention via data analysis.

Procedure:

1. Identify very precisely the behavior to be reduced and provide examples and non-examples to the student.
2. Collect baseline data on the frequency of target behavior throughout a designated interval (e.g., 30 minutes) that off-task or inattentive behavior is more likely (e.g., during reading). To accomplish this, simply count the number of times the student does not attend during the course of the interval for 3–5 days.
3. Explain the procedure to the students as follows:
    - Describe the rewards available at the end of the interval(s) for on-task and attentive behavior.
    - The student (or the class) receives 5 colored or numbered strips at the beginning of a designated interval. For students who have a higher frequency of misbehavior, provide more strips so they do not lose all of their strips (and thus their motivation) prior to the end of the interval.
    - Insert the paper strips in an envelope on each student's desk with the ends sticking out.
    - When off-task or inattentive behavior occurs, the teacher removes 1 strip of paper from the envelope.
    - At the end of the interval, each student takes their remaining strips, writes their name on them, and puts them in a lottery box.
    - Repeat this for other times of the day when students may become inattentive or drift off task.
    - At the end of the interval(s), the teacher draws one piece of colored paper from the lottery box. The winning student receives the day's reward.
    - The student with the most strips in the box stands the best chance of winning a reward.
4. Determine the effectiveness of this procedure by counting the number of times the target behavior occurs during the intervention and comparing it to the baseline.
5. As student on-task behavior increases, progressively increase the length of the interval (e.g., from 30 to 40 minutes).

References

Witt, J. C., & Elliot, S. N. (1982). The response cost lottery: A time efficient and effective classroom intervention. *Journal of School Psychology, 20*(2), 155–161. https://doi.org/10.1016/0022-4405(82)90009-7

Appendix 13: Junk Behavior

Attention-Seeking Behavior—Ignoring Junk Behavior

About the Procedure: Typical behavior from students that is annoying but not harmful.

Common Function(s) of the Behavior: Attention seeking. This is not for students whose behavior functions for peer attention (e.g., a student who makes jokes in class to make their peers laugh).

Works Best When: This procedure works best for low-magnitude behavior, and when the student can hear or see another student receive praise for desirable behavior. Do not use it for high-magnitude or aggressive behaviors.

Examples of the Behavioral Context:
- A student calls out an answer versus raising their hand while teacher instructs.
- A student rolls their eyes, mumbles, or sucks their teeth when redirected during class.
- A student chats with peers, mumbles, sucks teeth, and so forth during a silent transition.

Procedural Definitions:

Ignoring (extinction)—a procedure whereby a reinforcing consequence is no longer delivered for a behavior. In this case, the reinforcing consequence is teacher attention. Under these conditions, do not look at, talk to, or otherwise acknowledge the existence of the student when behavior occurs.

Pivot—the teacher turns away from the individual and attends to other students in the area who behave appropriately, then later, turns back to the individual and praises appropriate behavior. Via this procedure, the student now contacts positive reinforcement (i.e., teacher attention) for appropriate behavior instead of the misbehavior.

Procedure:

1. When the target student demonstrates this type of inappropriate, attention-seeking behavior, ignore the behavior. (Pivot away)

2. Turn attention away from the student (Pivot away) and do not deliver any eye contact. You may move away from the student.

3. Move toward, and attend to, the other students (Pivot to) who engage in appropriate behavior and demonstrate classroom expectations. Provide behavior-specific praise (e.g., "I love the way Kayla, Malik, Matt, and Kamal work quietly through their math problems").

4. Once the student engages in the appropriate behavior, (Pivot back) provide attention and behavior-specific praise to the student (e.g., "I like how you've gotten back on task to quietly complete your assignment. Keep it up").

Appendix 14: Behavior Contracts

About the Procedure: A contingency or behavior contract is one method that includes the student in the development and implementation of their intervention plan. A contract describes the goal for behavior change and specifies the reinforcers available contingent on meeting the behavior goal.

A contract should identify

1. the target behavior and the goal for the behavior
2. people involved in administering the contract
3. how and when behavior will be measured
4. reinforcers available and a schedule for delivering them

It also may identify consequences for failure to meet behavior goals, consequences for the emission of challenging behavior, and a bonus clause for exceptional performance. Contracts may be developed between the student, school personnel, and home; in addition, they may be developed for individuals, groups of students, or the whole class.

Common Function of the Behavior: Escape from teacher demands; attention seeking from the teacher. For these students, the activity or task that is selected is not necessarily aversive; rather, it is the teacher selection and the teacher presentation of the directive that is perceived as aversive.

Works Best When: A behavior contract works best for students who engage in continuous misbehavior and do not respond to redirection and prompts to change their behavior. Teachers implement a behavior contract for a student when misbehavior impacts other students' learning. Select the goals and appropriate behaviors collaboratively with and for the student. Rewards offered as part of the contract must be motivating enough so the student wants to earn them and ultimately cooperate with the contract versus engage in targeted misbehavior.

Sample Contract:

Room 513 Contract

Date: _____

During the week of: _____

I will: _____

If I do this, I will receive: _____

We agree to the above terms.

Teacher Signature: _____

Student Signature: _____

Witness Signature: _____

Procedure:

1. Refer to data collected on the problem behavior that prompts the need for a contract.
2. Create a list of the target misbehaviors that need to be reduced. The behaviors should be observable, measurable, and easily tracked.
3. Select two or three behaviors to focus on (pick the behaviors most in need of change).
4. Write out the goals with the student in a positive format. For example, instead of saying, "Jaime will stop shouting out during the math lesson," try, "Jaime will raise his hand to speak during math." This helps the teacher and student focus on the positive aspects of the behavior contract and sets up celebration of their accomplishments.
5. Explain the point, number, or picture system that tracks progress. Help the student understand what happens if they earn a certain number of points or all smiley faces (for example) for the day.
    - The teacher creates a list or matrix of available reinforcers for the student to earn.
    - The student makes the choice of reward to earn so they know what they will receive contingent upon the correct behavior.
6. Ask permission from the parent(s) before starting a contract. Parental support increases the likelihood the behavior contract will be effective, and it demonstrates the teacher and parent(s) working together for the student's success.
7. The student must agree to the contract. Honor requests for negotiation in the creation of the contract. If the student does not agree to engage in the behaviors outlined in the contract or the rewards, or even use the contract at all, the contract will not work.
8. Both the teacher and student sign the behavior contract. The teacher may ask the parent to sign the behavior contract as well.

References

Kern, L., Bambara, L., & Fogt, J. (2002). Class-wide curricular modifications to improve the behavior of students with emotional or behavioral disorders. *Behavioral Disorders, 27*(4), 317–326. https://doi.org/10.1177/019874290202700408

Appendix 15: ABC Recording

ABC Code Form				
Student Name:		**Teacher Name:**		**Time:**
Briefly describe behavior:				
Circle Code A O B				
"Before" Conditions			"After" Conditions	
Curriculum	**Delivery**	**Antecedents**	**Teacher Responses**	**Peer Reaction**
☐ English Language Arts ☐ Math ☐ Social Studies ☐ Science ☐ Music ☐ PE ☐ Media ☐ Technology ☐ Math/Science Resource ☐ Other:	☐ Independent center ☐ Independent practice ☐ Small group center ☐ Small group teacher ☐ Whole group ☐ Other:	☐ Attention given to others ☐ Difficult task/activity ☐ Demand/request ☐ Challenge or teasing by other students ☐ Corrective feedback ☐ **Not** engaged in activity ☐ **Not** receiving attention ☐ Object/activity removed ☐ Specific peer interaction ☐ Transition ☐ Given consequence ☐ Did not receive point ☐ Other:	☐ Change of seating ☐ Choice given ☐ Clarification ☐ "First-then" ☐ Pivot praise ☐ Planned ignoring ☐ Proximity control ☐ Redirection ☐ Demerit ☐ Time owed ☐ Other: **Progressive Consequences** ☐ 1st <u>warning</u> ☐ 2nd _____ ☐ 3rd _____ ☐ 4th _____ ☐ 5th _____	☐ Disapproval ☐ Encourage ☐ Ignore ☐ Laugh ☐ Praise ☐ Provoke ☐ Reprimand ☐ Retaliate ☐ Warn **Possible Motivation** ☐ Escape adult demand ☐ Escape peer attention ☐ Escape task/activity ☐ Obtain teacher attention ☐ Obtain student attention ☐ Access preferred item/activity

Appendix 16: Effective Classroom Management Planning Guide

Rationale: Students must learn classroom expectations, rules, and procedures as prerequisites to academic learning; and teachers must teach these just like core academics to create structure, set the tone, and foster a positive culture for the classroom. As with teaching core academics, there is a learning rationale and description of the expectation/rule/procedure using examples and non-examples to illustrate and teach. Students should practice the skill and demonstrate the appropriate, expected behavior; practice and repetition are key to learning. Once students demonstrate expectations without prompts, reinforce and correct behaviors until students engage in them independently and habitually.

Instructions: Use this as a guide to develop your own classroom management plan. You can directly apply many of the procedures outlined in the book and appendices to your plan. Your plan may not include all sections (e.g., School-Wide Expectations), and conditions may not be relevant for all classroom activities. Use what you need.

Developing Rules and Procedures

When developing rules and behavioral expectations for your classroom, you will need to consider the following:

What does the behavior look like?	What does the behavior sound like?	During what routine/activity will the behavior be used?
• How do students enter the class and begin work? • What occurs if a student is tardy?	• What volume can students use when speaking?	• Entering the classroom
• How do students predict the schedule?	• Is the activity silent or noisy?	• Independent work
• How do students ask for help? • Where can students move to? • Who can students talk with? • What can they talk about?	• Will you use individual or choral responding? • What kind of positive and respectful language do you want students to use?	• Whole group activities • Small group activities
• How to collect completed work?		• Transitions
• How do students take turns?		• Leaving the classroom
• What to do if a student is missing materials.		
• What to do if a student is bothering another student.		

Developing Rules: Checklist

Be sure your rules are observable, measurable, stated positively, understandable, and applicable to your classroom.

School-Wide Expectations	Classroom Rules	Observable?	Measurable?	Positive?	Understandable?	Applicable?
Safe	Keep hands and feet to self.	X	X	X	X	X
	Walk.	X	X	X	X	X
Responsible	Bring all materials to class.	X	X	X	X	X
	Complete and turn in assignments on time.	X	X	X	X	X
Respectful	Raise hand to talk.	X	X	X	X	X
	Use appropriate language with others.	X	X	X	X	X
Engaged	Stay on task.	X	X	X	X	X
	Ask questions and participate in discussions.	X	X	X	X	X

Positively Stated Classroom Rules

When you create classroom rules, outline the specific behaviors and procedures you want students to engage in while in the classroom. Select rules that meet the specific needs of your classroom. Here are some guidelines for creating classroom rules:

School-Wide Expectations	Aligning Classroom Rules
Be Safe.	Keep hands, feet, and objects to yourself.
Be Respectful.	Walk with voice level 0 to your area.
Be Responsible.	Turn in completed assignments on time.
Be Engaged.	Follow directions the first time they are given.

Sample school-wide expectations in alignment with sample classroom rules:

- Select a maximum of five positively stated rules. They should be simple and age-appropriate.
- Rules should be observable and measurable.
- Rules should be enforceable.
- Communicate desired and appropriate behaviors.
- Align classroom rules with school-wide expectations.

Classroom Expectations by Routines Matrix

School-Wide Expectation	Routine					
	Entering classroom	Independent work	Small group activities	Whole group instruction	Transitions	Leaving classroom
Be safe	Use kind words and manners. Maintain voice level 1.	Keep all chair legs on the floor.		Keep hands and feet to yourself. Keep all chair legs on the floor.	Clear your desk of all materials. Push chair under your desk.	Push chair under your desk.
Be respectful	Walk quietly to your desk.	Raise your hand if you need help. Stay in your own space.	Maintain voice level 1. Take turns. Use a positive, friendly tone when speaking with others.	Maintain voice level 0 when listening.	Maintain voice level 0.	Maintain voice level 0.
Be responsible	Place homework in basket folder on teacher's desk.	Start assignments within 1 minute.	Complete your part of the assignment.	Raise your hand to be called on. Use voice level 2 for responding. Actively listen.	Take all needed belongings with you. Leave space better than you found it. Bring what you need to be ready for what's next.	
Be engaged	Begin morning assignment quickly.	Stay on task. Complete task.	Actively listen.			

Performance Expectations: Considerations

Once you establish a general set of rules and expectations for all major classroom routines and activities, you must teach the students to engage in the behaviors you want to see: Teach students what to do and what not to do. Remember, teaching is not telling. Once you instruct students, you must consistently reinforce expectations and correct misbehavior to develop good classroom habits.

When teaching rules and expectations in the context of routines, think about the following:

1. How will I teach the behavioral expectations?
2. How will I model the behavioral expectations?
3. How/when will students have an opportunity to rehearse the behavioral expectations?

4. How/when will students receive regular feedback related to the behavioral expectations?
5. How will I measure acquisition of the behavioral expectations?
6. How will students practice the skill under conditions that closely mirror the natural environment?
    ◦ Students should experience simulated natural consequences related to following expectations and receiving a reward.
    ◦ Students should experience simulated natural consequences related to refusing to follow expectations and receiving a corrective consequence.
7. How will I measure students' knowledge of the behavioral expectations?
8. How will I measure students' skills related to the behavioral expectations?
9. How and when will pre-correction of behavioral expectations occur?
10. How and when will correction of behavioral expectations occur?

After teaching rules and expectations within the natural context and providing students with behavior-specific feedback, engage in active supervision. This means you circulate the classroom, interact with students, and provide behavior-specific praise to students who follow classroom rules and expectations. With active supervision, you can also consistently catch misbehavior and then calmly and privately provide corrective feedback.

Active Engagement: High-Quality Opportunities to Respond for Students

There are a variety of techniques that teachers can apply to actively engage students in observable ways. A powerful approach to student engagement in learning that simultaneously reduces misbehavior is to provide high rates of opportunities to respond, with varied individual and group responding throughout the lesson.

Consider the following ways to engage students:
- written responses
- writing on dry erase boards
- choral responding
- gestures (e.g., thumb up or down to indicate response)
- random pickers (e.g., popsicle sticks)

Provide Specific Feedback ...	Praise/Correction Examples:
... for desired behavior (praise)	• "Wow. You were very cooperative when you helped your friends gather their materials for small group reading." • "Class, I see you are engaged and ready to learn ... this will be a fun and important lesson."
... for undesired behavior (correction)	• "I see materials on desks. Group 3, please return to your area and show that you can leave the space even better than you found it." • "I see that not everyone participated in the group activity yet. Please lower your hand if you've responded, and be sure you are kind and give everyone a chance to share their ideas."

Pre-Correct Expected Behavior ...	Pre-Correction Examples:
... at the beginning of each activity	• "While I read, you can actively listen by keeping your hands and feet to yourself, voice level 0, materials down, and eyes on me."
... prior to the end of each activity	• "In 1 minute, we will move into our next learning center. Please be kind to your space: Put your materials away, sanitize your space, and leave it better than you found it."
... before each transition	• "Remember, as we walk, we will be kind, with voices quiet, and safe."

Acknowledging Appropriate Student Behavior: Strategies

Foster positive environments with frequent, consistent responses to students' correct responding and appropriate behavior or performance. When you provide praise, be specific and immediate. Tell the student exactly what they did well. Also, use a variety of praise statements; move away from just "good job." Positive responses must be sincere and authentic—how you say it is important when you praise. The tone of your voice, level of enthusiasm, and eye contact are important when you deliver positive responses. Eye contact suggests that you care, and that the response is specific for that student. Be aware of students' appropriate behavior during the day and respond accordingly. Catch your students being good! When teaching a new skill or behavioral expectation, it may be necessary to initially reinforce expectations at a higher rate (e.g., a 10:1 ratio) and then fade to a 4:1 ratio. Here are some strategies to consider for acknowledging appropriate behavior:

- Specific and contingent praise
  - Specific—tells the learner exactly what they did correctly
  - Contingent—immediately after the appropriate behavior
- Group contingencies
- Behavior contracts
- Token economies

Acknowledging Student Misbehavior: Strategies

Sometimes, traditional responses to misbehavior fail. Often, it's because the corrective responses we use require alignment with the classroom expectations or positively stated rules, or there is not a clear system to teach and reinforce expected behavior. As a teacher, you must determine an effective response to misbehavior to decrease the likelihood that the behavior will occur again. To facilitate behavior change in your classroom, you must use skills to intervene when misbehavior happens and also reward appropriate behavior. It's also important to collect baseline data to determine if your interventions work. When you respond to mild or moderate misbehavior in the classroom, consider the following continuum of strategies.

- Early intervention
  - Re-teaching the expectations
  - Re-teaching the rules
  - Changing seating arrangements
  - Holding a conference with student
  - Holding a conference with parent and student
  - Crafting student behavior contracts
- Error corrections
  - Give immediately after the behavior.
  - Specifically tell the student what they did incorrectly, and tell them what to do instead.
  - Make it brief! Redirect and move on.
- Pivot praise
  - Direct behavior-specific praise to reinforce a student who is on task as a prompt to a student who is off task.
  - When the off-task student returns to task, direct behavior-specific praise toward them.
- Planned ignoring
  - Behavior maintained by adult attention.
- Response cost
  - Withdrawal of specific amounts of reinforcer (e.g., loss of points or tokens).
- Time-out from reinforcement
  - Removal from a reinforcing activity; reinforcement is not available in the time-out environment (i.e., all attention and reinforcers are withdrawn).
- Demerits
  - Points awarded for misbehavior that lead to a corrective consequence.
- Time owed
  - Withhold access to reinforcement.
- Positive practice
  - Require the student to rehearse appropriate behavior.
- Restitution
  - Require the student return the environment to its previous state.

Teaching Behavior: Lesson Planning

1. Name the skill.
2. State the purpose of the lesson.
3. Identify specific routines and activities to teach expectations.
4. Create three teaching examples and non-examples.
5. Develop student activities.
6. Create follow-up/reinforcement activities.

Lesson Focus:

Demonstrate _____ (*expectation*) in the _____ (*setting/routine*).

Teaching Objective:

Following instruction, students will demonstrate _____ (*expectation*) in the _____ (*setting/routine*) by _____ (*describe behaviors*) across ___ out of ___ sampled opportunities (*criteria*).

Teaching Examples:

Positive Examples (*Looks, sounds, & feels like ...*)	*Negative Examples* (*Does NOT look, sound, & feel like ...*)
• • •	• • •

Lesson Materials:

Lesson Activities:

Model (I do):

Lead (We do):

Test (You do):

Follow-up Activities:

Strategies to prompt:

Procedures to reinforce context-appropriate behavior:

Procedures to correct errors (e.g., context-inappropriate behavior):

Procedures to monitor/supervise:

Procedures to collect and evaluate student data:

References

Center on PBIS. (2020, July). *Creating effective classroom environments plan template.* https://www.pbis.org/resource/creating-effective-classroom-environments-plan-template

Simonsen, B., Myers, D., Everett, S., Sugai, G., Spencer, R., & LaBreck, C. (2012). Explicitly teaching social skills schoolwide: Using a matrix to guide instruction. *Intervention in School and Clinic, 47*(5), 259–266. https://doi.org/10.1177/1053451211430121

Appendix 17: Emotional Regulation for Students

Training and Coaching

Emotional Regulation Training

Use this procedure until the student successfully demonstrates all components of emotional regulation skills during the training setting.

- Ask the student if you can speak to them about something important.
- If the student says yes, thank them and move on to the next step. If the student says no or refuses to respond, say "OK" and try again later.
- Ask the student to reflect on past misbehavior and the poor outcomes they produced.
- Tell the student if they feel upset, instead of misbehaving and experiencing poor outcomes, they can engage in other, more socially acceptable behaviors (replacement behaviors) that produce better outcomes like
  - Replacement behaviors (emotional regulation skills)
  - Ask for help
  - Problem-solving
  - Use "I" message to communicate how they feel
  - Write down their thoughts and feelings instead of saying them out loud
  - Take deep breaths
  - Other (behaviors appropriate to the specific situation or context)
- Have the student demonstrate the replacement behaviors.
- For each replacement behavior demonstrated correctly, praise the student. If not, provide corrective feedback and have the student demonstrate the behavior again until they do it correctly.
- Role-play situations in which the student was (upset, angry, sad, disappointed, etc.) in the past, and have them demonstrate one of the replacement behaviors. Do this for each replacement behavior chosen.
- During the role plays, provide praise or corrective feedback, as necessary.
- Ask the student what replacement behaviors they can use when they feel this way in the future.
- If the student answers correctly, praise; if not, provide corrective feedback.

Emotional Regulation Coaching: To Support Transfer of Skills Into the Natural Environment

Follow this procedure throughout the day and whenever you see that the individual is (upset, angry, sad, disappointed, etc.).

- If you see the student is (upset, angry, sad, disappointed, etc.), wait 10 seconds and see if they use the emotional regulation skills they learned.
- If the student does, praise and reflect on the positive outcomes that resulted from the emotional regulation skills they used.
- If not, prompt the student to engage in one of the emotional regulation replacement behavior/skills they learned.
- Once the student is calm, assist with problem-solving. If necessary, ask the student to reflect on their behavior and the outcomes it produced.
- Provide praise or corrective feedback, as necessary.
- Remind the student to use these skills when they become (upset, angry, sad, disappointed, etc.).

Appendix 18: Student Performance Diagnostic Checklist

Specify an academic task or behavioral expectation to improve. Walk through the questions from the viewpoint of the student. For any "No" response, identify a solution.

Antecedents and Information	Yes	No
1. Is there a written description telling *exactly* what is expected of the student regarding a particular academic task or behavioral expectation task?		
2. Has the student received adequate instruction (e.g., instructions like "Please line up quietly and only after I call your row," or "When adding or subtracting, be sure to line up the figures vertically")?		
3. Has the student received formal training on this academic task or behavioral expectation? If yes, check all applicable training methods. ☐ Instructions ☐ Demonstration ☐ Rehearsal ☐ Feedback		
4. Are there task aids visible **while** completing the academic task or behavioral expectation in question (e.g., reminders to prompt the task in the correct way at the correct time/duration; visual of expectations)?		
5. Can the student state the purpose of the academic task or behavioral expectation?		
6. Is the student ever reminded to use the academic task or behavioral expectation just before they are going to engage in it? If yes, how often? ☐ Each time ☐ Most of the time ☐ Sometimes ☐ Rarely ☐ Not at all By whom? Check all that apply: ☐ Peer ☐ Aide ☐ Teacher ☐ Other		
7. Are there frequently updated, challenging, yet attainable goals with which the student is comfortable, related to the academic task or behavioral expectation?		
8. Is the student "aware" of the mission of the school? If so, is the mission aligned with the student's values?		

Equipment and Processes	Yes	No
9. If equipment is required, is it available and operational (e.g., writing tools, calculator, computer, etc.)?		
10. Are equipment and environment optimally arranged in a physical sense (e.g., the arrangement of student desks)?		
11. In general, do larger processes perform well despite any incorrect academic/behavioral performance along the way (e.g., routines and procedures)?		
12. Are these processes and the related expectations written out and arranged in a logical manner for the student?		
13. Can the student implement the academic task or behavioral expectation without any obstacles (e.g., interruption by the intercom)?		

Knowledge and Skills—Training	Yes	No
14. Can the student tell you what they are supposed to do and how to do it related to the academic task or behavioral expectation?		
15. Can the student physically/verbally precisely demonstrate the academic task or behavioral expectation?		
16. Can the student perform the academic task or behavioral expectation at the appropriate speed?		

Motivation	Yes	No
17. Is the student motivated based on the outcomes following completion of the academic task or behavioral expectation? In other words, can they verbally describe the connection between shorter- and longer-term goals?		
18. Is the student aware (they can observe) of the more immediate positive outcomes of engaging in the academic task or behavioral expectations (e.g., getting a problem correct, improved grades, increased positive attention, decreased corrections from the teacher)?		
19. How often is the student monitored related to this academic task or behavioral expectation? ☐ < 5 mins ☐ < 15 mins ☐ < 30 mins ☐ < hourly ☐ ½ day ☐ daily		
20. Does the student receive feedback about their performance related to the academic task or behavioral expectation? If yes, By whom? _____ and How often? _____ How long of a delay for feedback from the academic/behavioral task? _____ Check all that apply: Feedback focus: ☐ Positive ☐ Constructive Feedback type: ☐ Written ☐ Verbal ☐ Graphed ☐ Other		
21. Is the academic task or behavioral expectation easy to implement?		
22. Do other academic tasks or behavioral expectations appear to take precedence over the targeted task or expectation?		

References

Carr, J. E., Wilder, D. A., Majdalany, L., Mathisen, D., & Strain, L. A. (2013b). Performance diagnostic checklist—human services. *PsycTESTS Dataset*. https://doi.org/10.1037/t32807-000

Gavoni, P., & Weatherly, N. L. (2024). *Deliberate coaching: Optimizing teaching and learning through behavior science*. KeyPress Publishing.

Witt, J. C., & Beck, R. (1999). *One-minute academic functional assessment and interventions: "Can't" do it or "won't" do it*. Sopris West.

Appendix 19: QUICK ACTion Plan A

Name: _____ Date: _____

A. **Briefly** describe your behavior:

_____
_____
_____

B. What impact can this behavior have on yourself or others?

_____
_____

C. **Options** *(List at least three possible solutions)*

1. _____ 2. _____

3. _____ 4. _____

5. _____ 6. _____

D. **Choose** *(Pick from one of your possible solutions)*

_____
_____

E. _____ _____
   Student signature   **Date**

   _____ _____
   Staff signature   **Date**

Appendix 20: QUICK ACTion Plan B

Why Me ... Why You?

Think about why you were removed from the classroom. Read the following questions and answer them as honestly you can.

What did you learn about adults and educators this year regarding misbehavior?

If a teacher or adult sees you do something inappropriate, should they ignore it? Why?

How do you think they should handle it?

What should adults do if you continue to misbehave?

What do you learn if a teacher or adult lets you "get away" with something?

How does removal from the classroom impact you?

How does your behavior in the classroom impact others?

What can you do next to avoid removal from the classroom?

Appendix 21: QUICK ACTion Plan C

Student: _____ **Date:** _____

Draw a picture of what happened.

Draw a picture of what you can do instead next time.

Draw a picture of how you will make up for what you did *(for example, clean up, apologize, help peer, etc.)*.

Appendix 22: ACT Matrix for Classrooms

The Acceptance and Commitment Training (ACT) Matrix, developed by Polk et al. (2016), is an effective tool designed to increase personal and group awareness, encourage thoughtful decision-making, and cultivate better habits. When used in a classroom setting, the ACT Matrix helps teachers and students work together to identify and commit to shared values, recognize behaviors that impede learning, and actively participate in activities that promote a positive learning environment.

With this matrix, the classroom community can openly address internal thoughts and feelings that may lead to disruptive behaviors. Together, they can devise committed actions that align with collective goals of respect, engagement, and mutual support. This process helps create a more harmonious classroom atmosphere and equips students with critical life skills in self-awareness, empathy, and proactive problem-solving.

Educators can effectively lead their students through a structured approach to self-improvement and group cohesion by integrating the ACT Matrix into classroom activities. This promotes an inclusive culture where every student feels valued and motivated to contribute positively, enhancing overall learning outcomes and interpersonal relationships within the classroom.

Sample Script for Teachers

This script is a guideline for engaging your students with the ACT Matrix activity. You may need to modify the wording in the script based on the grade level.

"Today, we will use the ACT Matrix, a simple but powerful tool to help us build a stronger, more supportive classroom environment. It will help us understand and improve how we work together as a class.

"The ACT Matrix helps us visualize our shared values as a learning community and identify behaviors or feelings that might prevent us from living up to these ideals. We will also explore how we might react when feeling stressed or unsure and then plan positive actions that align with our goals of supporting and learning from each other.

"The purpose of this activity is not just to make our classroom a better place to learn but also to help us become more effective and fulfilled individuals. This will teach us to handle challenges constructively and contribute to a positive learning atmosphere.

"I'm looking forward to seeing what we can achieve together and how this will help us grow as individuals and a community. Let's get started and see how we can all contribute to making our classroom a place where everyone feels valued and engaged!"

Using the ACT Matrix

When working with your students on the ACT Matrix, it's essential to have a large representation of the matrix visible, whether it's on a board, chart paper, or electronic display like PowerPoint or a smart whiteboard. You should capture the students' responses on the matrix as you work through it with the students. Make sure to include all the components, as shown below, when creating the matrix. Review each quadrant with the students and explain the meaning of each component. Provide examples, some of which are given below.

The ACT Matrix is divided into four quadrants. These quadrants will help you and your students categorize your private thoughts, feelings, and bodily sensations (covert behaviors) and actions others can see (overt behaviors). This process will assist you and the students in identifying whether your actions align with your values as a classroom community.

Procedure: Engaging Students in the ACT Matrix

Step 1: Values—What Is Important to Us (Lower Right Quadrant)

Description:

- Values are the chosen directions that influence the collective actions in the classroom and are not just endpoints. They represent what is important to the teacher and the students, providing everyone with collaboration, purpose, and belonging.
- The process involves reflecting on the qualities the teacher and students aim to embody as a learning community.

Start in the lower right quadrant. Explain to students that values are those ways of being and doing that give your life meaning. Values can also be considered reinforcers or important things to us. You might ask, what are some things you value or are important to you as a student in this class? What do you want for yourself and a member of this classroom community? What might be necessary to you to help you learn in this class? Here, you'll guide the students to identify and affirm shared classroom values that give the group a sense of purpose and direction.

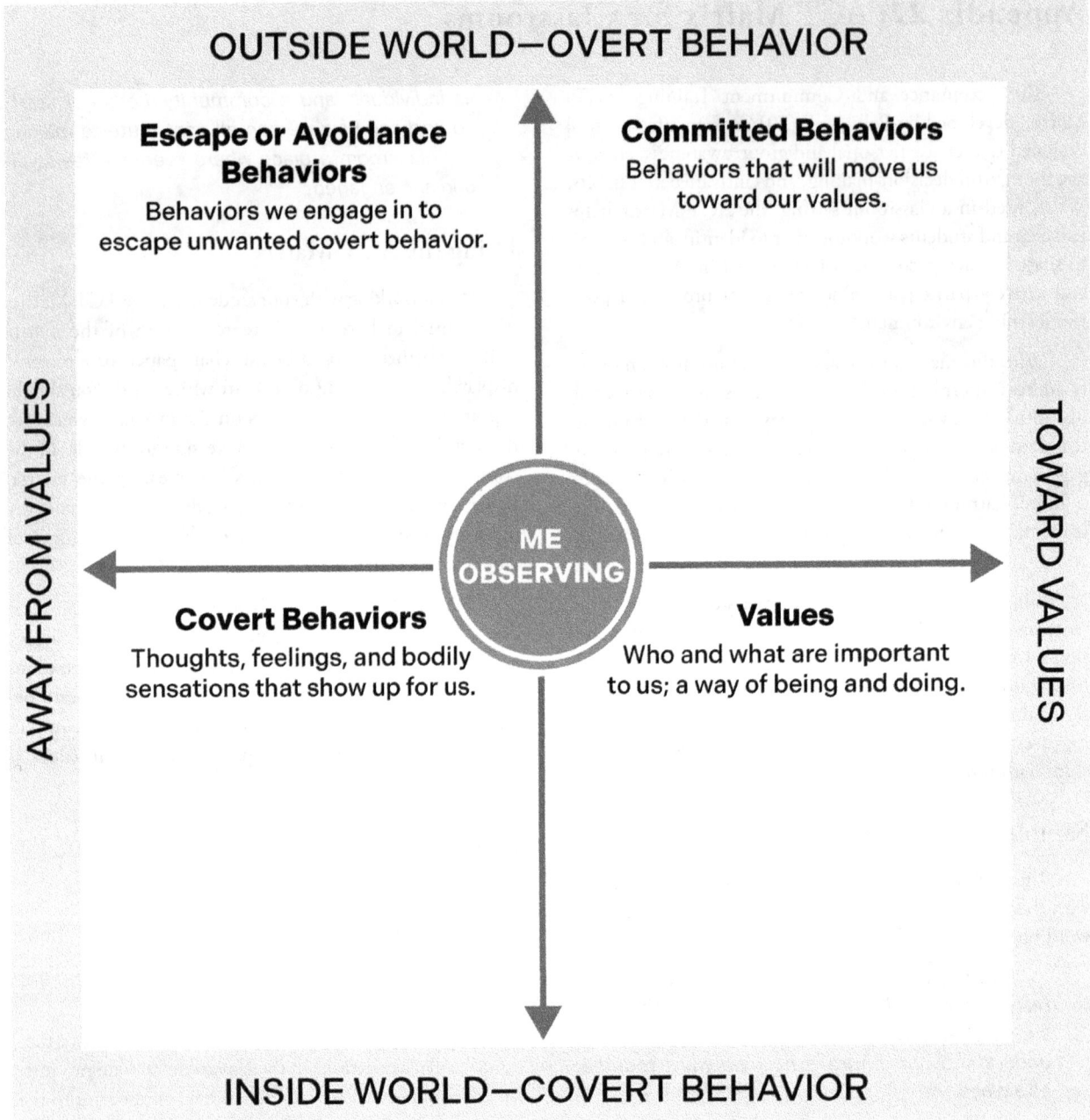

1. **Group Discussion on Values:** Facilitate a classroom discussion to articulate what is fundamentally important in their shared learning environment. This might include values like respect, curiosity, teamwork, or support.
2. **Reflection and Articulation:** Encourage students to contribute their thoughts and articulate shared qualities they value in their learning environment.
3. **Values Alignment:** Together, examine how current classroom behaviors and practices align with these stated values, identifying areas for realignment.

Values Examples:
- **Teamwork:** "In our classroom, we value respect for everyone's ideas and encourage active participation."
- **Respect:** "We want to support each other's learning by being focused during work times and on task so that we can respect the teacher when they are teaching, so everyone can learn."
- **Fun:** "We enjoy collaborating in groups and discussing our work. Class is fun when we play games and compete with our classmates."

Step 2: Covert Behavior—Getting Stuck (Lower Left Quadrant)

Description:

- Covert behaviors are internal experiences, such as thoughts and feelings; only students can observe them. These often involve getting caught up in our thoughts, where we let them control our actions, causing us to get stuck.
- These are the negative thoughts and feelings that "show up" when we are faced with difficult, challenging, or uncomfortable situations or environments. Covert behavior is negative statements or the things we say to ourselves about our behavior.

In the bottom left-hand corner, discuss and list the negative thoughts, feelings, and bodily sensations when the classroom environment is not good for learning. Have students reflect on the moments when they feel disengaged and don't want to be in class. Ask the students what thoughts and feelings arise when some students misbehave, and the class doesn't meet its daily goals. Reflect on feelings about when the class lacks cooperation and respect. Ask for examples of these negative thoughts and feelings. Discuss how negative thoughts and feelings may dominate the classroom's atmosphere and detract from the learning experience. Explore how these thoughts and feelings move the teacher and students away from their classroom values and impact the learning environment. Remember, these questions may be modified to fit the class level and situation.

1. **Creating a Safe Space for Sharing:** Remind students that this is a safe space to discuss their thoughts and feelings and that it is OK to be honest and authentic in sharing their feelings.
2. **Capturing Covert Behaviors:** When listing covert behavior in the bottom left-hand corner, write exactly the phrase or thought. See the examples below.
3. **Identifying Values Misalignment:** Ask students to reflect on how these negative thoughts and feelings might impact their behavior.

Covert Behavior Examples:

- "I don't even know what she wants us to do." "Every time someone asks a question, they get yelled at. I'm not asking anything!" "I'm just going to put my head down so I don't get in trouble."
- "I need to figure out how to get out of here; we're not doing anything anyway."
- "I'd rather be in the dean's office than in here."
- "She always catches me talking, but the students who always talk, she calls on them to answer questions all the time, and they never get in trouble."

Step 3: Escape and Avoidance Behavior—Problem Behavior (Upper Left Quadrant)

Description

- Engaging in escape or avoidance behavior is distancing yourself from negative thoughts and sensations.
- By engaging in certain behaviors and experiencing relief from those unpleasant thoughts and sensations, you effectively engage in escape behavior.
- While we all behave in ways that allow us to escape things that may be aversive, these behaviors move us away from what we value and often prevent us from reaching our goals.
- Engaging in these behaviors provides us with immediate but temporary relief.

In the top left corner, discuss with students the behaviors they may engage in when they get stuck in the cycle of those negative thoughts and feelings. List escape or avoidant behaviors as the students respond. Have the students reflect on when those negative thoughts and feelings show up—what their escape or avoidance behaviors are to eliminate those bad feelings about the situation. Record those behaviors that move students away from their values. Discuss the group's overt actions to alleviate the distress from covert behaviors and assess their alignment with core values.

1. **Mapping Group Behaviors:** List behaviors and actions the teachers and students engage in when experiencing stress, discomfort, or challenging situations.
2. **Values Alignment Evaluation:** Determine if these actions lead away from or toward the classroom's core values.

Overt Behavior Examples:

- Students engage in off-task behavior (e.g., sleeping, putting their heads down, scrolling on their phones, talking)
- Calling out during whole group activities
- Teacher sending students out of class for apparent classroom-managed misbehavior
- Major disruptive behavior (e.g., fighting, cursing, refusal to follow classroom expectations)
- Out of seat without permission

Step 4: Pinpointed Committed Behavior—Getting Unstuck (Upper Right Quadrant)

Description:

- This quadrant focuses on identifying and committing to specific behaviors that help the classroom collectively move toward its shared values, despite any emotional or cognitive challenges that may arise. It's about making conscious choices that contribute positively to the classroom environment.

- Pinpointed committed behaviors are actionable and deliberate, chosen to counteract the escape behaviors and foster a culture of respect, engagement, and mutual support. These behaviors are essential for cultivating a learning atmosphere where students feel included and empowered to participate.

In the top right-hand corner, discuss with the students the behaviors they can or should engage in when negative thoughts and feelings start to arise. Committed behaviors are the actions you engage in instead of the problematic behaviors. These behaviors will move you toward your values and the right side of the matrix. With the students, create a list of committed behaviors aligned with shared classroom values. Remind students that they should acknowledge those covert behaviors—and the negative thoughts and feelings when they show up—and remember those committed actions and behaviors they need to engage in instead.

1. **Identifying Committed Group Actions:** As a class, define specific, actionable behaviors that align with the classroom's values. This might include practices like actively listening to one another, offering constructive feedback, or supporting a peer through a challenging task.
2. **Implementation Planning:** Discuss as a group how these behaviors can be implemented in daily classroom activities. Plan together to anticipate any possible obstacles and develop strategies to address them effectively.
3. **Commitment as a Group:** Each classroom member commits to these behaviors, understanding their role in fostering a positive and inclusive learning environment.

Examples of Committed Behaviors:

- Students complete assignments on time.
- Addressing conflicts directly, respectfully, and privately.
- Students ask for help when needed.
- Students work together on group projects with defined roles, ensuring every student contributes to the task.

Step 5: Metrics and Evaluation (Continuous Review and Adjustment)

- Metrics serve as tangible indicators of progress and effectiveness, helping the classroom leader and students assess how well their behaviors align with their shared goals.

Establish clear metrics to evaluate the effectiveness of the classroom's actions in alignment with their shared values and committed behaviors. Check in with students frequently as a class for ongoing assessment. This check-in may occur daily initially and decrease as students start meeting the classroom expectations based on shared values.

Procedure:

1. **Identification of Relevant Metrics:** Collaborate with the student to determine specific outcomes to measure, such as the frequency of collaborative projects, improvement in class participation, or decreases in conflict incidents.
2. **Setting Baselines and Targets:** Determine the current situation and establish achievable improvement goals.
3. **Regular Data Collection:** Implement a schedule for collecting data on these metrics.
4. **Review and Adjust Actions:** Schedule regular classroom meetings to review the metrics and discuss progress.

Examples:

- Use a class-wide rating scale after activities and transitions. Gather feedback from students on their performance and adherence to expectations. Display the results for the students to review.
- Assess the students' current performance to determine the baseline. If the goal is to improve dismissal procedures as part of a shared commitment to following expectations, identify the behaviors in the dismissal procedure that need improvement. From there, the expectations are taught, and improvement is reinforced.
- Data collection should occur frequently and be analyzed often. Collect data to determine if adjustments are needed when teaching new behaviors, expectations, routines, or procedures. Then, share the data with the students.

References

Polk, K. L., Schoendorff, B., Webster, M., & Olaz, F. O. (2016). *The essential guide to the ACT matrix: A step-by-step approach to using the ACT matrix model in clinical practice.* Context Press.

Appendix 23: Performance Diagnostic Checklist for Coaching

Coachee name: _____ Coach assessing: _____ Date: _____

Briefly describe performance concern: _____

Antecedents and training	Yes	No
1. Did I provide the coachee with a written description telling *exactly* what I expect of the coachee for a particular instructional/behavioral strategy?		
2. Did I provide the coachee with adequate instruction about what to do? (Instructions like "I want you to do this and this before we leave today.")		
3. Did the coachee receive formal training on this instructional/behavioral strategy? If yes, check all applicable training methods. ☐ Instructions ☐ Demonstration ☐ Rehearsal		
4. Did I facilitate/ensure visible task aids **while** completing the instructional/behavioral strategy? (Reminders to prompt the strategy in the correct way at the correct time/duration.)		
5. Did I determine if the coachee can state the purpose of the instructional/behavioral strategy?		
6. Do I ever verbally, textually, or electronically remind the coachee to use the instructional/behavioral strategy? If so, how often? ☐ Hourly ☐ Daily ☐ Weekly ☐ Monthly By whom? Check all that apply: ☐ Peer ☐ Coach ☐ Administrator ☐ Other		
7. Do I frequently provide updated, challenging, and attainable goals the coachee is comfortable with related to the instructional/behavioral strategy?		
8. Did I make sure the coachee is aware of the mission of the school?		

Equipment and processes	Yes	No
9. Did I make any needed equipment available (e.g., computer, A/V, mic, etc.)? Does it work?		
10. Are the equipment and environment optimally physically arranged (e.g., the arrangement of student desks)?		
11. Did I check to ensure larger processes perform well despite any incorrect instructional/behavioral strategies along the way (e.g., routines and procedures, following schedules, etc.)?		
12. Did I determine if these processes flow in a logical manner (e.g., rotating the schedule with preferred and nonpreferred activities)?		
13. Have I made sure coachees are able to implement the instructional/behavioral strategy without any obstacles (e.g., interruption by the intercom)?		

Knowledge and skills	Yes	No
14. Can the coachee tell me what they are supposed to do and how to do it?		
15. Can the coachee precisely demonstrate the instructional/behavioral strategy for me physically/verbally?		
16. Can the coachee perform the instructional/behavioral strategy for me at the appropriate (quick) speed?		

Motivation	Yes	No
17. Is the coachee motivated based on the outcomes following completion of the task (e.g., using a behavior strategy will reduce misbehavior)?		
18. Do I help coachees see positive effects of implementing the instructional/behavioral strategy (e.g., increased learner engagement, increased assessment data, decreased misbehavior)?		
19. How often do I or my leadership team observe the coachee? ☐ Hourly ☐ Daily ☐ Weekly ☐ Monthly		
20. Does the coachee receive feedback about the performance? If so, By whom? _____ How often? _____ How long is the delay between the feedback and the instructional/behavioral strategy? _____ Check all that apply: Feedback focus: ☐ Positive ☐ Constructive Feedback type: ☐ Written ☐ Verbal ☐ Graphed ☐ Other		
21. Is the instructional/behavioral strategy particularly effortful or difficult?		
22. Do other instructional/behavioral strategies (elements) appear to take precedence over the targeted strategy? If yes, indicate the strategies below. Strategy: _____ Strategy: _____ Strategy: _____		

References

Carr, J. E., Wilder, D. A., Majdalany, L., Mathisen, D., & Strain, L. A. (2013b). Performance diagnostic checklist—human services. *PsycTESTS Dataset*. https://doi.org/10.1037/t32807-000

Appendix 24: Reducing Tardiness—Managing Late Arrivals

About the Procedure: This procedure targets the behavior of students who are chronically or selectively late. Tardiness disrupts the classroom environment and can affect the learning process for all students.

Common Function(s) of the Behavior: Tardiness often functions to avoid tasks or gain peer or teacher attention; or it is due to lack of routines.

Works Best When: This procedure is most effective when implemented consistently as part of a broader strategy to promote punctuality and accountability, reinforcing positive behaviors while providing natural consequences for tardiness.

Examples of the Behavioral Context:

- A student consistently arrives late during a specific subject or activity.
- A student is late in the mornings, missing the beginning of the school day.
- Selective tardiness observed when students feel less engaged or motivated.

Procedural Definitions:

- Punctuality reinforcement—a procedure whereby prompt arrival is consistently reinforced with a reward or privilege.
- Consequence for tardiness—involves implementing a natural or logical consequence for being late, such as missing out on a preferred activity or making up the missed time.

Procedure:

1. Reinforce Punctuality:
   - Reward on-time arrival with small privileges or acknowledgments (e.g., "Thank you, Maria, for being on time today!").
2. Implement consequences for tardiness:
   - Apply natural consequences for late arrivals, such as missing out on the start of an activity (e.g., "Since you were late today, you'll need to wait until after we finish this activity to join in.").
3. Minimize reinforcement of tardiness:
   - Avoid drawing undue attention to the tardy student, beyond the necessary communication of consequences.
4. Monitor and adjust:
   - Keep track of tardiness occurrences to assess the effectiveness of the intervention, and adjust strategies as needed.
5. Provide education on effects of tardiness:
   - Discuss the impact of being on time versus being late, emphasizing real-life implications and the importance of developing good habits.

Considerations: Ensure that consequences and rewards do not inadvertently reinforce the undesired behavior of being tardy. For example, suspending a student for tardiness may unintentionally reinforce the function of escape by removing them from the school environment, which could be the outcome they seek. Instead, the focus should be on creating a supportive environment that encourages punctuality through positive reinforcement, natural consequences, and strategies that address the underlying reasons for tardiness. This approach should also include ensuring that the student completes any missed work as part of the intervention, promoting both attendance and academic engagement.

In implementing this procedure, the aim is to reduce instances of tardiness, thereby minimizing disruptions and enhancing the learning environment for all students.

Appendix 25: Reducing Stealing Behavior With the "Green Dot" Procedure

About the Procedure: This approach is specifically designed to address and manage stealing behavior in the classroom, which can disrupt the learning environment and affect student relationships. It involves the use of a simple visual marker to help students self-monitor their behavior regarding personal and others' belongings.

Common Function(s) of the Behavior: Stealing often serves functions such as gaining access to desired items or seeking attention.

Works Best When: The procedure is consistently applied and clearly understood by the student. It is particularly effective for students who have shown a pattern of taking items from peers.

Examples of the Behavioral Context:

- A student repeatedly takes items that belong to classmates, such as school supplies or personal belongings.

Procedural Definitions:

- Green dot stickers—used to mark belongings that are legitimately owned by the student. Items without these markers are considered not owned and taken without permission.
- Systematic checks—regular checks of the student's belongings to ensure compliance with the rules set forth by the green dot system.

Procedure:

1. Definition and explanation:
    - Clearly define what constitutes stealing—possessing items without a green dot sticker. Explain the system to the student and ensure understanding.
2. Implementation of green dot system:
    - Place green dot stickers on all items that belong to the student. Ensure that any new items brought to school are also marked.
3. Regular monitoring:
    - Conduct checks of the student's belongings every 30 minutes. Record any items found without a green dot as stolen.
4. Rewards and consequences:
    - Reward the student with one point for every 30-minute check where only green dot items are found. Points can be exchanged for small rewards.
    - Impose a five-point fine for each item found without a green dot.
5. Progressive reduction of checks:
    - As the student begins to show improvement, gradually decrease the frequency of checks (e.g., hourly, every 2 hours, daily) while maintaining the reward and fine system.

Considerations: This procedure requires strict adherence and consistency to be effective. It might initially seem rigorous but is crucial for helping the student learn to control impulsive behaviors related to stealing.

Monitoring: Use a frequency count to track occurrences of stealing before and after implementing the green dot procedure to evaluate effectiveness.

References

Rosen, H. S., & Rosen, L. A. (1983). Eliminating stealing: Use of stimulus control with an elementary student. *Behavior Modification*, 7(1) 56–63. https://doi.org/10.1177/01454455830071004

Appendix 26: Reducing Tattling—Managing Reporting Behavior

About the Procedure: This procedure is designed to address and reduce unnecessary tattling among students, which often distracts from classroom activities and can create a negative classroom environment.

Common Function(s) of the Behavior: Tattling is typically motivated by a desire for attention from adults or peers.

Works Best When: The procedure is most effective when students are made aware of what constitutes inappropriate tattling and are encouraged to monitor their own behavior.

Examples of the Behavioral Context:

- A student reports minor issues between peers that do not require adult intervention.
- Tattling that occurs frequently and disrupts classroom activities or causes conflicts among students.

Procedural Definitions:

- Baseline measurement—collecting initial data on the frequency of tattling to understand the scope of the behavior.
- Behavioral feedback—providing the student with immediate feedback based on set criteria (good, OK, not good) to help them recognize and correct their behavior.

Procedure:

1. Define tattling:
   - Clearly define what tattling behavior looks like to ensure it is observable and measurable.
2. Collect baseline data:
   - Observe and record the frequency of tattling over a 5-day period to establish a baseline for intervention.
3. Initial feedback and goal setting:
   - Inform the student that tattling is problematic and set goals together to reduce it.
4. Implementation phases:
   - Phase 1: Direct feedback
     - Objective: The student receives direct feedback from the teacher after each predetermined time interval (e.g., 10 minutes) about their tattling behavior. This feedback categorizes their behavior as "good" (no tattling), "OK" (one incident of tattling), or "not good" (two or more incidents of tattling). This phase aims to help the student understand the behavioral expectations and the criteria for each category.
     - Duration: This phase is conducted over 5 consecutive school days to establish a consistent understanding.
   - Phase 2: Self-assessment and prediction
     - Objective: Transitioning from receiving feedback to self-monitoring, in this phase, the student is encouraged to predict the feedback they would receive based on their own assessment of their behavior during the same intervals.
     - Method: At the end of each interval, before the teacher provides any feedback, the student states their prediction of what they believe their behavior rating should be based on their understanding from Phase 1.
     - Reinforcement: The student earns points if their self-assessment aligns with the teacher's assessment. This method encourages the student to pay closer attention to their own behavior and promotes self-regulation.
     - Duration: This phase can continue for a longer period and is adjusted based on the student's progress and needs.
5. Reward System:
   - Allow the student to earn rewards from a pre-agreed list of reinforcers after accumulating a certain number of points.

Considerations: This strategy encourages self-regulation and is suitable for students capable of self-reflection. Adjust the time frames if necessary to better suit the classroom dynamics and the individual student's capabilities.

Monitoring: Evaluate the effectiveness of the intervention by continuing to monitor the frequency of tattling behaviors before and after implementing the procedure.

References

Robertson, S. J., Simon, S. J., Pachman, J. S., & Drabman, R. S. (1979). Self-control and generalization procedures in a classroom of disruptive retarded children. *Child Behavior Therapy*, 1(4), 347–362. https://doi.org/10.1300/J473v01n04_04

Appendix 27: Reducing Vocal Disruptions Procedure

About the Procedure: This strategy is intended to manage students who frequently speak out in a disruptive manner during class. Instead of eliminating all instances of talking out of turn, this approach aims to reduce these occurrences to a more manageable level, recognizing that some interruptions will naturally happen.

Common Function(s) of the Behavior: Talking out in class may serve functions such as gaining peer attention or avoiding instructional demands.

Works Best When: This procedure is most effective when consistently applied and when the student understands the expectations and potential rewards. It works well for students who regularly disrupt class with inappropriate talk-outs (vocal disruptions).

Examples of the Behavioral Context:

- A student frequently interrupts class discussions with irrelevant comments.
- The student talks over peers or the teacher in an attempt to be heard.

Procedural Definitions:

- Talk-outs—any verbal comment or noise made by the student that interrupts classroom instruction or peer interaction without permission to speak.
- Observation period—a randomly selected 1-hour period each day during which the student's talk-outs are tracked.

Procedure

1. Defining talk-outs:
    - Clearly define what constitutes an inappropriate talk-out so that it can be easily observed and measured. For example, any time the student speaks without being called on or interrupts classroom instruction.
2. Collect baseline data:
    - For 5 consecutive days, count the number of talk-outs the student makes during 1 hour of observation each day. This will provide a baseline for future comparisons.
3. Calculate the daily rate:
    - Determine the student's average rate of talk-outs per minute by dividing the total number of talk-outs in 1 hour by 60 minutes. For instance, if 20 talk-outs occur in 60 minutes, the rate is 20/60, or 0.33 talk-outs per minute.
4. Set a target rate:
    - Once the baseline rate is established, reduce it by 50% to set the maximum allowable rate of talk-outs. Using the previous example, if the baseline is 0.33 talk-outs per minute, the target rate would be 0.16 talk-outs per minute.
5. Inform the student:
    - Explain to the student that you will monitor their talk-outs daily and that if they can maintain the target rate or below, they will receive a reward.
6. Random monitoring and feedback:
    - Choose a random 1-hour period each day to observe the student's behavior, without informing them in advance which hour will be observed. Afterward, calculate the rate of talk-outs and compare it to the target rate. If the student stays within the allowable rate, reward them and provide positive feedback. If the rate is exceeded, explain that they didn't earn the reward for that day but will have another chance tomorrow.

Considerations: This method promotes moderation rather than complete elimination of the behavior, encouraging students to manage their talk-outs. The procedure is also adaptable for further shaping, allowing gradual reduction of the target rate over time, such as reducing by half initially, then by quarters, and so on.

Shaping Behavior: This procedure can be adjusted to gradually reduce talk-outs even further. For example, after achieving a 50% reduction, the target rate can be decreased by 75%, then by 87.5%, and so on.

Adaptability: This method can also be applied to other disruptive behaviors, such as reducing out-of-seat behavior or minimizing the time taken to transition between activities.

Monitoring: Use a frequency count of inappropriate talk-outs before and after implementing the procedure to evaluate its effectiveness. Consistent monitoring will help track the student's progress over time.

References

Dietz, S. M., & Repp, A. C. (1973). Decreasing classroom misbehavior through the use of DRL schedules of reinforcement. *Journal of Applied Behavior Analysis, 6*(3), 457–463. https://doi.org/10.1901/jaba.1973.6-457

Appendix 28: School-Wide Tardiness Reduction Procedure

About the Procedure: This school-wide initiative aims to address and significantly reduce student tardiness, ensuring that valuable instruction time is preserved. The School-Wide Tardiness Reduction Procedure, developed through the collaborative efforts of the school's site team, focuses on safe and timely transitions by actively supervising students, teaching clear behavioral expectations, enforcing consistent consequences for tardiness, and utilizing data-driven decision-making for continuous improvement.

Common Functions of the Behavior: Tardiness may serve multiple functions for students, including

- **Avoidance:** Delaying arrival to class to avoid challenging tasks or social interactions.
- **Attention:** Seeking attention from peers or adults through disruptive late entries.
- **Access to Tangibles:** Spending time in preferred locations outside of the classroom (e.g., hallways, bathrooms) before heading to class.

Works Best When: The intervention is most effective when all staff are committed to its implementation, expectations are clearly communicated, and consequences are consistently applied. Active supervision and data-based adjustments are crucial for addressing specific issues effectively.

Examples of the Behavior/Context:

- A student arrives 10 minutes late to class, causing the teacher to restart the lesson. This may function as avoidance of an unpreferred activity that begins each class period.
- Multiple students are tardy during the morning transition, chatting in the hallways, potentially seeking social attention.

Procedural Definitions:

- **Active supervision**—the strategic positioning and movement of staff in key areas during transitions to monitor and guide student behavior.
- **Behavioral expectations lessons**—structured lessons designed to explicitly teach students the expected behaviors during transitions.

Procedure:

1. **Data Collection and Analysis:** Collect and analyze tardiness data by grade level and instructional period to understand the scope and specifics of the issue.
2. **Staff and Zone Assignments:** Assign teaching and non-teaching staff to supervise designated zones that are identified as problematic.
3. **Communication of Expectations:** Define clear behavioral expectations for students during transitions, and communicate these through direct teaching.
4. **Implementation of Consequences:** Establish a tiered system of consequences for tardiness based on the school's policies and resources. For example:
    - **1 to 3 tardies:** Student completes a corrective action tardy form.
    - **4 to 6 tardies:** Lunch detention.
    - **7 to 9 tardies:** After-school detention with school service tasks.
    - **10 to 12 tardies:** Mandatory attendance on Friday afternoons.
    - **More than 12 tardies:** Parental conference and a meeting with a panel of community elders.
5. **Staff Training:** Conduct comprehensive training for all staff on the procedures and expectations, including practice sessions without students.
6. **Student Lessons:** Teach students the expectations through targeted lessons over 3 days, ensuring consistent delivery across all classes.
7. **Monitoring and Adjustment:** Monitor the fidelity of implementation and make necessary adjustments based on ongoing data analysis.

Implementation and monitoring: During transitions, ensure that staff provide active supervision both in hallways and at classroom entrances. After the tardy bell, teachers should immediately start instruction and manage late arrivals as per the established procedure. Administrators oversee the following procedural integrity during and after transitions:

1. Initial Encounter:
    - **Identify the tardy student:** As soon as a staff member notices a student arriving late, they should calmly approach the student.
    - **Verification:** Quickly verify the student's schedule to confirm that they are indeed late for the class they should be attending.
2. Communication:
    - **Discuss expectations:** Remind the student of the school's expectations regarding punctuality. This conversation should be brief but clear, aiming to reinforce the importance of being on time.
    - **Reason for tardiness:** Ask the student to briefly explain the reason for their tardiness. This step is crucial for understanding if there

is a recurring issue that needs addressing at a systemic level.

3. Documentation:
   - **Recording the incident:** Document the tardiness using the school's designated system (e.g., digital record, tardy slip). Include the time, the student's explanation, and any other relevant details.
   - **Tardy form:** Require the student to fill out a tardy form, which includes the date and time of tardiness, the reason provided, and what corrective action they will take to be on time in the future.

4. Consequences:
   - **Implement consequences:** Based on the number of times the student has been tardy, apply the appropriate consequence as outlined in the school's tardiness policy.

5. Escort to Class:
   - **Guidance to classroom:** Once the documentation is complete, and the appropriate action has been taken, escort the student to their classroom.
   - **Inform the teacher:** Briefly inform the teacher of the student's late arrival and any measures taken, ensuring minimal disruption to the ongoing class.

6. Follow-Up:
   - **Monitor behavior:** Keep track of the student's punctuality over the following days to see if there is improvement or if further interventions are needed.
   - **Feedback loop:** If tardiness persists, communicate this to higher level administration for possible further action or adjustment of the intervention strategy.

7. Continuous Improvement:
   - **Review procedures:** Regularly review and adjust these procedures based on feedback from staff and effectiveness in reducing tardiness.

Student Lesson Guide for Timely Class Attendance and Respectful Hallway Behavior

Educational Goals:

1. Conduct in Hallways:
   - **Walk:** Always walk in the hallways to maintain a safe and orderly environment.
   - **Continuous Movement:** Keep moving toward your classroom. If you need to converse, step aside to avoid obstructing the hallway.
   - **Volume Awareness:** Keep your voice at a conversational level to contribute to a peaceful hallway atmosphere.

2. Punctuality Standards:
   - **Pre-Class Preparedness:** Understand that the warning bell is your cue that you have X seconds to be inside your classroom.
   - **Definition of Tardiness:** You are officially tardy if not in your classroom when the final bell completes its ring.
   - **Start of Class Protocol:** After the final bell, teachers will shut the classroom doors and initiate the lesson.
   - **Procedure for Late Arrivals:** If you arrive after the classroom door is closed, please find and follow the staff member responsible for the "positive sweep."

Strategies to Avoid Tardiness:

Common Tardiness Excuses and Proactive Solutions:

1. **Unheard Bell:** Take personal responsibility for your time management; the bell serves as a secondary reminder.
2. **Delayed by a Teacher:** Secure a note from the teacher confirming the reason for your delay.
3. **Desire for Snacks:** Save snack time for lunch breaks, not during class transitions.
4. **Engaging With Peers:** Prioritize proceeding to your class immediately upon hearing the bell; social interactions can wait.

"Positive Sweep" Guidelines:

If You Are Late and Participate in a Positive Sweep:

1. **Follow the Staff Member:** Quietly accompany the staff member to the sweep room, adhering to their directions.
2. **Complete the Tardy Form:** Fill in the required details on the tardy form, including the reason for your delay and your plan to improve punctuality.
3. **Escort Back to Class:** Return to your class with the staff member, ensuring you re-enter quietly and promptly.
4. **Seamless Re-entry:** Once back in class, immediately engage in the ongoing activities without disruption.

Student Tardy Form

Date: _____ Student name: _____

Grade: _____ Homeroom teacher: _____

Time of arrival: _____ Class missed: _____

Reason for tardiness: (Please check the appropriate reason or write in your own words.)

- ☐ Did not hear the bell
- ☐ Detained by another teacher
- ☐ Needed to visit the restroom
- ☐ Obtaining snacks or beverages
- ☐ Conversation with peers
- ☐ Other: _____

Plan to improve punctuality: (Describe what steps you will take to ensure you arrive on time in the future.)

Improvement plan

Steps: _____

_____

_____

_____

Signatures:

Student signature: _____ Date: _____

Staff member signature: _____ Date: _____

Comments by staff member (if any): _____

_____

_____

Additional notes: _____

_____

Parent/guardian notification

- ☐ Yes, a copy of this form has been sent home.
- ☐ No, a copy of this form has not been sent home.

References

Sprick, R. (2003). *Safe transitions and reduced tardies (START) on time!* Pacific Northwest.

Tyre, A., Feuerborn, L., & Pierce, J. (2011). Schoolwide intervention to reduce chronic tardiness at the middle and high school levels. *Preventing School Failure: Alternative Education for Children and Youth, 55*(3), 132–139. https://doi.org/10.1080/10459880903472918

Appendix 29: QUICK Response Fidelity Monitoring Form

Date:															
Pick Up															
	Yes	No	Yes	No	Yes	No	Yes	No	Yes	No	Yes	No	Yes	No	Yes	No
Teacher called the correct code																
QUICK Team Members responded within 5 minutes																
Teacher discreetly informs the responding staff regarding the ABCs of the incident																
QUICK Responder provides directives in a business-like manner																
If a student refuses to follow direction, QUICK Responder uses setting limits procedure to present demand																
QUICK Responder minimizes conversation with student																

Date:															
Drop Off															
	Yes	No	Yes	No	Yes	No	Yes	No	Yes	No	Yes	No	Yes	No	Yes	No
Following QUICK Room placement, the QUICK Responder uses behavior momentum before student returns to class (e.g., "tuck your shirt in")															
QUICK Responder reminds student of expectations prior to the transition back to class															
Just before the student returns to class, the QUICK Responder reminds student about restitution (e.g., apology, clean up area)															
Just before the student returns to class, the QUICK Responder reminds the student to ask permission to return															
Teacher welcomes back the student when the student returns															
If the student refused to complete a task prior to removal, the teacher directs the student to the task															
QUICK Responder uses fading procedure (e.g., 1 minute in class, 1 minute by door, 1 minute outside door)															

Appendix 30: QUICK Room Fidelity Monitoring and Self-Assessment Guide

Date:									
	+	−	N/A	+	−	N/A	+	−	N/A
1. Students sign in									
2. Explain the rules									
3. Explain the point sheet in detail									
4. Give students the point sheet									
5. Assign students a timer									
6. Use proximity control when placing students at desks									
7. Score student point sheets every 10 minutes									
8. Give students action plans after the QUICK 10 minutes									
9. Require student to complete an action plan									

Date:									
	+	−	N/A	+	−	N/A	+	−	N/A
10. Use the Setting Limits procedure to present demands to a student who refuses									
11. If a student continues to disrupt, stop their time and mark consequence on the point sheet									
12. If student is highly and continuously disruptive, remove them briefly to an alternate time-out area									
13. Check the accuracy of the action plan before the student returns to class									
14. Return action plans and point sheets to the teacher									

Appendix 31: QUICK Response Social Validity Questionnaire

Position title: _____ Date: _____ Grade level(s) taught/served: _____

Questions	Agree	Somewhat agree	No opinion	Somewhat disagree	Disagree
1. The QUICK program at my school helps to improve the behaviors of my students.	5	4	3	2	1
2. I have a thorough understanding of the QUICK program.	5	4	3	2	1
3. Overall, the QUICK program is acceptable to me.	5	4	3	2	1
4. The QUICK program requires too much time/staff/effort to implement.	5	4	3	2	1
5. The school implements the QUICK program the way we learned to implement it.	5	4	3	2	1
6. School administrators support and value the QUICK program.	5	4	3	2	1
7. There is a noticeable difference in my students' behaviors since my school implemented the QUICK program.	5	4	3	2	1
8. My job is easier since my school implemented the QUICK program.	5	4	3	2	1
9. Overall, my school benefits from having a QUICK program.	5	4	3	2	1
General comments/suggestions:					

Appendix 32: Elopement Reporting Tips

If a student elopes off campus, staff should *verify* and provide law enforcement with as much information as available:

1. A current photo
2. A current address
3. Contact information:
    a. Guardian's name
    b. Guardian's phone number
    c. Other contact information that may be pertinent. For example:
        i. Family member
        ii. Counselor
        iii. Probation officer
4. Physical description including
    a. Approximate height and weight
    b. Hair color
    c. Type and color of clothes, shoes, and so forth
5. The direction the student heads
6. Current medications including
    a. Name of medication
    b. Dosage/schedule
    c. Purpose
    d. Problems or side effect associated with medication
7. Any behavior that law enforcement should be aware of
8. Tips for managing behavior
9. History of elopement that includes:
    a. Location student was found
    b. People student was found with
    c. Where student was returned to and *why*
10. Any other information that might assist law enforcement

Please note, staff should follow the laws, policies and procedures provided within your school or district.

Facts & Tips Sheet for Police Example: Billy

Billy is a 13-year-old White male with a variety of mental health diagnoses and intellectual disabilities. Since he presents as a typical 13-year-old, a stranger might view his behavior as him being "disrespectful" rather than as a result of his disabilities. Once he feels that he is "in trouble," Billy tries to manipulate situations with appropriate and inappropriate words. When engaged with police officers or other authority figures, he often makes threats, becomes physically or verbally aggressive, throws things, bites, and curses. It is important to approach Billy confidently, using clear requests. Allow about 30 seconds for him to act on your requests. Words other than brief, periodic instructions directed toward Billy are irrelevant and useless in controlling him or the situation.

POLICE INVOLVEMENT usually begins when Billy elopes from school, alone or with peers.

Hair: Blonde, shoulder length

Weight: 131 lbs.

Eyes: Blue

Medication	Dosage/schedule	Purpose	Problems or side effects
Invega	9 mg, 1 tab, QAM	Mood swings, psychosis	Nausea, rapid heart rate, headaches
Neurontin	300 mg, 1 tab BID; 2 tab QHS	Anxiety, aggression	Drowsiness, dizziness, and coordination problems
Clonidine	0.01 mg, 1 tab, PO, QID	Anxiety, aggression	Dry mouth, drowsiness, fatigue
Lamictal	200 mg 1 tab, PO, BID	Mood swings	Headache, blurred vision, coordination problems

Please be aware Billy:	CANNOT tell the difference between safe and unsafe actions; HAS NO fear of police/authority figures; DOES NOT respond to threats, reasoning, or lectures; DOES NOT always connect his actions with their potential consequences, CANNOT accurately describe what he has done wrong, nor why he has done it. **Bringing Billy to the Juvenile Detention Center or having him Baker Acted will have ABSOLUTELY NO EFFECT ON BILLY'S BEHAVIOR.**
When Billy:	**PLEASE do this:**
Runs away from school (alone or with friends)	Look for Billy in places he ran to in the past: Publix, Burger King. When found, RETURN Billy TO SCHOOL.
Tries to hurt others, hurt himself, or damage property (major)	Immediately act to keep him and others safe, if it is necessary to restrain Billy, release in gradual increments until he stops resisting, and return Billy to school.
Swears, makes personally degrading remarks, or threatens to hurt you or others	This may happen when you pick Billy up after an elopement or when you drop him off back at school. Resist the urge to respond to his words. Reduce his audience. Disperse onlookers and any others who do not need to be directly involved.
Relevant addresses	**Residence:** 321 North Happy Lane, Port St. Lucie, FL 34949 **School:** Stormy Oaks Middle School (SOMS), 827 Sunset Blvd., Ft. Pierce, FL 34957
Important contact info	Mr. Kay (School Principal), 772-528-5555; Joe Buller (Billy's dad), 772-555-5555; Wendy (Billy's Mental Health Counselor), 772-555-2220

Appendix 33: Problem-Solving for Students

Training and Coaching

Problem-Solving Training

Use this procedure until the student successfully demonstrates all components of problem-solving.

1. Ask the student if you can speak to them about something important.

2. If the student says yes, thank them and move on to the next step. If the student says no or refuses to respond, say "OK" and try again later.

3. Talk with the student and say, "I'm going to teach you how to problem-solve so that you can learn to appropriately get your needs met in the future."

4. Briefly review the following four steps:

   a. Statement of the problem (e.g., "Johnny keeps trying to talk to me while I'm trying to get my work done.")

   b. List possible solutions:

      i. Ignore Johnny

      ii. Politely ask Johnny to wait to talk until after your work is completed

      iii. Ask to move your seat

      iv. Tell the teacher Johnny is talking to you and you can't complete your work

   c. Pick the best possible solution (e.g., Politely asking Johnny to wait …)

   d. If that solution does not work, go back to the list and pick the next best solution.

5. Use an example of a time the student could have used the problem-solving steps and have them state each of the four steps of problem-solving they could have used in that example.

6. If the student states the problem-solving steps correctly, give praise.

7. Provide corrective feedback if the student states the problem-solving steps incorrectly.

8. Remind the student to use problem-solving for problems in the future.

Problem-Solving—Coaching to Support Transference of Skills Into the Natural Environment

Follow this procedure throughout the day and whenever you see the student struggle.

- If you see the student uses the problem-solving steps correctly, praise and reflect on the positive outcomes that occurred as a result of the problem-solving skills used.

- If not, prompt the student to engage in the problem-solving skills trained.

- If the student has a problem and does not use problem-solving skills, prompt them to engage in problem-solving skills (e.g., "Remember when we practiced problem-solving? See if you can work through the steps.").

- If necessary, prompt the student through the problem-solving steps.

- Provide praise for correct responses and corrective feedback for incorrect responses.

- Point out the positive outcomes of the solution selected and remind the student to use problem-solving skills in the future.

Appendix 34: QUICK Room Point Sheets

Daily QUICK Report

Student:_____ Date: _____

Time entered: _____ Time exited: _____ Time on task: _____ Time owed: _____

On-task behavior	Progressive consequences
☐ Remained quiet ☐ Head remained off desk ☐ Remained in seat ☐ Raised hand for help ☐ Completed 100% of assignment ☐ Earned 20 minutes of independent activity ☐ Earned 20% time reduction	☐ 1st: ineligible to work independent on activity ☐ 2nd: loss of 20% time reduction ☐ 3rd: remained in seat ☐ 4th: completed 100% of assignment ☐ 5th: referral/parent/guardian contact ☐ 6th: parent conference ☐ 7th: out of school suspension
Daily tracker	**Off-task behaviors**
	1	2	3	4	5	6	7 | |---|---|---|---|---|---|---| | | | | | | | | Each star indicates that the student followed all QUICK expectations for that hour. An X indicates that a consequence occurred.	☐ Talked without permission ☐ Out of seat ☐ Head down or slept ☐ Incomplete assignment

_____   _____
Staff signature   Parent signature

Hourly QUICK Report

Student: _____ Date: _____

Time entered: _____ Time exited: _____

	Remained in seat	Remained quiet	Raised hand for help	Head remained off desk
60-50				
50-40				
40-30				
30-20				
20-10				
10-0				
Extra time				

Progressive consequences	Off-task behaviors
☐ 1st: verbal warning	☐ Talked without permission
☐ 2nd: loss of 25% time reduction	☐ Out of seat
☐ 3rd: make up minutes required	☐ Misused materials
☐ 4th: removed to QUICK room	☐ Noncompliant
☐ 5th: parent contact	☐ Aggressive
☐ 6th: Saturday school or suspension	
Note: Student will still be required to serve their time within QUICK Room upon return.	

_____ _____ _____
Staff signature   Teacher signature   Parent signature

Appendix 35: Crisis Plan for Escalating Behavior

Escalation continuum	Behavior	Staff response (Refer to district crisis intervention procedures)
6. Physically acting out/ crisis	Continuous physical aggression Continuous self-injurious behavior, continuous high-magnitude disruption Continuous high-magnitude property destruction	Staff contact the crisis team and call the office for assistance. Staff do not talk, comfort, or attempt to teach new skills during a crisis. Attempt to get behavior under control in the environment in which it occurred, if possible; minimize attention. Student needs to deescalate and return to stable state. Provide minimal and low-intensity attention after a crisis. Otherwise, the behavior may continue if the function is attention. Additional staff should not provide attention after crisis.
5. Higher intensity, Pre-Crisis	Verbal/physical aggression Self-injurious behavior High-magnitude disruption High-magnitude property destruction	Staff seek assistance and put the rest of the crisis team on notice. Staff do not talk, comfort, or attempt to teach new skills.
4. Increased frequency of lower intensity / pre-crisis behavior	Uncooperative behavior (e.g., walks around the room; chooses preferred activities/items; major disruptions; throws items; inappropriate language, tone, cadence, volume)	Staff are directive and set limits. Staff minimize conversation, comfort, or attempts to teach new skills.
3. Low intensity / pre-crisis	Uncooperative (e.g., walks around the room, avoids academic demands, breaks pencils)	Staff redirects and reinforces appropriate behaviors. Remind student or prompt coping skills taught during an earlier time of on-task stable functioning. (Be careful: Hugs are probably not effective.)
2. Off task, pre-crisis / minor acting out / anxiety	Off-task behaviors (e.g., shuts down, overly quiet, overly talkative, minor perseverance on item activity)	Staff offer assistance, are supportive and empathetic. (Hugs are OK.)
1. On task / stable functioning	Cooperative, follows instruction, engages in behaviors targeted to excel	Staff reinforces, praises targeted behaviors, teaches coping strategies, etc. (Hugs are OK.)

Note: Escalation continuum based on Fleisig (2004).

References

Fleisig, N. (2004). *Professional crisis management: A cognitive-behavioral approach.* Professional Crisis Management Association. https://pcma.com/what-is-pcm.html

Appendix 36: ACT Matrix for Groups and Teams

The Acceptance and Commitment Training (ACT) Matrix, developed by Polk et al. in 2016, effectively enhances personal and group awareness, promotes thoughtful choices, and builds better habits. When applied among educators, the ACT Matrix facilitates a collaborative environment where faculty and staff can collectively identify and commit to shared professional values, recognize behaviors that hinder effective teaching, and actively engage in practices that enhance the educational environment.

This matrix allows faculty and staff to openly address internal thoughts and feelings that may impact their teaching effectiveness. Together, they can devise committed actions that align with collective goals of respect, engagement, and mutual support. This process not only aids in creating a more harmonious and supportive educational setting but also equips educators with essential skills in self-awareness, empathy, and proactive problem-solving.

Educators can effectively navigate through a structured approach to self-improvement and team cohesion by incorporating the ACT Matrix into professional development activities. This fosters an inclusive culture where every educator feels valued and empowered to contribute positively, thus enhancing overall teaching outcomes and relationships within the educational community.

Sample Introduction Script

This script is a guideline for engaging your group or team in the ACT Matrix activity. You may need to modify the wording based on your needs.

"Hello, everyone, and thank you for joining today's workshop. Our focus in this session will be on the ACT Matrix. This tool is designed to help us understand and align our actions with what truly matters to us in our educational roles. It's a simple yet powerful way to explore our professional behaviors and how they impact our teaching and students.

"The ACT Matrix will help us identify our shared values as educators—the principles that inspire and guide us daily. We'll also examine any internal experiences or behaviors preventing us from fully embodying these values. From there, we will outline specific, positive actions to enhance our effectiveness and satisfaction in the classroom.

"The goal is to improve our teaching practices and build a stronger, more supportive community of educators. Understanding our collective strengths and challenges can create a more cohesive and harmonious working environment.

"We'll work together to identify ways to support each other in making meaningful changes that benefit ourselves and our students. This is about turning our shared insights into concrete actions and fostering a culture of continuous improvement and mutual support.

"Let's begin by discussing what we all value most in our teaching and how we can make these values even more alive in everyday interactions. Are we all ready? Let's get started."

Using the ACT Matrix

When facilitating the ACT Matrix with faculty and staff, it's essential to have a large representation of the matrix visible, whether on a board, chart paper, or electronic display like PowerPoint or a smart whiteboard. You should capture the educators' responses on the matrix as you work through it with your team. Ensure you include all the components, as shown below, when creating the matrix. Review each quadrant with the educators, and explain the meaning of each component. Provide examples, some of which are given below.

The ACT Matrix is divided into four quadrants. These quadrants will help you and your team categorize your private thoughts, feelings, and bodily sensations (covert behaviors) and actions others can see (overt behaviors). This process will assist you and the team in identifying whether your actions align with your values as a school community.

Procedure: Engaging Teams in the ACT Matrix

Step 1: Values—Chosen Life Directions (Bottom Right Quadrant)

Description:

- Values are chosen life directions that influence our group actions and decisions but are not destinations themselves. They represent what is collectively important and give us a sense of purpose.
- The process involves reflecting on the qualities the group aspires to embody in their professional roles and the type of educators they want to be.

Start in the lower right quadrant. Explain to the team that values are those ways of being and doing that give your life meaning. Values can also be considered reinforcers or important things to us. You might ask, What things do you value or consider important to you as an educator. What do you want for yourself and a member of this school community? Here, you'll guide the educators in identifying and affirming shared personal and professional values that give the group a sense of purpose and direction.

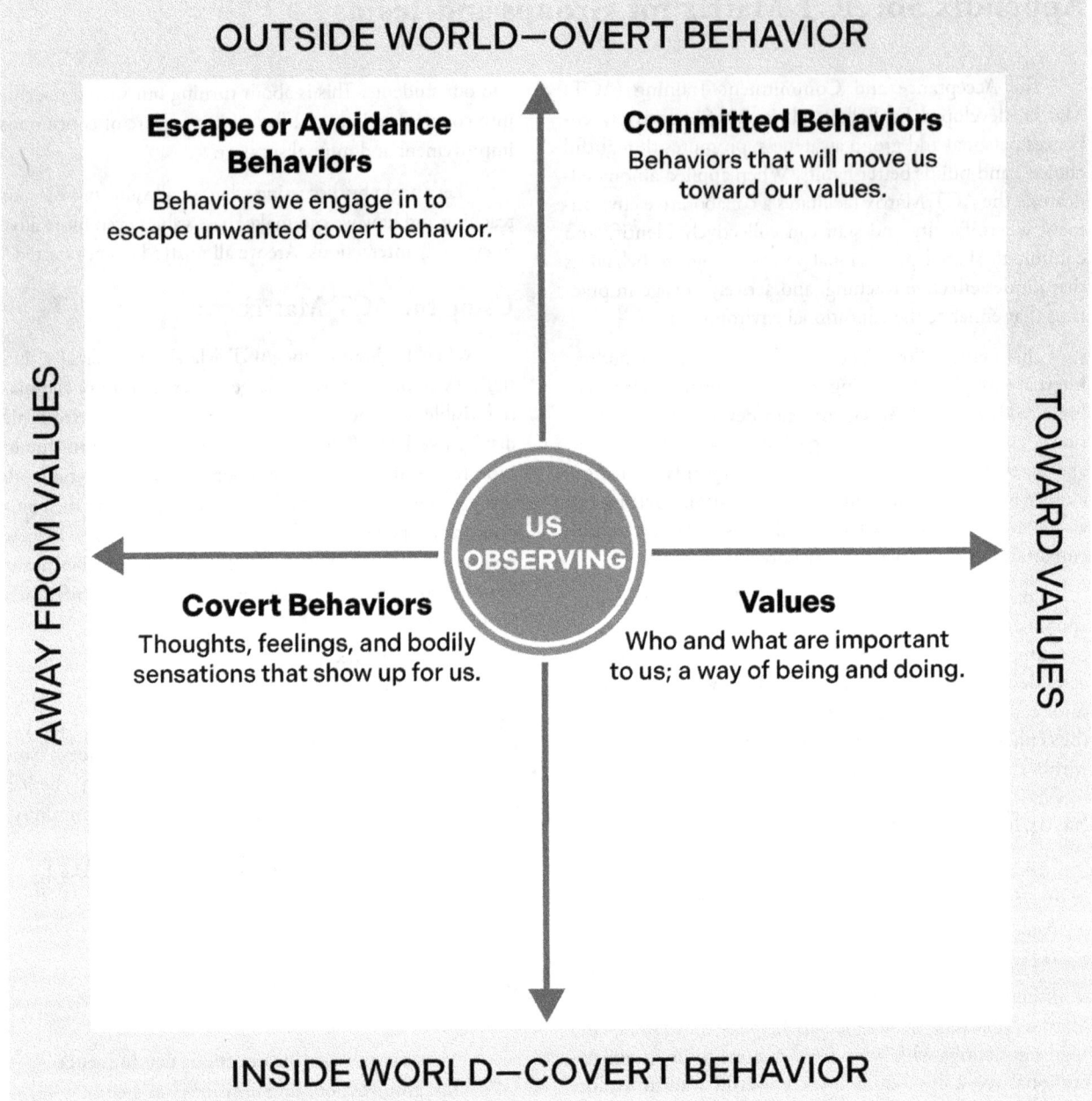

1. **Exploration of Shared Values:** Facilitate a discussion to articulate what is fundamentally important in personal and professional life. This might include effective communicators, supportive team members, or innovative educators.

2. **Reflection and Articulation:** Encourage the group to reflect on and articulate the shared qualities they value, such as kindness, compassion, authenticity, intelligence, and resilience.

3. **Values Alignment:** Together, examine how current behaviors and practices align with these stated values, identifying areas for realignment.

Values Examples:

- **Positive School and Learning Environment:** "As educators, we value fostering a nurturing environment that encourages student growth and confidence."
- **Continuous Learning:** "We strive to improve our teaching methods to better serve our students by being reflective educators."
- **Collaboration:** "We work together by sharing strategies during our professional learning communities, discussing ways to support struggling students through differentiated instruction,

and pooling resources to enhance classroom engagement and management."

Step 2: Covert Behavior—Getting Stuck (Bottom Left Quadrant)

- Covert behaviors are internal experiences, such as thoughts and feelings, that only each group member can observe for themselves. They often involve getting caught up in thoughts that lead to actions and behaviors that pull us further from our values.

- Common group experiences include ruminating about past mistakes, worrying about future failures, harsh judgments about themselves or others, and adhering rigidly to rules about how the school environment should be. These are the negative thoughts and feelings that show up when we are faced with difficult, challenging, or uncomfortable situations or environments.

In the bottom left-hand corner, educators should reflect on the challenges they face when the school environment is not conducive to teaching and learning. Educators may experience frustration, stress, or self-doubt when morale is low, there is disorganization, or they perceive a lack of support. When students seem disengaged or colleagues are not collaborative, educators might feel isolated, unappreciated, or anxious. These emotions are further compounded when school leadership or colleagues fail to provide the necessary support, especially when dealing with misbehaving students, insufficient resources, or inconsistent policies. This can lead to frustration, burnout, or a sense of helplessness. Facilitate discussion about those negative statements or the things we say to ourselves about our behavior, and list them in the lower left quadrant of the ACT Matrix.

1. **Creating a Safe Space for Sharing:** Remind faculty and staff they are in a safe space to discuss their thoughts and feelings and that it is OK to be honest and authentic in sharing their feelings.

2. **Capturing Covert Behaviors:** When listing covert behavior in the bottom left-hand corner, write exactly the phrase or thought. See the examples below.

3. **Identifying Values Misalignment:** Ask the team to reflect on how these negative thoughts and feelings might impact their behavior in the school environment and in the classroom.

Covert Behavior Examples:

- "I call for support, and no one ever comes!" "I have to deal with all this problem behavior with no help!"
- "I'm not cut out for this. I chose the wrong profession. I want to quit!"
- "The administration doesn't care, so why should I?"
- "Nothing will ever change! These kids are so bad. There's nothing I can do!"

Step 3: Escape and Avoidance Behavior—Problem Behavior (Upper Left Quadrant)

Description

- Engaging in escape or avoidance behavior is distancing yourself from negative thoughts and sensations.

- By engaging in certain behaviors and experiencing relief from those unpleasant thoughts and sensations, you effectively engage in escape behavior.

- While we all behave in ways that allow us to escape things that may be aversive, these behaviors move us away from what we value and often prevent us from reaching our goals.

- Engaging in these behaviors provides us with immediate but temporary relief.

In the top left corner, reflect on the behaviors we engage in when we get stuck in the cycle of negative thoughts and feelings within the school environment. In these moments, we might resort to escape or avoidant behaviors, such as withdrawing from collaborative efforts, delaying grading or lesson planning, or disengaging from staff meetings. As educators, we need to reflect on when these negative thoughts and feelings arise and recognize our own avoidance behaviors that attempt to eliminate the discomfort. These behaviors often move us away from professional values, such as fostering student growth or maintaining a positive learning environment. Discuss the group's overt actions to alleviate the distress from covert behaviors and assess their alignment with core values.

Escape and Avoidance Behavior Examples:

- **Minimizing student engagement** by relying on lecture-heavy lessons rather than incorporating more interactive, student-centered activities to avoid potential classroom management challenges.

- **Avoiding parent communication** by delaying or skipping difficult conversations with parents about a student's progress or behavior, especially when the discussion might lead to conflict.

- **Procrastinating on curriculum updates** or lesson planning, especially when faced with the need to modify or improve ineffective teaching methods.

- **Skipping professional development opportunities** to avoid confronting gaps in skills or knowledge, leading to stagnation in teaching practice.

- **Relying on punitive discipline** as a quick fix instead of addressing underlying student issues or working on behavior interventions because it's easier in the moment to maintain control.

Step 4: Pinpointed Committed Behavior—Getting Unstuck (Top Right Quadrant)

Description:

- Committing to actions that align with shared values is crucial, even in the face of challenging emotions or thoughts. This involves accepting emotions without letting them dictate actions—unhooking from unhelpful thoughts.
- The group emphasizes behavioral action that moves toward shared values, accepting emotions as they are and reducing their disruptive impact.

In the top right-hand corner, discuss with the team the behaviors they can or should engage in when negative thoughts and feelings arise. Committed behaviors are the actions you engage in instead of the problematic behaviors. These behaviors will move you toward your values and the right side of the matrix. Create a list of committed behaviors aligned with shared school values. Remind educators that they should acknowledge those covert behaviors—and the negative thoughts and feelings when they show up—and remember those committed actions and those behaviors they need to engage in instead.

1. **Identifying Committed Group Actions:** As a group, define specific, actionable behaviors that align with the shared values. This might include practices like actively listening to one another, offering constructive feedback, or supporting a peer through a challenging task.
2. **Implementation Planning:** Discuss as a group how these behaviors can be implemented. Plan together to anticipate any possible obstacles, and develop strategies to address them effectively.
3. **Commitment as a Group:** Each educator commits to these behaviors, understanding their role in fostering a positive and inclusive learning environment.

Examples of Committed Behaviors:

- **Incorporating interactive teaching methods:** Instead of relying on lecture-heavy lessons, actively engage students through group discussions, hands-on activities, or technology-based learning to enhance student involvement and participation.
- **Proactively communicating with parents:** Address concerns about student progress or behavior early on through regular updates, emails, or phone calls, fostering a collaborative approach with families to support student success.
- **Staying consistent with lesson planning and curriculum updates:** Set aside dedicated time each week to review and improve lesson plans or update curriculum materials, ensuring they meet students' needs and learning objectives.
- **Engaging in professional development:** Actively seek out workshops, courses, or peer collaboration to develop new skills and stay updated with teaching best practices, fostering growth and innovation in the classroom.
- **Implementing positive behavior interventions:** Instead of relying on punitive discipline, use proactive strategies such as positive reinforcement, restorative practices, or behavior contracts to address underlying student issues and encourage responsible decision-making.

Step 5: Metrics and Evaluation (Continuous Review and Adjustment)

Description:

- Metrics serve as tangible indicators of progress and effectiveness, helping the group quantitatively assess how well they manage their behaviors and achieve their goals.
- These metrics should be specific, measurable, achievable, relevant, and time-bound (SMART), providing a clear basis for ongoing evaluation and adjustment.

Establish clear metrics to evaluate the effectiveness of the group's actions in alignment with their shared values and committed behaviors.

Procedure:

1. **Identification of Relevant Metrics:** Collaboratively determine what specific outcomes the group wants to measure. This could include the frequency of engaged teaching practices, reductions in stress-related behaviors, improvements in collaborative planning and execution, or increases in student engagement and performance.
2. **Setting Baselines and Targets:** Establish baseline data for each metric, and set realistic targets for improvement. This might involve pre- and post-assessments of educator engagement, student feedback, peer evaluations, or other relevant data points.
3. **Regular Data Collection:** Implement a schedule for collecting data on these metrics. Decide who will be responsible for data collection and analysis and how often this will occur (e.g., monthly or quarterly).
4. **Review and Adjust Actions:** Schedule regular meetings to review the metrics and discuss progress. Use this data to decide whether current strategies are effective or need adjustment. Celebrate successes and collaboratively problem-solve areas where targets are not being met.

Examples of Metrics:

- **Engagement Metrics:** Number of active participations in team meetings and professional development sessions.
- **Performance Metrics:** Changes in student performance metrics pre- and post-implementation of new teaching strategies.
- **Well-Being Metrics:** Reduction in reported stress levels and absenteeism among educators.
- **Collaboration Metrics:** Increase in cross-departmental projects or joint lesson planning sessions.

References

Polk, K. L., Schoendorff, B., Webster, M., & Olaz, F. O. (2016). *The essential guide to the ACT matrix: A step-by-step approach to using the ACT matrix model in clinical practice.* Context Press.

References

Allen, S. & Hartman, N. (2008), Leader development: An exploration of sources of learning. *Development and Learning in Organizations, 22*(6), 75–88. https://doi.org/10.1108/dlo.2008.08122fad.003

Atkins, P. W., Wilson, D. S., & Hayes, S. C. (2019). *Prosocial: Using evolutionary science to build productive, equitable, and collaborative groups.* New Harbinger Publications.

Austin, J. (2000). Performance analysis and performance diagnostics. In J. Austin & J. E. Carr (Eds.), *Handbook of applied behavior analysis* (pp. 321–349). Context Press.

Balfanz, R. & Legters, N. (2004). *Locating the dropout crisis: Which high schools produce the nation's dropouts? Where are they located? Who attends them?* Center for Research on the Education of Students Placed at Risk, The Johns Hopkins University. http://jhir.library.jhu.edu/handle/1774.2/62930

Basile, M. (2012). The cost-effectiveness of socioeconomic school integration. In R. D. Kahlenberg (Ed.), *The future of school integration: Socioeconomic diversity as an education reform strategy.* Century Foundation Press.

Binder, C. (1996). Behavioral fluency: Evolution of a new paradigm. *The Behavior Analyst, 19*, 163–197. https://doi.org/10.1007/BF03393163

Borich, G. D., & Tombari, M. L. (1997). *Educational psychology: A contemporary approach* (2nd ed.). Addison Wesley Longman.

Carey, R. G., & Bucher, B. (1981). Identifying the educative and suppressive effects of positive practice and restitutional overcorrection. *Journal of Applied Behavior Analysis, 14*(1), 71–80. https://doi.org/10.1901/jaba.1981.14-71

Carr, J. E., & Wilder, D. A. (2016). The performance diagnostic checklist—Human services: A correction. *Behavior Analysis in Practice, 9*(1), 63. https://doi.org/10.1007/s40617-015-0099-3

Carr, J. E., Wilder, D. A., Majdalany, L., Mathisen, D., & Strain L. A. (2013a). An assessment-based solution to a human-service employee performance problem: An initial evaluation of the Performance Diagnostic Checklist—Human Services. *Behavior Analysis in Practice, 6*(1), 16–32. https://doi.org/10.1007/BF03391789

Carr, J. E., Wilder, D. A., Majdalany, L., Mathisen, D., & Strain, L. A. (2013b). Performance diagnostic checklist—human services. PsycTESTS Dataset. https://doi.org/10.1037/t32807-000

Center on PBIS. (2020, July). *Creating effective classroom environments plan template.* https://www.pbis.org/resource/creating-effective-classroom-environments-plan-template

Chandler, L. K., & Dahlquist, C. M. (2006). *Functional assessment: Strategies to prevent and remediate challenging behavior in school settings.* Merrill Prentice Hall.

Cheng, C., & Zhao, J. (2023). The impact of professional learning communities on pre-service teachers' professional commitment. *Frontiers in Psychology, 14.* https://doi.org/10.3389/fpsyg.2023.1153016

Chiesa, A., & Malinowski, P. (2011). Mindfulness-based approaches: Are they all the same? *Journal of Clinical Psychology, 67*(4), 404–424. https://doi.org/10.1002/jclp.20776

Childs, K. E., Kincaid, D., George, H. P., & Gage, N. A. (2015). The relationship between school-wide implementation of positive behavior intervention and supports and student discipline outcomes. *Journal of Positive Behavior Interventions, 18*(2), 89–99. https://doi.org/10.1177/1098300715590398

Conyers, C., Miltenberger, R., Maki, A., Barenz, R., Jurgens, M., Sailer, A., Haugen, M., & Kopp, B. (2004). A comparison of response cost and differential reinforcement of other behavior to reduce disruptive behavior in a preschool classroom. *Journal of Applied Behavior Analysis, 37*(3), 411–415. https://doi.org/10.1901/jaba.2004.37-411

Cooper, J. O., Heron, T. E., & Heward, W. L. (2020). *Applied behavior analysis* (3rd ed.). Pearson Education.

Daniels, A. C. (2000). *Bringing out the best in people: How to apply the astonishing power of positive reinforcement.* McGraw-Hill.

Daniels, A. C. (2016). *Bringing out the best in people: How to apply the astonishing power of positive reinforcement.* (3rd ed.). McGraw-Hill.

Daniels, A. C., & Daniels, J. E. (2004). *Performance management: Changing behavior that drives organizational effectiveness.* Performance Management Publications.

Daniels, A. C., & Rosen, T. A. (1989). *Performance management: Improving quality and productivity through positive reinforcement.* Performance Management Publications.

Darling-Hammond, L., Hyler, M. E., & Gardner, M. (2017, June 5). *Effective teacher professional development.* Learning Policy Institute. https://doi.org/10.54300/122.311

Dietz, S. M., & Repp, A. C. (1973). Decreasing classroom misbehavior through the use of DRL schedules of reinforcement. *Journal of Applied Behavior Analysis, 6*(3), 457–463. https://doi.org/10.1901/jaba.1973.6-457

Dunlap, G., Kern, L., dePerczel, M., Clarke, S., Wilson, D., Childs, K. E., White, R., & Falk, G. D. (1993). Functional analysis of classroom variables for students with emotional and behavioral disorders. *Behavioral Disorders, 18*(4), 275–291. https://doi.org/10.1177/019874299301800403

Eckert, S. A. (2013). What do teaching qualifications mean in urban schools? A mixed-methods study of teacher preparation and qualification. *Journal of Teacher Education, 64*(1), 75–89. https://doi.org/10.1177/0022487112460279

Ferguson, R. F. (2012). Can student surveys measure teaching quality? *Phi Delta Kappan, 94*(3). 24–28. https://doi.org/10.1177/003172171209400306

Fleisig, N. (2004). *Professional crisis management: A cognitive-behavioral approach.* Professional Crisis Management Association. https://pcma.com/what-is-pcm.html

Foxx, R. M. (1996). Translating the covenant: The behavior analyst as ambassador and translator. *The Behavior Analyst, 19*, 147–161. https://doi.org/10.1007/BF03393162

Gavoni, P., & Costa, A. (2023). *Quick wins! Using behavior science to accelerate and sustain school improvement* (2nd ed.). KeyPress Publishing.

Gavoni, P., Edmonds, W. A., Kennedy, T. D., & Gollery, T. (2017). Data on the data: A method for improving the fidelity of office discipline referral completion. *The Journal of Teacher*

Action Research, 3(2), 30–44. https://nsuworks.nova.edu/cps_facarticles/1804/

Gavoni, P., & Weatherly, N. L. (2024). *Deliberate coaching: Optimizing teaching and learning through behavior science.* KeyPress Publishing.

Greenberg, J., Putman, H., & Walsh, K. (2014). *Training our future teachers: Classroom management. Revised.* National Council on Teacher Quality. https://eric.ed.gov/?id=ED556312

Grissom, J. A., Egalite, A. J., & Lindsay, C. A. (2021). *How principals affect students and schools.* Wallace Foundation. https://wallacefoundation.org/sites/default/files/2024-09/how-principals-affect-students-and-schools.doi_.10.59656%252FEL-SB1065.001.pdf

Guinness, K., Detrich, R., Keyworth, R., & States, J. (2020). *Overview of corrective feedback.* The Wing Institute. https://www.winginstitute.org/instructional-delivery-feedback

Gunter, P. L., Shores, R. E., Jack, S. L., Rasmussen, S. K., & Flowers, J. (1995). On the move using teacher/student proximity to improve students' behavior. *TEACHING Exceptional Children, 28*(1), 12–14. https://doi.org/10.1177/004005999502800103

Hall, G. E., & Hord, S. M. (2011). *Implementing change: Patterns, principles, and potholes* (3rd ed.). Pearson.

Hirschfield, P. J. (2008). Preparing for prison? The criminalization of school discipline in the USA. *Theoretical Criminology, 12*(1), 79–101. https://doi.org/10.1177/1362480607085795

Iwata, B. A., & Bailey, J. S. (1974). Reward versus cost token systems: An analysis of the effects on students and teachers. *Journal of Applied Behavior Analysis, 7*(4), 567–576. https://doi.org/10.1901/jaba.1974.7-567

Johnson, D. A., Johnson, C. M., & Dave, P. (2023). Performance feedback in organizations: Understanding the functions, forms, and important features. *Journal of Organizational Behavior Management, 43*(1), 64–89. https://doi.org/10.1080/01608061.2022.2089436

Joyce, B. R., & Showers, B. (2002). *Student achievement through staff development* (3rd ed.). Association for Supervision & Curriculum Development.

Kern, L., Bambara, L., & Fogt., J. (2002). Class-wide curricular modifications to improve the behavior of students with emotional or behavioral disorders. *Behavioral Disorders, 27*(4), 317–326. https://doi.org/10.1177/019874290202700408

Kerr, M. M., & Nelson, C. M. (1989). *Strategies for managing behavior problems in the classroom* (2nd ed.). Merrill.

Kollerová, L., Květon, P., Zábrodská, K., & Janošová, P. (2023). Teacher exhaustion: The effects of disruptive student behaviors, victimization by workplace bullying, and social support from colleagues. *Social Psychology of Education, 26,* 885–902. https://doi.org/10.1007/s11218-023-09779-x

Larrivee, B. (1992). *Strategies for effective classroom management: Creating a collaborative climate (Leader's guide to facilitate learning experiences).* Allyn & Bacon.

Lerman, D. C., & Vorndran, C. M. (2002). On the status of knowledge for using punishment: Implications for treating behavior disorders. *Journal of Applied Behavior Analysis, 35*(4), 431–464. https://doi.org/10.1901/jaba.2002.35-431

Lewis, T. J., & Sugai, G. (2017). Effective behavior support: A systems approach to proactive schoolwide management. *Focus on Exceptional Children, 31*(6). https://doi.org/10.17161/foec.v31i6.6767

Liu, X. S., & Meyer, J. P. (2005). Teachers' perceptions of their jobs: A multilevel analysis of the teacher follow-up survey for 1994–95. *Teachers College Record, 107*(5), 985–1003. https://doi.org/10.1111/j.1467-9620.2005.00501.x

MacKenzie-Keating, S. E., & McDonald, L. (1990). Overcorrection: Reviewed, revisited and revised. *The Behavior Analyst, 13*(1), 39–48. https://doi.org/10.1007/BF03392516

Martella, R. C., Nelson, J. R., Marchand-Martella, N. E., & O'Reilly, M. (2012). *Comprehensive behavior management: Individualized, classroom, and schoolwide approaches.* Sage Publications. https://doi.org/10.4135/9781452243931

Martinez, S. (2009). A system gone berserk: How are zero-tolerance policies really affecting schools? *Preventing School Failure: Alternative Education for Children and Youth, 53*(3), 153–158. https://doi.org/10.3200/PSFL.53.3.153-158

Marzano, R. J., & Waters, T. (2009). *District leadership that works: Striking the right balance.* Solution Tree Press.

Marzano, R. J., Waters, T., & McNulty, B. A. (2005). *School leadership that works: From research to results.* Association for Supervision and Curriculum Development.

Matsumoto, D., Frank, M. G., & Hwang, H. S. (Eds.). (2013). *Nonverbal communication: Science and applications.* Sage Publications. https://doi.org/10.4135/9781452244037

McIntosh, K., Girvan, E. J., Horner, R. H., & Smolkowski, K. (2014). Education not incarceration: A conceptual model for reducing racial and ethnic disproportionality in school discipline. *Journal of Applied Research on Children, 5*(2), Article 4. https://doi.org/10.58464/2155-5834.1215.

McKevitt, B. C., & Braaksma, A. D. (2008). Best practices in developing a Positive Behavior Support system at the school level. In A. Thomas & J. Grimes (Eds.), *Best practices in school psychology V: Vol. 3* (pp. 735–747). National Association of School Psychologists.

Morris, E. W., & Perry, B. L. (2016). The punishment gap: School suspension and racial disparities in achievement. *Social Problems, 63*(1), 68–86.

Mosca, F. J., & Hollister, A. (2004). External control and zero-tolerance: Is fear of our youth driving these policies? *Educational Horizons, 83*(1), 2–5. https://www.jstor.org/stable/42926518

Musti-Rao, S., & Haydon, T. (2011). Strategies to increase behavior-specific teacher praise in an inclusive environment. *Intervention in School and Clinic, 47*(2), 91–97. https://doi.org/10.1177/1053451211414187

Noltemeyer, A. L., Ward, R. M., & Mcloughlin, C. (2015). Relationship between school suspension and student outcomes: A meta-analysis. *School Psychology Review, 44*(2), 224–240. https://doi.org/10.17105/spr-14-0008.1

Northouse, P. G. (2007). *Leadership theory and practice* (4th ed.). Sage Publications.

Obee, A. F., Hart, K. C., & Fabiano, G. A. (2022). Professional development targeting classroom management and behavioral support skills in early childhood settings: A systematic review. *School Mental Health, 15*(2), 339–369. https://doi.org/10.1007/s12310-022-09562-x

Oliver, R. M., Wehby, J. H., & Reschly, D. J. (2011). Teacher classroom management practices: Effects on disruptive or aggressive student behavior. *Campbell Systematic Reviews, 7*(1), 1–55. https://doi.org/10.4073/csr.2011.4

Organisation for Economic Co-operation and Development. (2023, September 12). Education at a glance 2023: OECD indicators. https://doi.org/10.1787/e13bef63-en

Owens, R. G., & Valesky, T. C. (2010). *Organizational behavior in education: Leadership and school reform* (10th ed.). Pearson.

Palardy, G. J. (2008). Differential school effects among low, middle, and high social class composition schools: A multiple group, multilevel latent growth curve analysis. *School Effectiveness and School Improvement, 19*(1), 21–49.

Parsons, M. B., Rollyson, J. H., & Reid, D. H. (2012). Evidence-based staff training: A guide for practitioners. *Behavior Analysis in Practice, 5*(2), 2–11. https://doi.org/10.1007/BF03391819

Perone, M. (2003). Negative effects of positive reinforcement. *The Behavior Analyst, 26*(1), 1–14. https://doi.org/10.1007/BF03392064.

Perry, B. L., & Morris, E. W. (2014). Suspending progress: Collateral consequences of exclusionary punishment in public schools. *American Sociological Review, 79*(6), 1067–1087. https://doi.org/10.1177/0003122414556308

Polk, K. L., Schoendorff, B., Webster, M., & Olaz, F. O. (2016). *The essential guide to the ACT matrix: A step-by-step approach to using the ACT matrix model in clinical practice*. Context Press.

Professional Crisis Management Association. (2022, February 24). *Why hands off policies are likely to compound issues and compromise safety* [Article]. LinkedIn. https://www.linkedin.com/pulse/why-hands-off-policies-can-compound-/?trackingId=VzKCvqkERsqbeYxu1UuABg%3D%3D

Robbins, S. P., DeCenzo, D. A., & Wolter, R. M. (2013). *Supervision today!* (7th ed.). Pearson.

Robertson, S. J., Simon, S. J., Pachman, J. S., & Drabman, R. S. (1979). Self-control and generalization procedures in a classroom of disruptive retarded children. *Child Behavior Therapy, 1*(4), 347–362. https://doi.org/10.1300/J473v01n04_04

Rosen, H. S., & Rosen, L. A. (1983). Eliminating stealing: Use of stimulus control with an elementary student. *Behavior Modification, 7*(1) 56–63. https://doi.org/10.1177/01454455830071004

Ruth, W. J. (1996). Goal setting and behavior contracting for students with emotional and behavioral difficulties: Analysis of daily, weekly, and total goal attainment. *Psychology in the Schools, 33*(2), 153–158. https://doi.org/10.1002/(SICI)1520-6807(199604)33:2<153::AID-PITS8>3.0.CO;2-S

Sailor, W., Dunlap, G., Sugai, G., & Horner, R. (2009). *Handbook of Positive Behavior Support*. Springer.

Shakespeare, W. (2012). *As you like it* (H. Dubrow, Ed.). Wadsworth Cengage Learning. (Original work published 1623)

Simonsen, B., Fairbanks, S., Briesch, A., & Sugai, G. (2006). *Classroom management: Self-assessment revised*. Center on Positive Behavioral Interventions and Supports. https://www.pbis.org/resource/positive-behavior-support-classroom-management-self-assessment

Simonsen, B., Myers, D., Everett, S., Sugai, G., Spencer, R., & LaBreck, C. (2012). Explicitly teaching social skills schoolwide: Using a matrix to guide instruction. *Intervention in School and Clinic, 47*(5), 259–266. https://doi.org/10.1177/1053451211430121

Skiba, R. J., & Peterson, R. L. (2000). School discipline at a crossroads: From zero tolerance to early response. *Exceptional Children, 66*(3), 335–346. https://journals.sagepub.com/doi/10.1177/001440290006600305

Skinner, B. F. (1956). A case history in scientific method. *American Psychologist, 11*(5), 221–233. https://doi.org/10.1037/h0047662

Skinner, B. F. (1984). The shame of American education. *American Psychologist, 39*(9), 947–954. https://doi.org/10.1037/0003-066X.39.9.947

Sprick, R. (2003). *Safe transitions and reduced tardies (START) on time!* Pacific Northwest.

Sprick, R., Knight, J., Reinke, W., McKale Skyles, T., & Barnes, L. (2010). *Coaching classroom management: Strategies & tools for administrators & coaches*. Pacific Northwest Publishing.

Strahun, J., O'Connor, A., & Peterson, R. L. (2013). *Behavior contracting strategy brief*. Student Engagement Project, University of Nebraska-Lincoln and the Nebraska Department of Education.

Tyre, A., Feuerborn, L., & Pierce, J. (2011). Schoolwide intervention to reduce chronic tardiness at the middle and high school levels. *Preventing School Failure: Alternative Education for Children and Youth, 55*(3), 132–139. https://doi.org/10.1080/10459880903472918

Valenti, M. W., & Kerr, M. M. (2015). Addressing individual perspectives in the development of schoolwide rules: A data-informed process. *Journal of Positive Behavior Interventions, 17*(4), 245–253. https://doi.org/10.1177/1098300714544405

Vilke, G. M. (2020). Restraint physiology: A review of the literature. *Journal of Forensic and Legal Medicine, 75*. https://doi.org/10.1016/j.jflm.2020.102056

Wagner, K. (2012, May 30). Coaching your way to safe habits. *Aubrey Daniels International*. https://www.aubreydaniels.com/blog/2012/05/30/coaching-your-way-to-safe-habits#sthash.C9YtaSMh.dpuf

Watkins, C. (2022, November 18). "I miss the old me": Family continues fighting for change 3 years after 6-year-old girl's arrest. *WESH*. https://www.wesh.com/article/orlando-six-year-old-arrested/41997860

Weddle, H., Lockton, M., & Datnow, A. (2023). Fostering, tailoring, negotiating: The complexities of collaborative coaching in schools under pressure to improve. *Educational Researcher, 52*(8), 482–490. https://doi.org/10.3102/0013189X231187372

Westling, D. L. (2010). Teachers and challenging behavior: Knowledge, views, and practices. *Remedial and Special Education, 31*(1), 48–63. https://doi.org/10.1177/0741932508327466

Winston, M. (2016). *Adventures in special education and applied behavior analysis: A practical guidebook for understanding and solving problem behaviors in school*. Sloan Educational Publishing.

Witt, J. C., & Beck, R. (1999). *One-minute academic functional assessment and interventions: "Can't" do it or "won't" do it*. Sopris West.

Witt, J. C., & Elliot, S. N. (1982). The response cost lottery: A time efficient and effective classroom intervention. *Journal of School Psychology, 20*(2), 155–161. https://doi.org/10.1016/0022-4405(82)90009-7

Glossary of Terms

A-B-C – A description of a response in terms of the Antecedent (**A**), Behavior (**B**), and Consequence (**C**). A three-term contingency analysis.

Acceptance and Commitment Training (ACT) – A mindfulness-based approach rooted in the science of human behavior. It encourages being present in the moment by helping people become better observers of their behavior, better observers of their behavior's impact on the environment, and better observers of the environment's impact on their behavior. This includes both the environment outside of their skin and inside of their skin.

Acquisition – The time during which a student learns a new behavior. Data collected on the rate (speed) and accuracy of the skill inform the interventionist working with an individual if the teaching procedures need adjustment.

Antecedent – The stimulus that comes immediately before the behavior and gets it going.

Applied Behavior Analysis (ABA) – The field of applying the science of learning to socially significant human behavior.

Aversive Stimulus – A stimulus that increases the rate of behavior that eliminates or reduces it. If behavior is strengthened when the stimulus is removed, it is an aversive stimulus. Aversive stimuli are idiosyncratic, meaning what is aversive varies from person to person. Also called a negative reinforcer.

Baseline Data – During observation, we gather data relevant to the behavior of interest before initiating intervention.

Behavior – Some action made by an individual. Behavior is the movement of a person in the environment.

Behavior Contract – A statement of contingencies. Contracts specify behavior to perform and outline reinforcement or rewards contingent upon the behavior. Contracts are set in advance and may involve the student in developing the contract.

Behavior Intervention Plan – A written description outlining how individuals should respond to decrease inappropriate behavior and increase appropriate behavior.

Board Certified Behavior Analyst® – A person who satisfied all requirements to acquire the BCBA® designation and can, therefore, call themselves a Board Certified Behavior Analyst. Requirements include a requisite number of hours of university-level course work in the science of behavior, internship under the supervision of a BCBA, and passing the required written examination. To maintain certification, there are continuing education requirements. There are currently two levels of certification: Board Certified Behavior Analyst (BCBA) and Board Certified Assistant Behavior Analyst® (BCaBA®). The exact requirements and most current information regarding how to become or locate a BCBA are available through the Behavior Analyst Certification Board® website, www.BACB.com.

Classroom Management Plan – A plan for specific skills and procedures for managing the classroom. A classroom management plan includes rules, outlined expectations, and procedures for activities and routines that occur in the classroom. The plan should also include how a teacher will teach, reinforce, and correct student behavior.

Coaching – The process of supporting the transference of learned skills into the school and classroom environment so they are maintained by naturally occurring reinforcement.

Committed Behavior – The actions you engage in that are not problematic behaviors. The actions that move you toward your values and the right side of the matrix.

Consequence – The specific, immediate result of a given behavior. The consequence may or may not alter how often the behavior occurs in the future. A reinforcing consequence increases the likelihood that the behavior occurs again. A punishing consequence reduces the likelihood that the behavior will occur again.

Covert Behavior – Internal experiences, such as thoughts and feelings, that are only observed by the individual. These often involve getting caught up in our thoughts, where we let them control our actions, causing us to get stuck.

Data – Quantitative information gathered to guide the progress of decision-making.

Data-Based Decision-Making – A set of rules based on relevant data that allows teachers to decide when to change programs or methods.

Duration – The time from the start to the completion of the action or behavior.

Error Correction – When misbehavior occurs, the student is reminded of the expectations. Error correction interventions should be brief, concise, and delivered without emotion or judgment.

Escape and Avoidance Behavior – Behavior that is distancing from negative thoughts and sensations. Effectively escaping by engaging in certain behaviors and experiencing relief from unpleasant thoughts and sensations. These behaviors provide immediate but temporary relief.

Extinction – To cease reinforcing a previously reinforced behavior to decrease the behavior's frequency.

Fading – Gradually remove extra prompts introduced into a teaching situation.

Feedback – An indication of the accuracy or the effectiveness of an action or behavior.

Fluency – A measure of the ability of an individual to complete a given number of responses accurately within a given time. High rates of fluency are associated with effortless and proficient performance.

Frequency – Refers to the number of target responses counted. For example, "the student made seven initiations to his peers."

Functional Behavior Assessment – A process to identify the events in the environment that maintain a response. Functional assessment helps to answer questions such as "Why does that behavior occur?" or "Under what conditions is that behavior more likely?"

Generalization – Refers to variation in response or setting. We strive to generalize across time, setting, people, and instructional materials.

Graphing – The representation of data on a grid to allow visual analysis. In other words, graphs that are easily understood help people make judgments regarding changes in behavior over time. Graphs make for easy summarization of trend, level, and variability in behavior. Graphs are used to assess learning progress and make teaching and/or treatment decisions.

Group Contingencies – The entire class or small group works together toward a goal. An individual's inappropriate behavior affects the reward for the entire class or group.

Menu of Consequences – A matrix of a continuum of defining and classifying behavior, and strategies for intervening and correcting misbehavior at various levels.

Natural Reinforcers – Reinforcers that are naturally present where the behavior occurs. Natural reinforcers occur when the behavior produces an environmental change that gives the person pleasure. A natural reinforcer is a consequence that results from the very performance of the behavior we want the student to learn; that consequence motivates the student to engage in those behaviors again.

Negative Reinforcement – Describes a relationship between events in which the rate of a behavior's occurrence increases when some (usually aversive or unpleasant) environmental condition is removed or reduced in intensity. It leads to an increase in the future probability of a given behavior. For example, when a student engages in tantrum behavior after the teacher asks them to perform a task, the teacher withdraws the request due to the tantrum. In such a case, the teacher has accidentally negatively reinforced the tantrum and unwittingly made it more likely to happen in the future.

Organizational Behavior Management (OBM) – A subdiscipline of applied behavior analysis. It involves the application of behavior-analytic principles and contingency management techniques to change behavior in organizational settings. OBM focuses on assessing and changing the work environment to improve employee performance and workplace culture.

Out-of-School Suspension (OSS) – Out-of-school suspensions are disciplinary actions that temporarily remove a student from the school environment due to violations of school policies or behavioral expectations. During the suspension, students are prohibited from attending classes, participating in school activities, or being on school grounds. While intended as a consequence for serious infractions, suspensions may also result in missed instructional time, reduced academic progress, and weakened connections with peers and school staff.

Pit to Paradise – A metaphor that illustrates conditions where a student is removed from class to a more reinforcing environment.

Pivot Praise – Praise or earned rewards used to reinforce other students engaging in appropriate behavior and expectations. Reinforcement is available to the target student once they engage in the appropriate behavior or expectation.

Planned Ignoring – The teacher ignores the student's misbehavior, given that the behavior is not dangerous and/or the behavior will not spread to other students.

Positive Behavior Supports (PBS), Positive Behavioral Interventions and Supports (PBIS) – A decision-making framework for basing educational procedures on student progress data. Requires evidence-based teaching practices for both academic and social behavior.

Positive Punishment – Behavior results from something being added (+) to the student's environment. A stimulus is added, and the probability of future behavior decreases. For example, if a student runs in the hallway and is required to walk back, in the future, the student will most likely refrain from running in the hallway.

Positive Reinforcement – Describes a relationship between events in which the rate of a behavior's occurrence increases when some (usually pleasant) environmental condition is added or increased in intensity. It leads to an increase in the future probability of a given behavior. As with other consequences, it is important to remember that a stimulus is only a positive reinforcer if, when presented, it increases the future probability of the behavior.

Premack Principle (aka Grandma's Law) – This is "first-then" contingency. Essentially, the student must work before play (e.g., "First complete your 10 math problems, and then you can have computer time").

Problem Behavior – Any action severe enough or frequent enough to endanger or impede a student's or peers' academic or social progress. It may also be referred to as target problem behavior, misbehavior, or challenging behavior.

Prompt – Makes the desired behavior more likely. Think of prompts as hints. When you use a prompt, you should think about how to fade it out. This allows the student to respond to environmental cues on their own. In instruction, the prompt occurs as part of the antecedent condition (before the behavior occurs).

Proximity Control – The teacher moves closer to the student that misbehaves. This often is enough for the student to stop the undesired behavior.

Punishment – A stimulus follows a response and decreases the likelihood that the response occurs again.

QUICK – **Q**uestioning; **U**nconditional positive regard; **I**ntermittent reinforcement; **C**onstructive; **K**eep it brief.

QUICK Responses – A menu of consequences for responding to student misbehavior.

QUICK Room – An alternative to out-of-school suspension, in-school suspension, detention, or time-out of class.

QUICK Team – A group of people who provide systematic and function-based responses to high-magnitude behaviors that require a student's removal from the classroom.

Rate – A measure of frequency across a specific time. For example, *a student gets out of their seat seven times per hour.*

Redirection – An attempt by one individual to interrupt a student engaging in a behavior (often an inappropriate behavior) and engage them in an alternate (generally more appropriate) behavior.

Reinforcement – A process that increases behavior, whether it is positive or negative. Describes a relationship between events in which the rate of a behavior's occurrence increases when some environmental condition is added or removed, or increased or reduced in intensity. It leads to an increase in the future probability of a given behavior. The adding or subtracting of stimuli that increases occurrences of behavior (be it desirable or undesirable) is known as positive or negative reinforcement. See also **Positive Reinforcement** and **Negative Reinforcement**.

Reinforcer – A consequence that increases the future probability of the behavior that immediately preceded it. The only way a reinforcer can be identified is by the effect it has on future behavior.

School-Wide Positive Behavior Supports (SWPBS) – A proactive process that supports the needs and culture of the school by assisting school administrators, teachers, and staff to adopt and organize evidence-based behavior interventions into an integrated system that enhances academic performance and social behavior outcomes for all students.

Shaping – Process used to create new behavior by differentially reinforcing successive approximations to a desired behavior (the target response).

Social Reinforcers – Reinforcers that consist of interactions with other individuals (high five, thumbs up, wink).

Time-Out From Positive Reinforcement – Often called "time-out" for short; refers to a collection of often misused techniques. Time-out is when a reinforcer is removed or withheld in some way for a short period, contingent upon some inappropriate behavior emitted by an individual. This can take the form of an individual going to a different setting (e.g., the common time-out chair). However, time-out need not take this form, and there are good reasons to avoid this use (e.g., accidentally reinforcing with attention, or accidentally reinforcing avoidance behavior). Time-out can be accomplished within the setting (e.g., a TV is turned off for 10 seconds following cussing while watching).

Values – Ways of being and doing that give our lives meaning. Who we want to be, and what we want our lives to be about.

About the Authors

Paul "Paulie" Gavoni, EdD, BCBA-D

Dr. Paul "Paulie" Gavoni, an esteemed behavior analyst, educator, and leader, has shaped human performance and organizational leadership since 1995. In roles such as COO, vice president, school administrator, school turnaround manager, district behavior analyst, clinical coordinator, and professor, he has unified his innovative approach through a dedication to human behavior science, aiming to enhance performance and leadership.

With a deep knowledge of organizational behavior science, Dr. Gavoni tackles real-world problems, candidly addressing the shortcomings in performance improvement and change management. His ability to identify practical solutions, all firmly grounded in behavioral science, emphasizes his unwavering integrity. He employs science to foster engaging and highly productive environments and adheres to a philosophy that cultivating excellence in employees naturally leads to an environment that supports the sustainable achievement of desired results.

Dr. Gavoni's reach extends internationally across education, behavior analysis, and human service organizations. He hosts the top-ranked *Crisis in Education* podcast and *Thoughts and Rants of a Behavior Scientist* podcast, and he is a *Wall Street Journal* and *USA Today* best-selling coauthor. His books, built on the principles of behavior analysis, balance technical depth with accessibility while providing fresh perspectives and actionable solutions to modern educational and performance challenges.

A sought-after international speaker, Dr. Gavoni blends professionalism with approachability and concentrates on tangible problems and realistic solutions. His authenticity and firsthand experiences facilitate a strong connection with audiences and allow him to express concerns about educational systems and the adverse effects of certain methodologies, while concurrently offering positive, science-based alternatives.

Beyond his work in education and human services, Dr. Gavoni is a Golden Gloves champion and highly respected striking coach in combat sports. Coach "Paulie Gloves," as he's known in the mixed martial arts community, has trained world champions and UFC vets using technologies rooted in the behavioral sciences.

Dr. Gavoni holds a bachelor's degree in social work from Florida Atlantic University, a master's degree in social work from Barry University, a specialist degree in educational leadership from Nova Southeastern University, and a doctorate degree in organizational leadership from Nova Southeastern University.

Anika Costa, MSEd, BCBA

Anika Costa was first introduced to applied behavior analysis (ABA) in 2000 while working as a speech therapist. This experience sparked a passion that has driven her career for over 2 decades in behavior and performance support. Anika has worked in educational, private, and community-based agencies, providing effective interventions and leading initiatives to enhance individual and organizational performance.

Anika's experience in education as a classroom teacher, instructional coach, and behavior analyst allows her to work effectively with educators and school leaders to enhance classroom and school-wide outcomes. She specializes in integrating behavior-analytic technologies and organizational behavior management principles to elevate professional development and educational practices. As an instructional designer, she is skilled at designing and delivering training that results in significant changes and process improvements across all educational levels. Anika strives to empower leaders at every educational level to implement meaningful, lasting improvements.

In addition to her fieldwork and consulting, Anika is an accomplished author, having coauthored two best-selling books: *QUICK Responses for Reducing Misbehavior and Suspensions: A Behavioral Toolbox for Classroom and School Leaders* (1st ed.) and *Quick Wins! Using Behavior Science to Accelerate and Sustain School Improvement* (2nd ed.).

Anika is also a dedicated advocate for behavior science dissemination. She served as the United States Ambassador for the World Behavior Analysis Day Alliance (WBADA) and contributed to the Development Committee for the B. F. Skinner Foundation.

Eric Gormley, MEd, BCBA

Driven by a deep commitment to helping others, Eric Gormley has dedicated his career to education, particularly in specialized schools for students with severe behavioral challenges. In his decades-long career, Eric has focused on supporting children and teens who struggle in traditional classroom settings. His contributions include refining the QUICK Room approach, which has led to a significant reduction in student suspensions across multiple schools.

Eric's experience as a special education teacher motivated him to earn a master's degree in special education and become a Board Certified Behavior Analyst (BCBA). His passion for fostering community participation and enhancing social skills for individuals with special needs has driven him to develop plans for a private school tailored to students with diverse exceptionalities.

In addition to his work in schools, Eric is also a behavior analyst, providing ABA services to individuals with special needs in both home and community environments.

Andrew Houvouras, MA, BCBA

"Science is a gift to humanity." While Andrew Houvouras does not claim to be the originator of this phrase, it encapsulates his appreciation for science in general and the many benefits derived from the science of human behavior, ABA. As a master's student, Andrew was introduced to ABA by his graduate school advisor, Joe Wyatt. Andrew commented that "Like so many clinicians and teachers, I was looking for answers about how I could help people. The books I was reading at the time weren't providing me the inspiration or answers. When I learned about ABA, I knew I had found my way."

After graduating, Andrew became a BCBA. He began applying behavior science to help reduce problem behavior, teach adaptive skills, and develop systemic changes to promote positive behavior change. He worked with both children and adults in residential treatment and spent over 17 years working in the public school system. Andrew has also served as the Director of Experiential Training of the world-renowned School of Behavior Analysis at Florida Institute of Technology.

Andrew enjoys writing, consults and speaks nationally and internationally, and continues to pursue research. He is the author of the book *The Lives of the Silent*, and he notes that "Systems and procedures based on ABA have a real chance to create special environments marked by positive reinforcement, enjoyable learning, and achieved outcomes."

An avid surfer, paddleboarder, and bodysurfer, Andrew also enjoys hiking and playing and watching sports. He likes reading, movies, and walking on the beach to capture sunrises.

Frank Krukauskas, MA, BCBA

With more than 25 years of experience in educational settings, Frank continues to successfully utilize his knowledge of the science of human behavior to support students, clients, staff, and parents in a variety of environments, including private homes, group homes, day-treatment programs, children's shelters, intensive care facilities, and public and private schools.

Frank has had many roles, including program director, principal, behavior analyst, teacher, case manager, and instructor/trainer for several crisis management programs. He has assisted individuals and families struggling with the most challenging behaviors. He served as a principal of a small private school, providing support for 20 to 35 students with emotional behavioral disabilities for 4 years, and focused on addressing challenging behaviors in the setting without the use of suspensions.

Frank has also presented at state and national conferences and published his study "Using Auditory Feedback to Improve Striking for Mixed Martial Artists in Behavioral Interventions" in 2019. He is employed with Martin County Schools in Stuart, Florida, as a behavior analyst.

Discover More Books for Educators

From *QUICK Responses* authors Paul Gavoni and Anika Costa—

QUICK Wins!

Grounded in Organizational Behavior Management (OBM), or the science of human behavior for making a positive difference in any school or organization, the book's goal is to be a school leader's "grab and go" resource for building momentum for change. Though it is written from the perspective of a school leader, you don't have to be a school leader to leverage the power of *QUICK Wins*. Whether you are a school district official, principal, assistant principal, dean, guidance counselor, behavior analyst, or a school consultant, or you hold any administrative position where you engage people to implement change, this book is intended for you.

 Chapter download and bulk pricing available only from KeyPress Publishing.

QuickWinsBook.com

Paul Gavoni and Nicholas Weatherly—

Deliberate Coaching

Deliberate Coaching transforms organizations by applying concepts and tools, based on the science of behavior, to enhance leader effectiveness and organizational performance. Unlike traditional coaching guides, this book delivers a science-based approach with practical proven strategies for lasting positive change, addressing the inefficacy of conventional training and performance-improvement methods and offering alternatives that can be applied quickly and easily. *Deliberate Coaching* clarifies the proper use and everyday role of behavioral consequences and organizational systems, advocating for a precise, purposeful, and systematic coaching strategy.

Chapter download and bulk pricing available only from KeyPress Publishing.

DeliberateCoachingEdu.com